WELFARE STATE
TO
WELFARE SOCIETY

Restructuring New Zealand's Social Services

ANGELINE BARRETTA-HERMAN

GARLAND PUBLISHING, INC.
NEW YORK & LONDON / 1994

Library of Congress Cataloging-in-Publication Data

Barretta-Herman, Angeline, 1945–
Welfare state to welfare society : restructuring New Zealand's social services / Angeline Barretta-Herman.
p. cm. — (Children of poverty)
Includes bibliographical references and index.
ISBN 0-8153-1545-7 (alk. paper)
1. Public welfare—New Zealand. 2. Social service—New Zealand. 3. Human services—New Zealand. I. Title. II. Series.
HV515.5.B37 1994
361.993—dc20 93-32456
CIP

Printed on acid-free, 250-year-life paper
Manufactured in the United States of America

DEDICATION

to my colleague and husband, Randy,
and to my children, Christopher and Amanda

CONTENTS

FIGURES

TABLES

ACKNOWLEDGEMENTS

I wish to thank the social workers in New Zealand's Department of Social Welfare for their willingness to participate in a study that by design could offer only limited confidentiality. Their openness and cooperation was instrumental to the completion of the project. Drs. Graeme Fraser, Chris Wilkes and Nancy Kinross of Massey University read, commented and challenged this project though its initial stage. I am grateful for their consistent and persistent guidance and support. The faculty in the Department of Social Work at Massey University, including Mary Nash, Mary Ann Baskerville and Mark Tisdell, and the faculty in the Department of Social Work at the University of St. Thomas, particularly Dr. Barbara Shank, were unselfish in giving their time to edit, proof and comment on the manuscript. Dr. Brad Sheafor of Colorado State University and Dr. Dugald MacDonald of Canterbury University provided insightful comment and encouragement to bring this research study to press. The final stages required the skills and dedication of Susan Schell and Terri Kloch. I am eternally grateful for the personal support given by my colleagues Barbara Newcombe, Jane Brook and Terry Moore. Finally, I am grateful to Garland Publishing for making it possible that the lessons of the New Zealand experience are available to a wider audience of scholars, social policy analysts and social workers.

INTRODUCTION

CHALLENGES TO THE WELFARE STATE

The welfare state crisis of the last two decades forced a reevaluation of long-standing principles that guided the development and implementation of economic and social policy legislation in the welfare states around the world. Each welfare states' response is a reflection of the unique history of the individual country and, significantly, the conservative, free market ideologies dominating economic and social thought. This study of the New Zealand response to its welfare state crisis was prompted by the apparent ease with which the Fourth Labour Government elected in 1984 was able to reject a nearly one hundred year legacy of progressive social legislation and to 'restructure' social policies based on principles of the 'free market', deregulation and individual responsibility. The primary focus for this study was on social work practice, specifically on social work practice within New Zealand's Department of Social Welfare. The Department literally dominated the social services as the nation-wide bureaucracy responsible for implementation of social policy and its delivery since its creation by the legislature in 1971.

The study revealed an opposing tradition that questioned the assumptions upon which the welfare state was built and challenged the perception of New Zealand as an egalitarian, non-classist, non-racist society based on a strong, shared sense of community responsibility. This contradictory tradition was splintered into several factions. The factions most influential in the social services opposed the dominance of the centralized hierarchy of the well-developed and, allegedly, entrenched state bureaucracy. The Department of Social Welfare effectively controlled the fledgling voluntary and private social services agencies through its legal mandate and extensive funding programs to the non-statutory sector. The Department was criticized for ignoring the *Tangata Whenua*, the indigenous Maori people despite their disproportionate representation in negative social indicators such as admissions to mental hospitals and applications for welfare benefits.

The tradition opposing the welfare state found expression in the economic ideologies of the conservative 'right' and in what is argued here, in the social policy principles associated with a welfare society. Welfare society principles emphasize decentralized welfare bureaucracies, local community responsibility, delivery system 'pluralism' while de-emphasizing the role of the professional and of the state in service delivery. The Fourth Labour Government was able to maximize the force of this opposing tradition to effect its dramatic restructuring efforts that marked the beginning of the dismantling of the welfare state in New Zealand.

This study of developments in New Zealand assumed a three tiered research design. It began with a content analysis of the official documents, reviews and reports, published by government departments and voluntary agencies during the period 1969 to 1988. Any document that addressed the social services, specifically its development, structure, or relationships within the sector was examined and analyzed. The year 1969 was chosen because the discussions held that year on the creation of a centralized government department for the social services led directly to the passage of the Department of Social Welfare Act of 1971. Data was gathered through 1988. Developments since 1988 confirm that the process of the dismantling of the welfare state continues unabated by successive New Zealand governments.

The second tier of the study drew on the observations and experiences of the Regional Executive Officers of the Department of Social Welfare. Their positions were created by the first wave of restructuring of the Department in 1986 and were filled primarily with career civil servants, most of whom were social workers by training or experience. The third tier of study, on changes in social work practice with clients in an urban and rural district social work teams, elicited information on how the large scale policy changes were affecting social work practice with clients.

This study is important because it documents dramatic changes in social welfare policy from three perspectives, at the time of the change not confounded by subsequent events or the benefit of hindsight. The New Zealand social service sector prior to 1986 had little resemblance to the system in 1988 and even less today. The welfare state to welfare society framework utilized in this study offers a comprehensive perspective for studying not only the events in New Zealand but a useful framework for analyzing on-going developments in the welfare states of the western world.

Current debate on the welfare state centers on its irreversibility and on the benefits of welfare pluralism.[1] Some scholars, citing gross expenditure figures for social services, argue that expenditure under the conservative governments of the 1980s has increased rather than decreased.[2] The same is true of Britain where public expenditure rose under Thatcher from 39.5% of GDP in 1979-1980 to 42.5% at the end of the Thatcher years.[3] Because of the level of welfare expenditure over the last decade it may appear that the restructuring efforts of the 1980s has not appreciably changed the welfare state. However, as Mishra[4] points out the gross welfare expenditure figures, inflated as they are by the high level of unemployment benefits, mask the significant shifts in expenditure from universal benefits to targeted benefits. Scholars acknowledge that obvious radical changes in the welfare states have not occurred to the extent the restructuring language implies. However, the cumulative effect of the incremental change in the numerous subtle shifts to trim back universal coverage and means test additional categorical benefits will exert significant impact in the future on the form and character of the welfare states. These shifts challenge the claims that the welfare states are irreversible.

The debates on welfare pluralism are more complex. Welfare pluralism with its emphasis on service provision from voluntary, private, state and informal service providers is essentially anti-statist. Welfare pluralists view the state as an inefficient and ineffective service provider.[4] Under the 'free market' ideology which swept the welfare states, privatization, including privatization of the social services, is seen as the most effective and efficient way of producing and distributing goods and services. Proponents of welfare pluralism extol the virtues of competitive private enterprise as the means to reduce the role of the state while generating services despite the lack of evidence that private enterprise can provide quality service to meet the quantity of demand. Moreover, privatization of the social services, can "become an important instrument for weakening the universalist structure of these services"[5] as has been the case in education and health. The moves in New Zealand toward decentralization, devolution and increasing the level of contracting out for service provision to voluntary agencies and private providers as documented in this book, is noted by Freidman, Gilbert, and Sherer[7] as the most significant trend in the delivery of American publicly funded services.

Wilding in his carefully articulated assessment of the legacy of the Thatcher years in Britain argues that the legacy of Thatcherism lies in its challenges to the basic belief system upon which the welfare state is based. "Thatcherism has questioned, and substantially damaged, the credibility of the two basic instruments of collectivist welfare policy--bureaucracy and professions".[8] Attacks on the welfare bureaucracy and the profession of social work in New Zealand were so strong and pervasive that neither were able to effectively defend the existing form and structure of the welfare state.

Despite the damage that has been inflicted on that belief system, recent assessments of public attitudes toward welfare state provisions seem to indicate continued strong support of specific universal services, such as social insurance, in Sweden and in the U.S. and Israel. [9] The implications of this recent line of inquiry for harnessing public support for social service retention and development are immense. It points to the demand for higher levels of sophistication in the consideration and debate about the future of the welfare state and requires effort to build "a measure of consensus over desired ends and the means for achieving them" [11] that supersedes class interests and moderates the polarization of wealth and its concentration in the hands of a few.

The intensity and pace of change in New Zealand stands as a singular example of the rejection of the welfare state in favor of welfare society principles and welfare pluralism. The research study delineated in the following pages offers an explanation of how and why welfare society principles and welfare pluralism were adopted with so little apparent resistance in New Zealand. The meaning, benefit and service structure, and the expectations of the state were radically transformed in that island country despite its previous exemplary history of progressive social legislation. The transformation is seen as so dramatic that prompted one social policy analyst was prompted to exclaim: "Kiwis can now boast the dubious honour that they led the world in both the creation and dismantling of the welfare state".[12] The implications for New Zealand and a discussion of the meaning of the New Zealand case example for scholars, policy analysts and students of social work are threaded throughout this book and summarized in the final chapter.

FORM OF THE BOOK

This introduction has set out the central argument of the research study. Chapter One develops the theoretical framework used to analyse the macro social policy changes from a welfare state to welfare society. The two major debates in social work, professionalization and the definition of the social work task, are addressed and the organizational setting as the locale of the interface between policy and practice is examined. Chapter Two provides an overview of New Zealand in the mid-1980s, defines terms and gives background on the Department of Social Welfare and the social work profession in New Zealand. The research design is described in Chapter Three which also includes a summary of the demographic characteristics of the research respondents. The analysis of the publications, reviews, papers and reports that document the debates on the aspects of social service delivery systems germane to this research study are reported in Chapter Four. Chapter Five reports the perceptions of the restructuring of the Department by the eleven Regional Executive Officers who held nationwide responsibility for implementation of an alternative model of service delivery within the newly named Social Service Divisions. It is in Chapters Six and Seven that the responses and observations of the social work teams, as the front-line workers with the responsibility of interfacing with clients and the community are reported. Chapter Eight, 'Processes and Prospects', presents an analysis of the findings of the research, delineates implications for further research and the prospects for the future of the welfare state in New Zealand.

NOTES

1. Paul Wilding, *Professional Power and Social Welfare* (London: Routledge and Kegan Paul, 1992); Ramesh Mishra, *The Welfare State in Capitalist Society: Policies of Retrenchment and Maintenance in Europe, North America and Australia* (Toronto: University of Toronta Press, 1990).

2. Note: Social Welfare expenditure as a percentage of New Zealand Gross Domestic Product did increase from 5.9 % in 1971 to 12.1% in 1988 to 12.9% in 1989 (Department of Social Welfare, *Report Department of Social Welfare for the year ended 30 June 1990*, Wellington: Department of Social Welfare, 1990b).

3. Mishra, 34.

4. Ibid., 34·

5. Norman Johnson, *The Welfare State in Transition: The Theory and Practice of Welfare Pluralism* (Brighton, Sussex: Wheatsheaf Books, 1987).

6. Mishra, 35.

7. Robert R. Freidman, Neil Gilbert, and Moshe Sherer, eds., *Modern Welfare States: A Comparative View of Trends and Prospects* (New York: New York University Press, 1987).

8. Wilding, 202.

9. Victor A. Pestoff, "Third Sector and Co-Operative Services--An Alternative to Privatization," *Journal of Consumer Policy* 15 (1992) : 21-45; Ram A. Cnaan, Yeheskel Hasenfeld, Avital Cnaan, and Jane Rafferty, "Cross Cultural Comparisons of Attitudes Toward Welfare-State Programs: Path Analysis with Log-Linear Models, " *Social Indicators Research* 29 (1993) : 123-152.

10. Mishra, 11.

11. Charles Waldegrave, "Budget '91: Monetarist Dream Citizen's Nightmare, " *Social Work Review* 4 : 2-3 (1991) : 33-34.

Welfare State
to
Welfare Society

I

WELFARE STATE TO WELFARE SOCIETY: THEORY AND MODELS

To analyze field social work practice within the Department of Social Welfare, it is necessary to begin with an examination of the concepts 'welfare state' and 'welfare society' and to review the explanations offered in the literature for the crisis of the welfare state in contemporary Western societies. It is argued here that it is the broad directions of state responsibility that guide statutory organizational strategies for social service funding, provision and service delivery. Hence, the second major section of this chapter examines models of social service delivery by comparing and contrasting the features of the welfare state model as articulated by Titmuss[1] with the features of the welfare society model promulgated by Hadley and colleagues.[2] Issues of organizational design are considered in this second section which proposes that the welfare state model of social service delivery led to the development of a centralized, bureaucratic state system. Conversely, the welfare society model demands an organizational design characterized by a decentralized delivery system, pluralism in service providers and participation of the community in planning and service provision. Just as there is a relationship between the strategies of service provision and the characteristics of the organization designed to implement the model of social service delivery, these two elements are related to organizational performance. As conceptualized here, performance considers both the tasks to be accomplished by social workers and the qualifications required to perform those tasks. The last section of this chapter, analyzes these critical social work performance issues as the professionalization of social work and the definition of the social work task.

Although the relationship between strategy, design and performance is conceptualized as sequential for the purposes of explanation in the Pearce and Robinson[3] model, the relationship is more complex and dynamic. Pearce and Robinson acknowledge the significance of the environment especially in times of change. It is this extra organizational environment that contemporary organizational theorists argue has been insufficiently considered in the study of organizations.

The analytical framework presented and the research methodology used in the present research reflects the influence of the contemporary organizational theorists who contend that a paradigm shift is occurring which fundamentally alters both the 'world view' of organizational analysis and organizational research.[4] Advocates of the naturalist paradigm reject the positivist emphasis on rationality, planning and linear causality. The naturalists' view of the world is one of complexity, indetermination and mutual causality. They argue for an organizational analysis that adopts a 'holistic' approach and addresses the major criticism of system theories approaches which have dominated organizational analysis for thirty years. This criticism is exemplified in the comments of Scott who contends that open systems theories have not been adequately utilized to examine the relationship between: naturalist paradigm contrasted with positivist paradigm

> 'Internal' features and 'external' forces . . . to analyse how societal events push, pull and permeate organizational structures and processes.[5]

Lincoln reiterates this perspective when she calls for an organizational analysis that expands the boundaries of the organization and recognizes the organization in its immediate task environment *and* considers the organization within its broadest societal context. Such an analysis includes what she terms both 'horizontal' and 'vertical' organizational relationships.[6] The naturalists dismiss the 'retrospective rationality' of the positivist paradigm which they argue is "rare in organizations"[7] and the deliberation assumed in the planning function as "fostered for public consumption while a different set of procedures is used to get the work done."[8]

The influence of this emerging paradigm is evident in the analytical framework used in this present research. This framework considers societal or vertical relationships in the examination of social work within a particular organizational context, as well as the internal and external horizontal relationships of the organization.

WELFARE STATE TO WELFARE SOCIETY

Two views of the welfare state dominate the literature: the ideological view which focuses on the welfare state as a set of beliefs and values and the programmatic view which examines the benefits and services provided by the state. Ideologically, the term welfare state connotes an assumption of 'collective responsibility'. The term conveys a benevolent state attitude toward the well being of all its citizens and denotes "universal entitlement of a number of welfare provisions as a matter of right for the members of a nation state."[9]

Kaufman[10] proposes four dimensions for comparison of welfare states: (a) the ideological dimension which addresses the scope and limits of state responsibility for individual and collective welfare; (b) the institutional dimension which addresses the degree of state influence in the provision of services and in the redistribution of wealth; (c) the organizational dimension which examines the organized forms and the degree of centralization; and (d) the performance dimension which analyses the kind and amount of resources allocated to different public programmes. Furniss and Tilton,[11] on the other hand, contend that it is state intervention in economic and social policy which is the central feature of welfare states. Their view encompasses the ideological and organizational dimensions in Kaufman's schema. Furniss and Tilton argue that it is the form and goals of state interventionist policies along a continuum from minimalist to pervasive that provides the primary criteria for distinguishing one welfare state from another. Halsey in his discussion of the rise of welfare state policies in the Organisation for Economic Co-Operation and Development (OECD) countries, describes these policies as 'interferences':

> The rise of the Welfare State constitutes what was originally called 'interference' in the exchanges between the family and the economy. . . The more elaborate these 'interferences,' the more developed the Welfare State.[12]

The description 'Welfare State', then, can describe quite different perspectives and quite different patterns of social welfare policies and programmes provided by a particular government. It does not necessarily denote pervasive government intervention. It may not even accurately reflect the spirit of collective responsibility and altruism so often ascribed to it.[13] William Oliver[14] suggests that the welfare provisions established in New Zealand were more a response to economic depression that threatened national stability than a commitment to social justice. In New Zealand, however, the term welfare state is generally accepted as referring to a benevolent state attitude and to the comprehensive system of government-provided benefits and services as originally formulated in the Social Security Act provisions of 1938, codified by the 1972 Royal Commission on Social Security, 1972 and reconfirmed by the Report of the Royal Commission on Social Policy released in April of 1988.[15]

Initial formulations of the term 'Welfare Society', conversely, referred to industrial societies with highly developed universal services with few "distinctions between welfare and other types of social institutions."[16] The 'Welfare Society' as envisaged by Wilensky and Lebeaux was the culmination of the development of extensive institutionalized welfare programs. More recent formulations of the term[17] stand in direct contrast to this early conceptualization. Now the concept of a welfare society includes notions welfare society early conceptualizations of individual and local community responsibility and rejects notions of collective responsibility, particularly as exemplified in state provided services and benefits.[18] The term Welfare Society as it is used by 'anti-collectivists'[19] and welfare pluralists[20] emphasizes the responsibilities of primary social institutions such as the family (including the extended family network) and the local community in providing care. Proponents of a Welfare Society reject state provision of universal services because, they contend, such services foster dependency and inefficiency. They propose welfare pluralism as the means for encouraging and supporting the provision of services in both the voluntary and commercial sectors. From this perspective, the state is seen as providing only services of last resort, that is, services that can not be offered by the other sectors.

This conception of welfare society gained acceptance among both the political left, who were arguing for decentralized, responsive and localized services, and the political right, who sought both a justification for, and a way of circumventing the growth of welfare state expenditure as New Zealand began the painful process of dealing explicitly with its welfare state crisis.

THE WELFARE STATE CRISIS

The Organisation for Economic Co-Operation and Development in the preface to their report of the 1980 conference proceedings contended that it was the lower growth performance of the OECD economies since the 1970s that led to the disruption of the "continuing extension of programmes and the growth of benefits"[21] and, consequently, to the crisis in the Welfare States. The economic frailties of the post-industrial Western World were highlighted in the oil crises of 1973 and 1979; in the growing deficit and trade imbalances which meant that these countries were buying more and exporting less; in the rising unemployment which threatened the creation of the permanently unemployed, and in the high inflation rates which threatened fiscal security.[22] Robson argued that "Britain is trying to have a welfare state without a welfare society".[23] He perceived the difficulties Britain was facing with the Welfare State in the mid-1970s was a reflection of the absence of wide-spread popular support for the basic assumptions of the Welfare State which were fundamentally:

> A devotion to the well-being of the whole society; it is as much concerned with maintaining or improving conditions for those who enjoy a good life style as with raising the standard of living of those who fall below an acceptable national minimum.[24]

To Robson, a precondition of welfare state policies is a welfare society which, he describes as embodying heartfelt notions of caring among all members of society (thus, blurring the distinction between a welfare state and a welfare society). Robson lamented the centralizing trend in welfare states, the growth in the state bureaucracy and the increasing alienation of both the general public and the consumers from state provided social services. It was these ideological and economic factors that prompted Mishra to declare "the Welfare State throughout the industrialized West is in disarray."[25] New Zealand, like other Western nations in the economic recessions of the 1970s, vigorously questioned the assumptions of Keynesian economics and whether the country could any longer afford the welfare state. Brodkin argues:

> With the emergence of the welfare crises in the 1970's, there began a transition from a prevailing concern with poverty's causes and cures to an overriding concern with welfare costs and mismanagement.[26]

Essentially then, the question changed and economic concerns predominated.

However, the challenges to the Welfare State in the 1970s were not solely economic. Much debate questioned if the objectives of the welfare state had been unrealistically been expanded. Eisenstadt (1985) declared that the major if not the primary objective of the welfare state was the assumption that:

> Each individual is entitled to a decent standard of living, to education, housing, medical care and welfare service . . . [and that] through universal services would come elimination of poverty, the advancement of underprivileged groups and narrowing gaps in income, education and employment.[27]

This view was challenged by Abel-Smith, Kaufman, and George and Wilding[28] who contended that the objective of the Welfare State was much narrower: it was to establish a minimum level of rights and services. It was the expansion of this basic objective in Britain, as a case in point, that gave rise to expectations among many groups in society for the constant improvement in and the extension of welfare services. The Barclay Report[29] points to these rising expectations as exacerbating the fiscal shortage during the British economic stagnation of past two decades. Rising expectations led to criticisms of the British welfare state as failing to meet the ever expanding needs of society. As well, challenges to the provisions of the welfare state arose in the alleged efficiency gaps that distributed benefits to the middle and wealthy classes and the secondary negative side effects of service provisions, e.g. encouraging dependency on the state services or benefits.[30]

The concept of a welfare society was, on the other hand, associated with notions of welfare pluralism, decentralized systems responsive to local needs, community participation in service planning and provision, family responsibility and, particularly in New Zealand, the rights and ability of the indigenous peoples to 'take care of their own'.[31] One objective of the 1980 OECD Conference was to stimulate discussion on the emerging trend of reasserting the social roles of primary institutions, such as the family and the local community, as providers of social caring. The OECD discussions focused on providing commentary in answer to the question "Are we moving from a Welfare State to a Welfare Society?" The Secretary General of the OECD argued in his opening address that the major changes occurring in Welfare State policies deserved acknowledgment and encouragement:

> The emerging social needs and aspirations in contemporary post-industrial society [seek] new relationships between state and private action . . . new agents for welfare and well-being . . . [new emphasis on] the responsibilities of individuals for themselves and others . . *the emergence of the Welfare Society is both inevitable and desirable* [italics added].[32]

The concept of a welfare society was seen to emphasize individual and familial responsibility rather than the collective responsibility implied in a welfare state; thus it was a better fit with the monetarist policies in Western societies and the efforts to curtail state welfare expenditure. A number of economists and politicians began to consider liberal economic philosophy and monetarist principles as the optimal strategy for future development. Political support for monetarist policies was evident in the landslide victory elections of Ronald Reagan (1981 and 1985) in the United States and in Margaret Thatcher's hold as Prime Minister in Britain for the decade following her rise to power in 1979.

> Reagan and Thatcher . . . offer an export package of resurgent pro-capitalist economic policies shrouded under the ideological cloak of diehard conservatism that rejects the Keynesian foundation of the welfare state and espouses deregulation, privatization, tax reform and 'cash limit' financing . . . Both Reagan and Thatcher have attempted to transform society according to their ideological convictions and visions.[33]

In New Zealand, the reassessment of economic and social policy led to acrimonious debate. The major issues of the 1984 election addressed ways public expenditures could be curtailed, particularly how to contain the escalating costs of the welfare state. Dalziel[34] contends that the adoption of liberal economic philosophy and a monetarist perspective by the New Zealand Treasury occurred in the early 1980's and was clearly evident in the briefing papers to the incoming Minister of Finance in 1984. Rogernomics, as a variant of monetarist macroeconomics and commercialist microeconomics was set into place after the Fourth Labour Government took office. It was the intention of Roger Douglas to apply Rogernomics to both the economic and social policy arenas. A crucial debate erupted over which of the two policy areas should be New Zealand's first consideration. The 1988 Royal Commission on Social Policy argued that there can not be any separation of the two policy arenas. Roger Douglas, as the first Finance Minister of the Fourth Labour Government was seen to agree "except he argues that economic policy drives social policy rather than the reverse."[35]

MODELS OF SOCIAL SERVICE DELIVERY

The Welfare State Model

The concept of a welfare state with its emphasis on collective responsibility and the provision of a minimum level of benefit and services is contrasted with the concept of a welfare society' which places a heavier emphasis on individual and community responsibility and notions of welfare pluralism. These concepts have strong parallels in the institutional and residual models of welfare as conceptualized by Wilensky and Lebeaux.[36] The welfare state and the welfare society perspectives on social services have direct implications for the model of social service delivery implemented. It is not to be assumed that during the period of welfare state dominance that aspects of a welfare society were not evident. On the contrary, individual examples of social services patterned on welfare society principles can be noted, for example, in the state's dependence on the voluntary sector for specific programs. In New Zealand, for example, the state depended on a private agency, the Society for Intellectually Handicapped, for all services to this specific population. Private and voluntary agency delivery systems reflecting welfare society characteristics grew in scope, number and influence as the shift from a welfare state towards a welfare society model of service delivery gained momentum in New Zealand.

In a welfare state model of social service delivery, the state plays the key role as both funder and provider. As Mohan[37] points out, international comparisons between welfare states reveals wide variations in the application of the key role of the state as "State intervention in human affairs has always been a source of strain among conflicting ideologies and interests."[37] Richard Titmuss was a vigorous proponent of the view that the state had *the* primary responsibility in the provision of social services as an expression of collectivism and in the interests of social justice. Although Titmuss was not the architect of the British welfare state "he soon made himself its ideologue."[38] Titmuss view of the welfare stateTitmuss argued that the marketplace was unable to fulfil the ideals of social justice.

> [Titmuss had] a profound mistrust of the market and [urged] use of the state to redistribute resources in favour of equality. The state, he argued, should play a strongly integrative role, in particular compensating for the adverse effects of social and economic change.[39]

Titmuss supported the view that benefits and services should be universal, provided as of right and based on need not on an individual's ability to pay. He rejected a dual system of welfare based on means testing because he was convinced that a dual system would stigmatize recipients[40] and because means testing would both deter people from applying for services and would operate to restrict demand.[41]

Reisman claimed that Titmuss had a strong belief in the

effectiveness and efficiency of centralized decision making and of the ability of the state bureaucracy to delivery of social services.

> Titmuss believed that social policy is social action in accordance with widely held social values and had particular confidence in the sensitivity of politicians and administrators to the wish of the majority. . . [he] overestimated the accountability of politicians to public opinion and underestimated the extent to which they see themselves, once elected into office, as an independent estate in the 'land'.[42]

Titmuss argued that if services were to be available universally and without stigma, the state was essential. State provided social services recognized the failure of the market in the provision of services. Titmuss supported the role of professionals in the provision of social services, describing professions as "repositories of a very special kind of knowledge" and with whom the state must negotiate a "proper relationship" to insure the future of quality social services.[43]

While the state would be the primary funder and provider of social services, there is no indication in the writings of Titmuss that he rejected voluntary service provision. On the contrary, Titmuss acknowledged the role of the voluntary sector in providing specialist services and innovative responses to needs that the more cumbersome state funded services were less able to provide. For Titmuss, voluntary organizations had a 'vanguard' role in the identification of a response to unmet needs. Once the voluntary sector had developed a viable programme the state could take over provision. In this regard, Titmuss viewed the role of voluntary organizations as supplementary to, not a substitute for, state provided social services. Indeed Titmuss, and the Fabian socialists with whom he was associated, took the view that the development of extensive private services would "increase inequality in service provision, undermine altruism, weaken the public service, concentrate power in private hands and through direct and indirect methods, drain the public purse."[44] It is this philosophy, exemplified in the work of Titmuss, that is the welfare state model of social service delivery which dominated the pattern of service delivery in Britain and New Zealand from post World War II until the 1980s.

Given the secondary role relegated to the voluntary sector under the welfare state model, precisely establishing the contribution of the voluntary sector is problematic. While there was a parallel contribution to social service provision by the voluntary sector in the 'welfare states' which developed after World War II, the contribution of the voluntary sector remains largely unresearched. This was because of the preoccupation with state provision and the lack of comprehensive documentation that could substantiate the contribution made by the voluntary sector despite the contribution of voluntary organization research bodies.[45] This has been noted to be particularly true in New Zealand .[46]

The Welfare Society Model

Alternatives to state dominated social service delivery models were offered by the 'anti-collectivists', exemplified by advocates such as F. A. Hayek and Milton Friedman and by the welfare pluralists, such as Hadley, Hatch, and Mocroft.[47] The anti-collectivists:

> See welfare state policies as threatening or damaging to central social values and institutions--the family, work incentives, economic development, individual freedom, for example--and in general they are opposed to provision which is more than minimal.[48]

Other conceptualizations of a social service system not dominated by the state refer to 'mixed economy of welfare'[49] or to welfare pluralism. Both conceptualizations refer to statutory, voluntary, profit-oriented and informal service providers involved at varying levels in the financing and delivery of benefits and services.[50] The concept of a mixed economy of welfare attempted to draw attention to *existing providers other than the state.* A mixed economy of welfare emphasizes not only the existence of other providers but their potential for further development and utilization. Welfare pluralism refers to the provision of social services from the four sectors: statutory, voluntary, commercial and informal but "implies a less dominant role of the state."[51] Johnson contends that the lack of precision in definition of both the notion of a mixed economy of welfare and welfare pluralism hides its underlying 'anti-statist' philosophy:

> Welfare pluralism, as presently propounded [sic], is anti-statist; it wishes to see a substantial shift in the balance of provision from the state to the other three sectors.[52]

Johnson describes welfare pluralism as basically anti-bureaucratic and anti-professional and reliant on notions of decentralization and participation. Because Johnson does not assess welfare pluralism as neutral, he fears that welfare pluralists and their models "will serve to legitimate cuts in public expenditure and the development of market provision" [53] to the detriment of comprehensive universal services.

As welfare pluralists, Hadley and Hatch proposed recognition and support of the contribution of the four sectors in service provision. Within their model, pluralism and decentralization formed the two pronged strategy for "a reappraisal of the role of the state in social welfare." [54]

It is important to note that Black and colleagues[55] argued that in Britain throughout the 1970s, a high priority was placed on raising levels of social services provision and providing a minimum stock of statutory service provision. This contributed to an apparent disregard for the voluntary sector. These researchers went on to suggest that:

> This thrust seems to have permeated the very heart of social work practice ideology . . . [it] seemed rarely to take account of wider conceptions of welfare pluralism .[56]

The analysis undertaken in Chapter Four aims to show that these criticisms of the welfare state model of social service delivery were leveled against New Zealand's welfare state. Indeed, when Roger Hadley was invited to New Zealand in 1982 to discuss his ideas on the delivery of social services, he articulated an alternative model that addressed these perceived shortcomings and disadvantages of the centralized, bureaucratized welfare state model.

Hadley and Hatch had been closely associated with the voluntary social services in Britain: Roger Hadley as a Professor of Social Administration at the University of Lancaster, Stephen Hatch as a Senior Research Fellow in the Policy Studies Institute and Head of its Voluntary Organisations Research Unit. This association began in 1977 when Hadley and Hatch contributed to the Wolfenden Report on *The Future of Voluntary Organisations* [57] in Britain. Hadley and Hatch argued that the Committee had not gone far enough in its critique of the way social policy had evolved since 1945 and subsequently called for a re-evaluation of the role of the state. Hadley and Hatch asserted that the state's dominance in provision of social services had resulted in poor performance in the highly centralized, bureaucratized, and heavily funded state services. They argued for a pluralist, decentralized and participatory pattern of services which would be more accessible and more responsive to local needs. Such a restructuring of services would implement the aspirations for community development and the promotion of reciprocal relationships and mutual aid within the community advocated in the 1968 Seebohm Report.[58] Hadley and Hatch asserted that the recommendations of the Seebohm Report went unheeded because they were stifled by the centralization and bureaucratization of local authority departments.

> What seems to be needed now is a pluralist strategy which looks beyond the conflict over the commercial sector and seeks to develop roles for each of the sectors and, in particular, to maximize the voluntary and informal contributions.[59]

Such a strategy would require an alternative to the prevailing system of social service organization which Hadley and Hatch describe as a *representative* form of government. In such a form of government, the elected minister is seen as responsible for the design and implementation of social services through civil servants advised by professional 'experts.' The client is assumed to have a largely passive role, and is expected to accept the services provided.

> Representative systems of government in which all power is vested in the elected members of parliament or local authority logically exclude the right of the citizen to participate directly in the management and delivery of public services . . . [social services] are designed to carry out policies determined by [the Minister] Administration and professionals are . . . servants of the representative assembly.[60]

In Hadley and Hatch's *participatory* model of democracy, the general directions of social policy would still be determined by the elected members of government but:

> The ways in which the policies are developed and applied are open to discussion and amendment by both social services staff and clients, for their involvement is regarded as indispensable if available resources are to be maximized and variations in need/demand are to be recognized.[61]

Instead of bureaucratized social service organizations offering predetermined services to well-defined targeted groups, a participatory model of democracy would result in social service agencies with much wider terms of reference that would, in turn, encourage a co-operative and entrepreneurial approach. Such an approach, Hadley and Hatch asserted, would confine professional authority to areas where their expertise is a legitimate claim while affording opportunity for others, such as families, neighborhood groups and volunteers, to participate in a meaningful way in the provision of formal and informal caring. The state would continue to play a central role in policy development, program monitoring and evaluation but would share service delivery with other sectors.

The model proposed by Hadley and Hatch retains the role of the state as central in funding, planning and evaluation but emphasizes provision of services in the voluntary, private and informal care systems. Table I sets out a comparison of selected aspects of the social service organizational characteristics of the bureaucratic and participatory systems. Broadly speaking, the bureaucratic system approximates the principles and characteristics of the welfare state model discussed previously whereas, the participatory system approximates the features of a welfare society model for the delivery of social services.

Table I

Characteristics of social services organization in bureaucratic and participatory systems

Characteristics	*Bureaucratic*	*Participatory*
Function of system	Delivery of pretermined service to clearly defined client groups	Facilitation of feasible service in collaboration with staff, clients and the community
Main source(s) of authority	The organisation; training -expertise of individual staff	The organisation; the expertise of the team; negotiated relationships with the users/ community
Organisation structure	Hierarchical, large units	Flat organisations, small units
Model of decision-making	By individual, pressure to pass up the hierarchy	By team, pressures to push down to front line
Role of worker/ staff	Clearly defined and bounded	Flexible
Organisation of ancillary, volunteers	Segregated	Integrated
Role of client/user	Expected to be passive	Encouraged to be active

Characteristics	*Bureaucratic*	*Participatory*
Character of relationships between staff and user	Strives to be neutral, disinterested	Strives to be empathetic
Contracting work out to non-statutory agencies, volunteers, etc.	Low	High
Innovation in management of the organisation from within the agency	Rare	Frequent
Principal indicators of performance	Input indicators (e.g. buildings, hospital beds, meals delivered)	Output indicators-user satisfaction, as defined by user
Accountability	Upwards, to chief officer and representative body	Two-way: upwards (as representative); downwards - to users and staff
Definitions of professionalism	Mastery of body of knowledge; application to individual cases	Expert knowledge plus capacity to work with 'non-expert' in team, etc., to maximise effectiveness

adapted from Roger Hadley and Stephen Hatch
Social Welfare and the Failure of the State,
(London: Bedord Square Press, 1981)

According to Hadley and Hatch, three strategic changes are required if their approach to service delivery is to be implemented. First, strategy must be developed for creating rights that give individuals and community groups the power to take initiative in the development of service delivery programs. To ensure a degree of success, these initiatives must be supported by resources, staff, finances and information from the state welfare bureaucracies. Second and parallel to the development of the right to take initiatives outside statutory organizations must be the recognition of the right of clients, referred to as 'users' by Hadley and Hatch, to have voice in the management of the statutory services themselves. Not only do they advocate the participation of clients in decision making of statutory organizations, but they propose that participatory mechanisms must also be introduced for staff.

> The creation of rights for users should be matched with opportunities for staff of the social services to share in the management of their organisation.[62]

The issue of staff participation was also addressed by George and Wilding who noted that experiments of participation in social services demonstrated that participation is costly, problematic in its implementation and lead to systemic organizational and personnel issues.

> For example, if users of services are to participate in their organisation and management, this raises very sharply the question of staff participation, which in turn raises questions about traditional patterns of authority in bureaucratic organisations.[63]

The third essential change recommended by Hadley and Hatch was directed at the infrastructure of service delivery and required the extensive decentralization of social services with local control. Such decentralization was based on geographical 'patches' with relatively small population groupings of not more than 10,000 people. The patch system was designed to maximize organizational responsiveness and support of informal care systems.

The model proposed by Hadley and Hatch addressed the criticisms of the welfare state from both the political right and the political left. Indeed, features of this alternative model paralleled the key elements of a welfare society model of social service delivery. Moreover, it is a model which appears to exemplify the principles of the restructuring of the Department of Social Welfare in New Zealand.

The first structural feature Hadley and Hatch delineated involved *plural provision* of social services by voluntary, private, for-profit agencies, groups and individuals. Such an approach is the antithesis of the welfare state model with its state funded and provided centralized services. According to this feature, predetermined centrally mandated services are replaced with community initiatives focusing on local services for local needs. Plural provision also implies a redressing of the alleged imbalance in the statutory-voluntary service provision and in so doing explicitly acknowledges the role of non-statutory service providers in the planning and delivery of social services.

The decentralization and community orientation of statutory services is the second feature of the Hadley and Hatch model. These two interrelated features were intended to create responsive, integrated services predicated on a high degree of community input in both the planning and delivery of services. Such input is only possible, Hadley and Hatch argue, in decentralized structures. When *essential services* are provided by the state (one has to assume Hadley and Hatch are referring to child protective services and, perhaps youth justice), the predominant mode would be a community-oriented system characterized by a policy of *reinforcement* as opposed to *replacement* of informal sources of care. That is, statutory services provide support, referral and tangible services (e.g., finances, equipment, professional expertise) to supplement, not substitute for, community-based voluntary or informal care.

The third structural feature entailed contractual accountability to replace hierarchical accountability through the funding and contracting out of services to the voluntary sector. Accountability would be achieved through the use of negotiated contracts requiring explicit evaluation criteria. This contractual accountability would replace the hierarchical accountability that, Hadley and Hatch claimed, led to the gross inefficiency and ineffectiveness of the welfare state models of social service delivery. A significant consequence of this new system of accountability was predicted to be an increased role for statutory agencies in monitoring and inspection.

The last feature of the Hadley and Hatch model was the creation, development and support of participatory mechanisms designed to involve users and all providers in planning, decision-making and evaluation of statutory services to ensure their responsiveness and effectiveness in meeting social needs.

Critics of Hadley and Hatch attacked their reliance on informal helping systems. Feminists contended this reliance would further prohibit women from taking their place in the economic life of society and would contribute to the "redomestication of women."[64] Other critics contended that Hadley and Hatch's model used the liberal values of participation and community in an attempt to make the dismantling of the welfare state palatable to social work.[65] And more damaging, it offered a model that could be utilized by monetarists to further reduce the role of the state in providing care for its people.[66]

> [Community oriented models] can also be seen as a cheap alternative, a means by which families can provide at little or no cost to the state, services otherwise financed by taxpayers.[67]

Pinker questioned how the revised responsibilities of central government for funding and monitoring could be reconciled with "increased delegation of power to local authorities and increased devolution to the neighbourhoods."[68] Rowe questioned how community social work models addressed the issues of continuity of care during "those many periods when the enthusiasm or skills of its supporters ebb away or prove inadequate."[69] Others attacked what they termed as 'gross generalities' of the model. For example:

> One of the major dilemmas that confronts the 'patch' protagonists is that the participatory experiments have emerged from the self same 'inflexible' bureaucracies which they condemn.[70]

Critics focused on the assumption of a caring community of informal systems that would be both willing and able to assume more responsibility for caring. They pointed out that formal services were created *because* informal care systems were not operating or were non-existent.[71] They pointed out the realities of contemporary urban life and the prevailing patterns of family living suggest that systems of family support are neither as universal nor as extensive as the proponents of the welfare pluralism contend.

> A revitalization of community spirit and consequent care for the disadvantaged via informal caring networks seems an unlikely occurrence in a society whose economics emphasize individualism and competitiveness; whose politics emphasize duality and conflict; whose history shows division; and whose society provides little evidence of the ability to mobilize beyond particular campaigns or single self-interested issues.[72]

Commentary on the model proposed by Hadley and Hatch soon became intertwined with critiques of the Barclay Report with which Hadley served as a Working Party Member. The Barclay Report recommended a decentralized, localized and community oriented delivery system that seeks to "tap into, support, enable and underpin the local networks of formal and informal relationships"[73] reflected the principles of the patch approach which Hadley and Hatch advocated. These ideas were encapsulated in Barclay Report's call for "community social work."[74]

Hadley responded to criticism of the participatory approach to social service delivery in his co-authored report of a large scale study of community-centered teams. Hadley contended that the approach was not compatible with the proposals of the political right to dismantle the welfare state and shift service provision to voluntary organizations and the market place.

> On the contrary, the community-centred approach is built on the assumption of the continuation of large-scale investment by local and central government in the welfare services . . . Nor is the practitioner of community-centred methods likely to accept the view that his [sic] approach is bound to reinforce the traditional role of women as carers . . . [the] principle concern [is] to optimise the use of resources in a manner which is more equitable than the existing system.[75]

Hadley argued that the approach maximized the use of local resources by emphasizing a team approach that extended beyond the statutory agency's door. The cooperative, collaborative principle of the community-centered approach, or patch system, was reflected in the three central organizational features: localization, integration of services within the team, and integration within the patch to ensure continuity of care. Emphasis is placed on the:

> Development of methods and roles which reflect the stress laid on working with the local community and understanding the problems of the area.[76]

Workers are expected to work closely with voluntary and informal helping systems with the aim of strengthening, not usurping, those systems.[77]

As previously noted the four structural features of the community-centred approach advocated by Hadley and Hatch bear striking similarity to the four principles utilized in the restructuring of the Department of Social Welfare: regionalization, decentralization, devolution and partnership with the community. The essential point is that the Hadley and Hatch model appears to have provided the rationale for the changes proposed in the social service delivery system that were initiated under the Fourth Labour Government.

ORGANIZATIONAL DESIGN

The complexity of organizations as a phenomena is reflected in the proliferation of theories, models and approaches to organizational analysis.[78] Early organizational analysis focused on the features, characteristics and interrelationships internal to the organization and assumed the organization could be understood as a self-contained entity.[79] Later theoretical developments in organizational analysis followed two traditions. The British organizational analysts concentrated on organizational structure and processes while their American counterparts were more interested in the affect of informal and work group relationships on productivity.[80] Organization analysts of the 1960s and 1970s applied an open-systems approach that demanded organizations be viewed through their interrelationships with their 'environment'.[81] Environment was defined generally as the complex of exchanges an organization has with those outside their organization for the acquisition of raw materials, for sanction or license to operate, and for distribution of their outputs or products in both competing and complementary relationships.[82] Contemporary organizational analysts have extended the concept of environment to include a consideration of the broad societal context in an attempt to show a relationship between the macro-environmental and characteristics of the organization.[83] It is such a perspective that is utilized in this research through the consideration of the macro-environmental shift from a welfare state toward a welfare society.

Contemporary models for incorporating the multiple perspectives of organizational analysis draw on the broad systems approach tradition of organizational analysis and the development of the contingency theory of organizations which attempt "to specify the appropriate functional 'fit' between environmental settings and the internal organizational structures" they require.[84] The Pearce and Robinson model is one such example. Using a management perspective, Pearce and Robinson argue for planned 'fit' between the strategy of an organization, its design and desired performance. Strategy is defined as the desired objectives or outcomes of the organization. The design of an organization is conceptualized as the interrelationship between five key elements: structure, decision and reward systems, tasks, people and informal organization and culture. It is these five key factors which are of paramount importance in shaping the organization's design. The essential point is that an optimal 'fit' is essential for maximum performance. In addition, Pearce and Robinson postulate that not only are all of the elements interrelated but also "it is important that a match be achieved between each pair of elements."[85] Structural alternatives in shaping organizations are contingent on the organizational environment, the technology utilized by the organization and the size of the organization. Pearce and Robinson that organizational design is dynamic, i.e, for optimal 'fit' organizational designs must change over time. As well, distinct organizational designs may be required in different parts of the organization. Their schema is shown in Figure Two.

Figure One

KEY CONSIDERATIONS IN ORGANIZATIONAL DESIGN

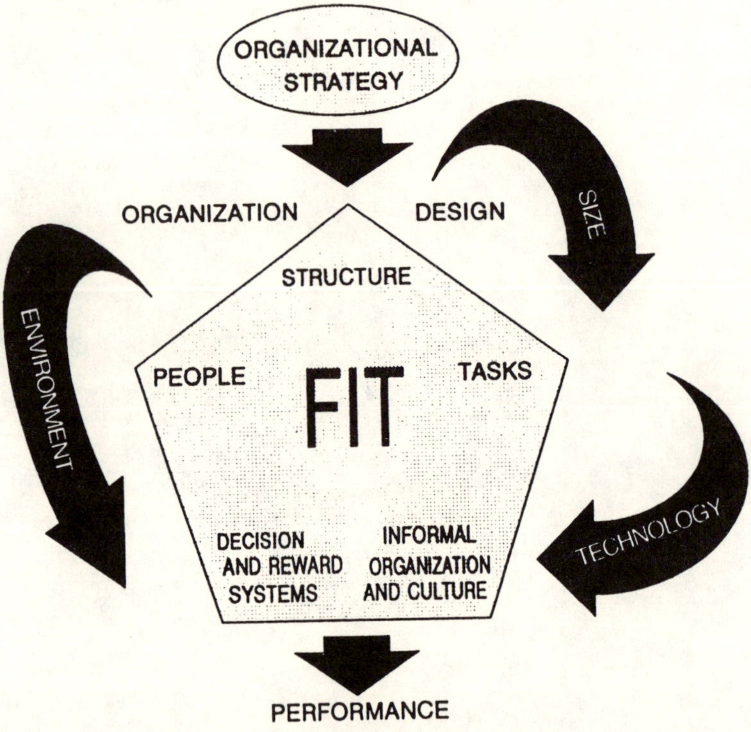

adapted from J. A. Pearce and T. A. Robinson, 1989, Management, Singapore: McGraw-Hill International Press.

The change from a welfare state toward a welfare society (strategy), from a centralized bureaucracy to a decentralized organization (design), from professional social work services to a pluralist system of providers (performance), can be explored using the Pearce and Robinson model. As the discussion of the models of service delivery demonstrated, each model is associated with specific organizational arrangements designed to facilitate its implementation. The welfare state model was associated with a centralized state bureaucracy.

Statutory and non-statutory providers were in an unequal balance of state domination in service provision with a reliance on expert professional workers. Pearce and Robinson postulate that "organizational design must be consistent with strategy."[86] A strategy of centralized, standardized services based on the principles of equality and universality demands an organizational design exemplified by centralized decision making systems, formalized and standardized task expectations, professional staff and an organizational culture characterized by deference to bureaucratic authority and a service ethic for optimum fit.

Likewise, if the strategy is for a decentralized, locally responsive, flexible organization, Pearce and Robinson would argue that the elements of organizational design must reflect the principles of the strategy to support maximum performance. Hence, since the welfare society model is associated with decentralized systems, pluralism of providers and participation of the community in decision making and service provision, the elements of the organizational design must offer support to this 'strategy' to ensure maximum performance. Therefore, a decentralized structure, is indicated with delegated decision making, participatory systems, complexity in staff composition (i.e., staff with wide variations in training, expertise and professional affiliation), and an organizational culture and reward system that encourages personal initiative and creativity. Their model acknowledges that the establishment of an organizational design to support a particular strategy is seldom an exclusively rational, planned activity. This recognition is consistent with the view of the proponents of the naturalist paradigm. Pearce and Robinson contend that changes in organizational design may occur either through an evolutionary process that takes place in a political, economic, cultural and social environment over time or a radical response to crisis in the organization's internal or external environment.

Four elements of the Peace and Robinson model are specifically addressed in this study. The first is organizational structure: the formal patterns of authority, task responsibility and coordinating relationships. The second is decision-making systems conceptualized in the present research as the dilemmas of centralization/decentralization and management style. Participation is addressed as an aspect of both structure and the decision-making system and is given more emphasis and a wider conceptualization in this study than in Pearce and Robinson model. Pearce and Robinson do point out, however, that design elements are "interrelated . . . [their relationship] should emphasize consistency and reinforcement."[87] The concept of participation, as already indicated, may refer to a plurality of service providers or to systems of involvement by clients, the wider community and /or staff in planning, decision making and monitoring of services. Participation is dependent on the styles of management in an organization and on the decision making systems established as part of the organization.[88]

The third and fourth elements of the model, 'tasks' and 'people', are considered in the discussion of the tasks of social work within the Department and the desired level of professionalism. The fit between these two elements and performance reflects the dynamic interrelationship conveyed in the model.

The next section will address organizational structure and decision making systems through an exploration of structure, the centralization/decentralization dilemma, management style and participation. Then the discussion will proceed to explore the relationship between performance and social work task and professionalism.

Structure

The structure of organizational patterns of authority, task responsibilities and coordinating relationships is most often depicted in an organizational chart. The chart denotes formal power centers in the organization, the status of the various positions and the title designations of each position. The organizational structural chart is often the first consideration in analysing an organization because it provides a wealth of information about the organization at a glance[89] and because it is "a major manifestation of the organization's design."[90] Of the various conceptualizations of organizational structure two types are outlined here. They have specific relevance for understanding New Zealand's Department of Social Welfare: the functional structure and the divisional structure.

An organization with a functional structure groups similar tasks or activities as separate units within the organization. This type of structure permits the development of specialized expertise. Functional structures are prevalent in many of the welfare services such as schools (primary, elementary, secondary), hospitals (coronary care, paediatrics, rehabilitation) and social services (child protection, services to the elderly, family services). The functional structure, while delegating operational, day to day decision making to the units, nevertheless retains centralized policy making in the chief executive manager or in the management group. Functional structures can, however, promote narrow specialization, rivalry and conflict between the functions for clients and resources, and create problems of coordination and integration across the functional divisions.[91]

A divisional structure can be a preferred pattern when the organizational strategy is to provide distinct services to a particular locale or when the organization serves a large geographical area. The divisional structure provides the organization with several distinct sub-units with considerable autonomy. This structural type allows for rapid and differentiated response to local environmental demands, focuses accountability and retains a degree of functional specialization. Because the divisions are semi-autonomous and can be made clearly accountable for expenditure and performance; however, competition, rivalry and dysfunctional jealousies can develop between divisions. Also, because each division must obtain selected resources from central office and accept central management costs (e.g., research and development), the negotiation processes can become inefficient and acrimonious. Most importantly semi-autonomous divisions may lead to policy inconsistencies which are particularly problematic for social service organizations.

Centralization and Decentralization

In common with other authors, Pearce and Robinson postulate that decision making systems must reflect the goals, tasks, staff, and culture of the organization.[92] Hence, if the organization aims at accomplishing large scale tasks of a relatively uniform nature, then this should be reflected in the organization's design. The centralized decision-making characteristics of bureaucracy are seen as ideally suited to the completion of large scale tasks with an assurance of equality of outcome and stability over time.[93] The growth of welfare services following World War II was characterized by the growth of welfare bureaucracies, as the organizational form of choice.[94] The bureaucratic organizational form became prevalent in twentieth century industrialization because:

> Bureaucracy, as a form of organization, enabled enterprises to transcend the limits of direct, extensive

> and formal control in commerce and business either by paternalistic owners, or, in governance more specifically political, the role of traditional or charismatic persons.[95]

With the growth of welfare services and the legislation enacted to provide universal, integrated and comprehensive services,[96] centralized bureaucracies grew as the organizational form best suited to accomplish large scale tasks in a spirit of equality and impartiality.[97]

One of the key characteristics of bureaucracy is its centralization of power and authority. Centralization refers to the "distribution of power among the actors in a social system"[98] and involves four separate but related issues: who participates in the decision making process, how widespread is the participation, at what level in the system are the decision makers and how concentrated is the distribution of authority to make decisions. In social service organizations, decentralization, the distribution of authority to the lowest level required for accountability, is argued to be imperative to ensure responsive service delivery.

> Decentralized units would be far more likely to develop routines consistent with responsive and efficient client treatment, than authorities removed from the scene, particularly if outside audits are continually able to draw attention to issues of service quality.[99]

Wineman offered additional support for decentralized social service systems by postulating that centralization, with its tendency to homogenize and to produce mass culture, was "unresponsive to local indigenous cultures and community life"[100] in comparison to more decentralized systems.

A high degree of decentralization, however, can weaken commitment to organizational goals as the decentralized units emphasize their sub-unit goals. If the sub-units are expected by the organization to be responsive to the needs of their local clientele, the sub-units are subject to the demands of strong interest groups or influential individuals to the detriment of other legitimate groups. Personnel in subunits can become so specialized that their contribution to the parent organization becomes limited. In the delivery of social services, decentralization gains in responsiveness to local needs what it loses in universality and standardization of services.[101]

> When delegation occurs in organizations this tends to increase the amount of training in specialized competencies. Also delegation increases the difference between organizational goals and achievement and thereby allows for more delegation. . . [This] can lead to increased conflict among the sub-units of the organization so that the content of decisions depends upon internal strategy. Even greater differences arise then between the goals of the organization and achievement so that there is further delegation.[102]

An important task of organizational managers in social service agencies is to achieve the best balance between centralized and decentralized features to meet the changing goals of the organization. Managers of public welfare organizations are cognizant of the conflicting goals of equality and equity and notions of responsiveness to special group or individual needs. Hollingsworth and Hanneman in their international study postulated that:

> Centralization has strong effects on distributional equality. More centralized systems . . . tend to generate more equal outcomes than less centralized structures . . . [because] centralized systems tend to treat social groups in a standardized manner for reasons of administrative 'rationality' and 'efficiency'. . . [they] tend to distribute resources across regions more equitably then decentralized systems . . . [they] have a far greater capacity to redistribute resources than less centralized ones . . . This 'relative autonomy' gives centralized systems a capacity to distribute resources and rewards according to policy preference, rather than in response to 'market' pressures.[103]

They contend that with a high degree of centralization both increased bureaucratization and professionalism occur. As a consequence of these two processes, Hollingsworth and Hanneman observed a decline of broad participation in the governing process, a view which is consistent with Hadley and Hatch's assertions[104] regarding participation in representative systems discussed earlier. In centralized and bureaucratized systems, highly specialized and influential interest groups, e.g., professional associations and specialist experts are the participants in the governing process, rather than clients or the community.

Management Style

Decision making systems and participation are linked through the exercise of management style. This can be defined as the way in which managers spend their time, what they do and how they go about doing it.[105] Scientific Management Theory placed decision making in the hands of the designated managers. Clegg and Dunkerly argued the rationality of bureaucracy was embodied in Scientific Management Theory because:

> This system was the apotheosis of the modern system of capitalism . . . the bearer of the underlying and defining spirit (geist) of modernity: rational organization.[106]

Scientific Management Theory, as developed by Taylor early in the 20th century, emphasized the division of labour, work measurement, individualized work, the development of management thinking, managerial control of the work process and the separation of manual and non-manual labour. It was a theory of management well suited to the bureaucratic form of organization. Scientific Management Theory also emphasized the role of the manager as distinct from the worker. It was the manager's responsibility to discover the 'one best way' to accomplish a task to maximize work efficiency. The theoretical development of Scientific Management and related theories was guided by the view of people as an economic one, motivated primarily by economic incentives. The role of management was seen as concerned with efficiency and motivating the worker through monetary reward and coercive power.

The Administrative Management School, as a splinter school of Scientific Management, further developed the conceptualizations of the functions of the executive (referred to in the acronym POSDCORB) and designated three types of personnel in organizations: line, staff and support. Line personnel are employees with the authority and responsibility to carry out the main objective of the organization. Staff personnel advise, counsel and provide technical expertise to line personnel and top executives. Support staff provide the housekeeping or auxiliary service required by the organization.[107]

An opposing view of the role of management, although little heeded until after the period of the classical theory development (1900s-

1920s), was promulgated by the Human Relations Movement whose emphasis:

> Shifted from the formal structure to the informal patterns of behavior caused by the physical and social conditions surrounding the participants in the work situation.[108]

The Human Relations Movement drew attention to the organization as a social entity comprised of individuals with their own needs and desires, of individuals as members of informal groups, and as individuals as members of groups with intergroup relationships. Human Relations Theory postulated that management styles and leadership patterns must be conceptualized so as to include democratic, as opposed to authoritarian, styles of management. In particular, Human Relations Theory, emphasized the importance of employee participation in work planning and design within an effective communication/feedback system. These two major schools of management which provide the base source material for contemporary theories of management, were heavily debated within the Department of Social Welfare, particularly following the release of the Report of the Administrative Review Committee[109] which recommended the Department move from an 'administrative' to a 'participatory' style of management.[110]

Participation

Hollingsworth and Hanneman argued that centralization and participation should be conceptualized as distinct and independent approaches to the study of power in organizations. They contend that although centralized systems may limit direct participation of individuals outside the organization in decision making, they do not necessarily limit the influence and pressure that groups are able to bring to bear on decision makers. They argue that participation in decentralized systems may not be what it seems because of the four elements they delineated: who participates in the decision making process, how widespread is the participation, at what level in the system are the decision makers and how concentrated is the distribution of authority to make decisions. The answer to each element must be thoroughly considered before the degree of participation in decision making by individuals both inside and outside the organization can be evaluated.

> Thus, once higher levels of decision making exist in a delivery system, the capacity of groups to participate effectively in the decision-making process is inversely proportional to system size, the degree of social heterogeneity in the society, and the degree of technological complexity in the system.[111]

Decentralization can then effectively decrease participation in decision-making as the level of participation increases. This occurs when the scope of the decision is narrowed (e.g., for only a small spatial segment of the society at the local level), or when the parameters of the decision are so limited as to render the degree of choice severely circumscribed.

Barber argues that one fundamental characteristic of strong democracy is broad participation. Democracy is:

> Politics in the participatory mode: literally, it is self government by citizens rather than representative government in the name of citizens . . . Self government is carried on through institutions designed to facilitate on-going civic participation in agenda-setting, deliberation, legislation and policy implementation.[112]

This offers a possible explanation for the unprecedented growth of participatory mechanisms created in New Zealand and pledged as part of the platform for the Labour Party Campaign in 1984.[113] This followed years of strong leadership by the National Party Prime Minister, Robert Muldoon and the dominance of expert opinion exemplified in the passage of the National Development Bill. This Act effectively curtailed public participation and increased the power of the executive in decision-making in the planning process for works of national importance while relegating the judiciary to an advisory role.[114]

Another perspective on participation and relationship with leadership and expertiseis offered by Gilbert and Specht who contend that participation, leadership and expertise compete for governance in the management of community affairs. The essential relationship between participation, leadership and expertise is competition; this is because the ascendancy of one of the three is inversely related to the other two. Deference to strong leaders or professional 'experts' will over time lead to a sense of alienation from government and social agencies followed by demands for greater participation. A high degree of participation over a period of time will lead to the identification of a leader or a growing reliance on experts particularly if the issues being dealt with are perceived to be 'technical' or 'intractable'.

> Participation becomes the primary value in community governance when leadership or expertise are perceived to be unresponsive to those being led or served.[115]

Resistance to decentralization of services and participation by clients, client groups and the wider community is based in part on the deference given to expert professional social service workers in planning for the provision of services. It is also based on the assumption that standards and universality of service are inherent in centralized social services.

> The assumption behind post-war welfare policy has been that uniform models of administration will produce equitable access to services. There has been an inherent resistance to any great decentralization or diversity in administering state benefits and services.[116]

Bamford reflects this resistance to decentralization in his work on social service management by arguing for the retention of centralized planning and policy making in the name of equality and accessibility.[117] In the Hadley and Hatch Participatory Model of Social Service Delivery,[118] the client is seen having an active role in the social service delivery system as a recipient, planner and provider. The role of the professional as 'expert' is limited to the professionals' immediate area of expertise. The professional is seen as part, but only a part, of the team.

Hadley and Hatch argue for participation in decision-making for staff. For them, it is only through participatory mechanisms that creative, innovative, effective and efficient service delivery can be assured. However, staff participation within organizations can have multiple meanings:

> To the workers, it may suggest increased autonomy, more control over resources and greater collaboration with peers in designing work activities. To the manager, participation may mean nothing more than consultation on matters of minor importance, or

> from the workers' perspective, co-optation and tokenism.[119]

Weatherley[120] places responsibility on the manager to clarify the meaning and exercise of participation with staff to avoid worker dissatisfaction and the lowering morale.

These issues of organizational design will be discussed in the New Zealand context. The final section of this chapter examines the two issues of social work practice addressed in the analytical framework and conceptualized in the Pearce and Robinson Model as related to organizational performance: social work professionalism and the social work task.

SOCIAL WORK PRACTICE

It is argued that it is social workers, who as the identified occupational group within the social service system, are charged with the responsibility of implementing the models of social service delivery. This is not to diminish their role in formulating and implementing models of social service delivery but to emphasize that social service delivery is accomplished primarily through the efforts of social workers at the front line and subsequently through the efforts of other human service or social service personnel. The nature of the relationship between professional social workers and their employing agency has consistently been an issue in the social work literature.[121]

From this extensive literature, two aspects of the nature of the relationship between social workers and their employing organizations were deemed to be central to the present analysis: the professionalization of social work and the definition of the social work task. This latter issue is concerned with the balance of social work activity devoted to individualized casework interventions (considered as primarily ameliorative or remedial) and those activities devoted to community work, community development and social action (considered as primarily preventative). A review of social work literature revealed ongoing, and frequently acrimonious debates about the professionalization of social work, on 'the purpose of social work' and the predominance of casework or community work as the focus of social work practice.[122] In these debates, radical social work theorists were prompted to contend that social work had become "an arm of the state."[123] The following discussion will examine these two issues.

Professionalization of Social Work

The terms profession, professional, and professionalization have multiple and indistinct meanings. Profession refers to an occupational group and professional to either an individual in that occupational group or work performed competently, to at least a minimum standard.[124] Professionalization may be viewed as the process through which an occupation acquires the traits associated with the status of a profession or "the socialisation process by which individuals are drawn into the institutional context of a particular occupation."[125]

Initially academic debate concerned itself with establishing the meaning of the term 'profession' and attempts to delineate the traits or characteristics of a profession in order to determine whether or not a given occupation could be rightly described as a profession.[126] Such endeavours led to a confusing array of lists, claims and counterclaims about the validity of the claim to professional status. The trait approach assumed that professional work could be deemed substantially different from other work, that an archetypal or ideal type exists, and that the status of traits can be clarified. However, no empirical work could substantiate the assumptions.[127]

The trait model of professionalism and its application to social work can be traced to a 1915 conference paper by Flexner who contended that social work was not a profession.[128] Fifty years later, Ernest Greenwood argued on the basis of the five distinguishing attributes of a profession that he assembled (systematic theory, community sanction, authority, an ethical code and a professional culture) that social work had acquired professional standing in society. But, he warned:

> The attainment of professional prestige, authority and monopoly by social workers will undoubtedly carry disturbing implications for the social action and social reform components of social work philosophy.[129]

Greenwood recognized that the professionalization of social work through the acquisition of those traits associated with professions, would have secondary effects on the pursuit of social work's dual commitment to individual and social change.

Wilding argues that the trait approach fails to consider the "the essential reality of professionalism-privilege and power."[130] It is this reality that lies at the heart of the critical perspective of professions.

The critical perspective on professions, exemplified by theorists such as Friedson, Johnson, and Wilding[131] addressed the questions of why an occupational group aspires to achieve professional recognition, why a particular occupation group gains or is granted special privileges by the state and what effect that recognition has on the relationships of the occupational group with recipients of services, with society and with other professions. The authority granted to professions by the state enable the more powerful professions to establish institutionalized forms of control over both their members and their clients. Professions represent to Friedson the winners in a societal conflict struggle for power and control. He argues that professions by virtue of their expertise can seek to gain control of their own terms of work, entry into the profession, regulation of their members and sole evaluation of their performance.

Johnson[132] proposed a typology for the critical analysis of professions based on the power and control dynamic between the producer and the consumer. The first type of producer-consumer relationship rests on collegiate control and is most similar to what is termed 'traditional' professionalism. In this relationship it is the producer, who along with the professional association, who defines the needs of the consumer and the manner in which these needs are met. The consumer is viewed as passive and considered to be virtually ignorant of the service provided.

Under patronage, it is the consumers who define their needs and the manner in which they are to be met. The consumer is seen as holding the power and control over the type of service to be provided and under what conditions the provision will take place. The producer provides the service or product directly to the consumer. The consumer can be a community or a corporation. In the third type of producer-consumer relationship, a third party mediates the relationship between the producer and the consumer, often assuming wide powers in defining needs and the manner in which they can be and are to be met. Johnson argues state mediation in the social services has led to the establishment of universal benefits and services regardless of means.

> The effect of state mediation has been to extend services to consumers who are defined on the basis of 'citizenship' rather than social origin or the ability to pay fees.[133]

Johnson acknowledged that it was possible for the mediated relationship to acquire the characteristics described in a patronage or in a 'traditional' professional relationship. Such an acknowledgment, he argued, demonstrates the dynamic quality of power and control relationships. He argued that within social work, the power relationship existing between practitioner and client:

> May be such . . . as to enable the practitioner to increase social distance and his [sic] own autonomy and control over practice by engaging in a process of 'mystification'.[134]

Johnson's typology offers a method of analyzing changes in the professional relationship between social workers as 'producers' and their clients as 'consumers' in the two models of social service delivery discussed here. In the welfare state model, the centralized bureaucracies fostered the growth of social work professionalism through its reliance on experts and by encouraging a more traditional professional relationship between social workers and their clients. Conversely, the welfare society model emphasizes (a) negotiated relationships between the social worker and the clients, (b) participation in service planning and (c) client evaluation and monitoring of services. Characteristics of this relationship between social workers and their clients in the welfare society model approaches the patronage type of relationship Johnson delineated.

Wilding extends the power and control arguments of Friedson and Johnson by contending that a state does not permit the transfer of power to a professional group, which he describes as basically a self-interest group, without assurances.

> Professionals have to show that, by their social standing or through their work, they help to support and maintain and strengthen the existing economic, social and political order.[135]

Hence, Wilding argues that the privileges of professional status are the result of an alliance between the state and the profession in which the profession performs important social functions for the state. These functions include standing as an expression of state concern for private troubles which have been accepted as public issues, legitimizing state action and providing status jobs for the elite and middle classes. The state in turn enforces both licensing and monopoly. The reciprocity of the relationship is clear in the medical profession.[136] The tenuousness of this relationship is evident in the case of social work.[137] Because of social work's commitment to social action, justice, equity and equality, social work has not consistently supported dominant state interests.

This both helps to explain why social work has not received universal acceptance of its claim to professional status and why the state has been reluctant to establish and enforce licensing of social workers.[138]

Because the professions stand as an expression of state concern for private troubles, Wilding argues that the expansion of welfare state policies have played a major role in corresponding growth in the welfare professions of medicine/health, education and social services/social work.

> The professions are not an unimportant part of the state machine. They operate essentially as a force for social control in its broadest sense. . . to locate the causes of delinquency and deviance safely within the individual rather than in the economic and social system.[139]

For social work, the implications are profound since the concentration on the private troubles of individuals is seen to lead "to a narrow view of the professional task and a neglect of what are equally proper professional responsibilities."[140] The task of social work (which will be discussed in the next sub-section) has always been seen as two-fold: individual and social change. It is the practice of social change responsibilities that has generated heated debate within social work exemplified in the work of the radical social work theorists.

Radical social work theorists[141] criticize the growth of professionalism in social work as deflecting social work from its commitment to social action by emphasizing singular interventions based on individual pathological explanations for social problems. Galper defines radical social as social work that:

> Contributes to building a movement for the transformation to socialism in and through the social services.[142]

Thus, to Galper radical social work is inherently socialist and critical of what is seen as an alliance with the dominant interest of the state as a precondition of professional status. However, as Timms and Timms point out:

> Radical social workers share neither the same political philosophy nor the same vision of an altered social work practice.[143]

Radical social workers also criticize self-imposed strictures on professional relationships with clients, colleagues and society that accompany professional training. It is those parameters on client-worker relationships that the radical social work theorists argue constrain effective participation of clients.

The participation of the client in the helping process is problematic for social work professionalization because professionalism is built on the assumption of expertise, monopoly and confidentiality. Social work has as one of its basic values that of self-determination which implies that the client has a central role in determining the form, content and outcome of social work intervention. Timms and Timms drew on the work of Keith-Lucas in their discussion of the principle of self determination. They defined self-determination as containing two distinct principles: client participation in the solutions of problems and the non-interference of the social worker except in essentials. Such a value, Timms and Timms argue compromises professionalism in its traditional sense, thus, making problematic social work's continued pursuit of professional status while attempting to retain the commitment of social work practice to social justice.

Efforts to promote social work professionalism may be further impeded by the organizational base in which social work typically is practiced. Black and colleagues argue that rather than conceptualizing social service organizations as bureaucratic where formal authority, backed by well-defined rules and procedures, is vested higher up the managerial hierarchy, "social service departments appear to have more in common with matrix organizations."[144] In matrix organizations the normal vertical hierarchy is overlaid by lateral authority, in this case professional discretion, which gives workers at the lowest levels of the hierarchy decision making authority. Whilst the literature suggests matrix organizations are appropriate in managing situations of uncertainly or rapid change typical in the personal social services, Black and colleagues raise the caution that where executive decision-making is decentralized to workers in front-line units, uncertainties and conflict may arise from imbalances between professional and bureaucratic authority.

> Moreover, whilst social workers have a considerable measure of professional autonomy, they are at the very periphery of their employing organizations and distant from the source of bureaucratic power.[145]

The debate is carried further in the work of Lipsky who argued that even with a high degree of centralization:

> The decisions of street-level bureaucrats [e.g., social workers], the routines they establish and the devices they invent to cope with uncertainties and work pressures, effectively *become* [sic] the public policies they carry out.[146]

Lipsky asserts the existence of a discrepancy between policy declaration and policy implementation at the interface of the client and the practitioner (whom he describes as the 'street level bureaucrat'). This discrepancy has its roots not only in the contradictory value system of the bureaucracy and the professional but in the "contradictory impulses of the society the agency serves."[147] Lipsky contends that "it is easier to change articulated policy from the top than to change practice from below."[148] Practice is rooted in a professional value system and in defense mechanisms developed to ensure survival on the job. This is further compounded in times of 'fiscal crisis' when employees are faced with revenue limitations and/or hiring freezes which result in the distribution of tasks among those remaining without reducing responsibilities they currently hold or without increased compensation.

> If qualitative aspects of service delivery are neglected, cost reductions and volume receive more attention as workers and managers accommodate their behavior to agency signals of priorities. This contributes to the self-fulfilling prophecy of the ineffectiveness and ultimate irrelevance of social services, even though the human needs for nurturing, protection, support, and assistance remain unanswered. Thus the tones of the fiscal crisis may linger, even if the budgetary alarms of the current period are eventually quieted.[149]

It is clear from this review that a direct relationship between articulated policy from the top and practice at the front line is far from assured. Practitioners at the front line are ultimately responsible for the implementation of policy but their performance is subject to many forces including professional values and the realities of their workload.

As was discussed earlier in the chapter in the section on models of social service delivery, the welfare state model is associated with the further development of social work professionalization. The welfare society envisions a role for the professional social worker as an input but the boundaries of that role are strictly confined. The professional social worker is seen as only as one member of the team. This positioning implies minimizing the power differential between client and worker through recognition and utilization of the client in service planning and provision.

The Social Work Task

Morales and Sheafor entitled their text on social work, *Social Work: A Profession of Many Faces*[150] to exemplify the range of social science knowledge involved in the diverse tasks, skills, and competencies encompassed by the term social work. Despite the problems surrounding the definition of social work, social work theorists do agree that its practice is concerned with individuals in their social environment. Social work is seen as a process of planned change that requires intervention in the personal, familial and societal spheres of a person's life.[151] The balance of emphasis on individual change efforts and change efforts aimed at the social environment varies in the definitions and in practice over time. Note the differences in emphasis evident in the following two widely quoted definitions:

> Social work seeks to enhance the social functioning of individuals, singly and in groups, by activities focused upon their social relationships which constitute the interaction between man [sic] and his environment. These activities can be grouped into three functions: restoration of impaired capacity, provision of individual and social resources and prevention of social dysfunction.[152]

> Social Work is concerned with the interaction between people and their social environment which affects the ability of people to accomplish their life tasks, alleviate distress and realize their aspirations and values. The purpose of social work, therefore, is to (1) enhance the problem-solving and coping capacities of people, (2) link people with systems that provide them with resources, services and opportunities, (3) provide the effective and human operation of these systems, and (4) contribute to the development and improvement of social policy.[153]

Although the shift in balance may be subtle, it is none the less significant because of its implications for social work practice and the tasks that constitute that practice. The second definition lays responsibility on social work to both consider, and to engage in changing, social policy as it affects on a client's life. It is the lack of social action that lead Hunt to argue, as do the radical social work theorists, that:

> Traditional social work is about adaptions, it is a form of social control rather than social change, it is manipulative, profoundly conservative, it colludes with the injustice of a divided and profoundly unequal society.[154]

Yet, social work historically has a firm base in social action and social change. Social work traces its beginnings back to the Settlement House Movement which was essentially a social change movement aimed at the amelioration of the poverty and unemployment made prevalent in the cycles of economic recession associated with early twentieth century industrialization.[155] The emphasis in social work shifts periodically to emphasise on the individual as the system of intervention. The shift to individual interventions in the 1940s and 1950s was due in part to the relative prosperity in the West and to the development of empirically tested, scientific theories of intervention with the individual and small groups. However, social work theorists maintained their theoretical commitment to social change.

> Social work is in danger . . . of failing to make its proper, distinctive and appropriate contribution to the alleviation and prevention of social ills through participating in the formulation of social policy, the development and modification of social welfare programs and through the distinctive methods conceived as ways of implementing social agency programs.[156]

Middleman and Goldberg[157] were specific in their conceptualization of the dual focus of the social work task when they contended that social workers had the responsibility as practitioners to address themselves to changing oppressive economic and social structures. Heated debate within social work centered on how to fulfil the dual commitment of social work. This is exemplified in Chambers' directive that the client's surroundings demand "every bit as much care and attention from the working professional as family, community, psychological and work factors"[158] and in the call for radical social change evident in the writings of Corrigan and Leonard, Galper, and Bailey and Brake.[159] The social work crisis in the 1970s was a reflection of the imbalance evident by the dominance of casework as *the* social work method of choice and of the empirical studies that questioned the effectiveness of social work.

> Thus, not only has professional casework failed to demonstrate that it is effective, but lack of effectiveness appears to be the rule rather than the exception across several categories of client' problems, situations, and types of casework.[160]

One extensive study into the practice of social work in statutory agencies was completed by Black and colleagues in Britain. They found that not only did social workers feel ambivalent about community work and social action as an integral part of social work, but only one of the trained social workers in their study felt equipped to engage in this level of intervention. Thus raising questions about the professional training of social workers emphasizing individual interventions at the expense of social action skills knowledge. Furthermore, they concluded that social worker's function in the political context as employees in large state bureaucracies with defined, statutory duties.

> Thus, the reluctance of social workers to depart from a relatively narrow interpretation of their role simply reflects the occupational mandate they have been given and their accountability to their employer. . . . The management system and the workload pressures meant social workers neither had the time nor were given the encouragement to innovate or challenge policy or practice.[161]

The constraints of the agency[162] and the limitations imposed on social work practice in statutory agencies has been noted repeatedly.[163] It was these constraints that Black et al. argued contributed to a case-by-case approach with clients.

Hadley and McGrath in the introduction to their study of community-centred teams lamented the dominant 'client-centred' philosophy of most of Britain's Social Service Departments. Hadley and McGrath contend that the client-centred approach reflects three main factors:

> The social worker's view of the individual user's web of personal relationships in contemporary society; the second concerns the dominant models of professionalism in social work and other social services occupations and related attitudes to the job; the third is the effect of the legislative framework of the personal social services and the character of the political system of which they form a part.[164]

Stein, in her discussion of the efforts to build a unified social work theory in the late 1960s into the 1970s, concluded:

> This conceptual framework was expected to advance and unify social work theory and practice resulting in the dissolution of traditional method compartmentalizations.[165]

Such efforts continued throughout the 1970's. Siporin, in the introduction to his text, *Introduction to Social Work Practice*,[166] which was widely use in the United States[167] and in New Zealand articulated:

> A generic framework for the scientific practice of social work. . . . It offers bridges between social work, clinical and therapeutic orientations and activities, and those of community planning, social policy and administration and social action.[168]

Despite professional and theoretical commitment to the dual focus of social work, despite the fervent calls for re-evaluation of casework and implementation of radical social work.

> Professionalism, epitomized by individually focused case-work and its principles and methods, remains at the heart of social work practice.[169]

Black and colleagues contend that social work practice is constrained by the statutory organization's power of legitimizing practice modalities and the entrenched accountability system of the state bureaucracies. This situation will worsen, they argue, because of the increasing implementation of quantitative managerial systems which will further entrench quantitative individualistic interventions. There is some contrary empirical evidence to support the proposition that social workers in small, voluntary agencies are more likely to engage in community work and social action than their counterparts in the statutory sector.[170]

The function of organizational strategic policy is to set the goals, objectives, standards, and methods of practice within broad guidelines. The degree of specification in the guidelines differ from agency to agency, and in fact may differ within agency programmes. Those programs delivering services mandated by legislation/statute are governed more closely by detailed policies and procedures, e.g. child protective services as compared with services to the elderly. Lipsky argues that 'street-level bureaucrats', defined as "public service workers who interact with citizens in the course of their jobs and who have substantial discretion in the execution of their work"[171] are not passive functionaries to agency policy.

> Not only do street-level bureaucrats exercise discretion to such an extent that they are not easily affected by policy articulation from the top. . . . The character of worker-client and worker-supervisor relations, no matter what the articulated organizational policy, is likely to reflect the dominant bureaucratic relations of the society, no matter what the administrative guidelines provide.[172]

This theme is repeated by Gilbert and Specht in their discussion of the relevance of policy for practitioners:

> Experienced practitioners often exercise considerable discretion in executing broad directives and so shape as well as discharge the requirements of organizational policies. . . . The importance of the direct-service practitioner's discretion for policy interpretation increases as organizations grow larger and more complex.[173]

These observations highlight the centrality of the relationship between strategy (i.e. policy) and performance (in this instance the social work task) as postulated in the Pearce and Robinson model (1989). It is at the interface between the practitioner and the client in the final analysis that policy is articulated. In this regard it is anticipated that there will be a measure of congruence between the overall strategy as set out in the organizations goals and the objectives pursued by practitioners.

SUMMARY

The influence of the emerging paradigm in organizational analysis is evident in the emphasis of the analytical framework on vertical and horizontal contexts and in the qualitative research techniques that form the research methodology to be described in Chapter Three. The analytic framework utilized the multi-level explanatory model developed by Pearce and Robinson[174] to explore the relationship between organizational strategy, design and performance. The first level analyses the meanings of welfare state and welfare society and proposes that a shift has taken place. Several factors that contributed to the shift were explored. The proposed shift was explored through the debates on the crisis of the welfare state and in the consideration of alternative models of social service delivery that purported to address the criticisms and fiscal constraints affecting welfare state policies.

Two models of social service delivery were compared: the welfare state model as articulated by Titmuss[175] and a welfare society model as promulgated by Hadley and colleagues.[176] The role of the state in service provision and role of the voluntary sector in each of the models was examined. Characteristics of organizational design were discussed in the second level of analysis which addressed aspects of organizational design including organizational structure, the dilemmas of centralization/decentralization, management style and participation

It has been argued that a strategy designed to implement a welfare state model of social service delivery would demand an organizational design based on centralized services and a professionally-trained staff responsible for the provision of services. Staff performance would focus on pre-determined services with minimal participation of clients in the planning and provision of services: moreover the definition of the social work task would be clearly aligned with organizational expectations. Although, aspects of performance in social work are not as clearly articulated in the welfare society model, social workers were expected to alter their performance by addressing issues of responsiveness to client needs, promoting higher levels of client participation and to redefining professionalism with a view to reducing the power differential between client and worker. These issues of performance will be discussed as the implementation of the welfare state strategy and New Zealand is explored.

The next chapter will describe New Zealand, the Department of Social Welfare and social work in the 1980s.

NOTES

1. Richard Titmuss, *Social Policy: An Introduction*, ed. Brian Abel-Smith and Kay Titmuss (London: George Allen and Unwin Ltd, 1974); Richard Titmuss, *Essays on 'The 'Welfare State'* 3d ed (London: George Allen and Unwin Ltd, 1976).

2. Roger Hadley and Stephen Hatch, *Social Welfare and the Failure of the State: Centralized Social Services and Participatory Alternatives* (London: George Allen and Unwin Ltd, 1981; Roger Hadley and Morag McGrath, eds., *Going Local: Neighbourhood Social Services* National Council for Voluntary Organisations, Occasional Paper 1 (London: Bedford Square Press, 1984); Roger Hadley, Peter Dale and Patrick Sills, *Decentralising Social Services*, National Council of Voluntary Organisations (London: Bedford Square Press, 1984).

3. John A. Pearce, II and Richard B. Robinson, Jr., *Management* (Singapore: McGraw-Hill International Editions. 1989).

4. Yvonna S. Lincoln, ed., *Organizational Theory and Inquiry: The Paradigm Revolution* (Beverly Hills: Sage Publications, 1985); Egon G. Guba, "The Context of Emergent Paradigm Research," in *Organization Theory and Inquiry: The Paradigm Revolution*, ed.Yvonna S. Lincoln (Beverly Hills: Sage Publications, 1985), 79-105; Karl Weick, "Sources of Order in Underorganized Systems: Themes in Recent Organizational Theory" in *Organization Theory and Inquiry: The Paradigm Revolution*, Yvonna S. Lincoln, ed. (Beverly Hills: Sage Publications, 1985), 106-136; Michael Reed, *Redirections in Organizational Analysis* (London: Tavistock Publications, 1985).

5. W. Richard Scott, "Health Care Organizations in the 1980's: The Convergence of Public and Professional Control Systems," in *Organizational Environments: Ritual and Rationality*, eds. John Meyer and W. Richard Scott (Beverly Hills: Sage Publications1983b), 99-114.

6. Lincoln, 9.

7. Weick, 109.

8. Ibid, 111.

9. H. Y. Siddiqui, "Social Policy in the Third World: A Third World Perspective," (Palmerston North: Massey University, Department of Social Policy and Social Work, 1987).

10. Franz-Xaver Kaufman, "Major Problems and Dimensions of the Welfare State," in *The Welfare State and Its Aftermath*, eds. S. N. Eisenstadt and Ora Ahimer (London: Croom Helm, 1985).

11. Norman Furniss and Timothy Tilton, *The Case for the Welfare State* (Bloomington: Indiana University Press, 1977).

12. A. H. Halsey, "Some Lessons from the Debate: A Sociologists Viewpoint," in *Organisation for Economic Cooperation and Development: An Account of the Conference on Social Policies in the 1980's* (Paris: OECD, 1981), 21.

13. Titmuss, *Social Policy;* Titmuss, *Essays;* Kaufman, "Major Problems"; William Oliver, "Social Policy in New Zealand: An Historical Overview", in *The April Report,* Royal Commission on Social Policy, Vol. I (Wellington: Government Printer, 1988), 3-45; Margaret Tennant, *Paupers and Providers (*Wellington: Allen and Unwin, N.Z. Limited, 1989).

14. Oliver, *Social Policy.*

15. Brian Easton, *Social Policy and the Welfare State in New Zealand* (Auckland: George Allen and Unwin, 1980).

16. Harold L. Wilensky and Charles N. Lebeaux, *Industrial Society and Social Welfare* 2d ed. (New York: The Free Press, 1965), 147.

17. Organisation for Economic Co-Operation and Development (OECD), *The Welfare State in Crisis: An Account of the Conference on Social Policies in the 1980s* (Paris: OECD, 1981); Vic George and Paul Wilding, *Ideology and Social Welfare* 2d ed. (London: Routledge and Kegan Paul, 1987).

18. Norman Johnson, *The Welfare State in Transition: The Theory and Practice of Welfare Pluralism* (Brighton, Sussex: Wheatsheaf Books, 1987).

19. George and Wilding.

20. Johnson.

21. OECD, 5.

22. Brian Easton, "The Unmaking of Roger Douglas" In *The Making of Rogernomics,* ed. Brian Easton (Auckland: University Press, 1989), 171-187; OECD; Ramesh Mishra, *The Welfare State in Crisis* (Brighton: Wheatsheaf, 1984); Kaufman.

23. William A. Robson, *Welfare State and Welfare Society* (London: George Allen and Unwin, Limited, 1976).

24. Robson, 175.

25. Mishra, xiii.

26. Evelyn Z. Brodkin, *The False Promise of Administrative Reform: Implementing Quality Control in Welfare* (Philadelphia: Temple University Press, 1986), 24.

27. S. N. Eisenstadt and Ora Ahimeir, eds. *The Welfare State and Its Aftermath* (London: Croom Helm, 1985), 2.

28. Brian Abel-Smith,"The Major Problems of the Welfare State: Defining the Issues." In *The Welfare State and Its Aftermath*, eds.

S. N. Eisenstadt and Ora Ahimeir (London: Croom Helm, 1985), 31-43; Kaufman; George and Wilding.

29. Barclay Report, *Social Workers: Their Role and Tasks* (London: Bedford Square Press, 1982).

30. For a discussion of the efficiency gaps and alleged secondary negative effects of the welfare state see Titmuss, *Social Policy,* Kaufman or Eisenstadt.

31. OECD; New Zealand Planning Council (NZPC), *Directions* (Government Printer: Wellington, 1981); New Zealand Planning Council (NZPC), *Who Makes Social Policy?* (Wellington: Government Printer, 1982); Peter Flora, "On the History and Current Problems of the Welfare State," in *The Welfare State and Its Aftermath,* eds. S. N. Eisenstadt and Ora Ahimeir (London: Croom Helm, 1985), 11-30.

32. OECD, 12.

33. Brij Mohan, *The Logic of Social Welfare: Conjectures and Formulations* (New York: St. Martin's Press, 1988), 82.

34. Hugh Oliver, "The Labour Caucus and Economic Policy Formation, 1981-1984" in *The Making of Rogernomics,* ed. Brian Easton (Auckland: University Press, 1989), 11-52.

35. Easton, 182.

36. For a complete discussion of these concepts see the 1965 work of Wilensky and Lebeaux.

37. Mohan, 40.

38. David Reisman, *Richard Titmuss: Welfare and Society* (London: Heinemann, 1977); Titmuss, *Social Policy.*

39. Hadley and Hatch, 1.

40. Reisman.

41. George and Wilding.

42. Reisman, 38.

43. Titmuss, *Social Policy,* 27.

44. George and Wilding, 90-91.

45. Susan A. Ostrander, Stuart Langton and Hon Van Til. eds. *Shifting the Debate* (New Brunswick: Transaction Books,1987).

46. Both Oliver in his work with the Royal Commission on Social Policy and Tennant have discussed this point with regard to New Zealand social services.

47. Johnson.

48. George and Wilding, 35.

49. Neil Gilbert and Harry Specht, *Dimensions of Social Welfare Policy* 2d ed. (Englewood Cliffs, NJ: Prentice-Hall, 1986), 35; Ken Judge, "The British Welfare State in Transition," in *Modern Welfare States: A Comparative View of Trends and Prospects,* ed.

Robert R. Freidman, Neil Gilbert, and Moshe Sherer (New York: University Press, 1987), 2.

50. Paul Spicker, *Principles of Social Welfare: An Introduction to Thinking About the Welfare State* (London: Routlege, 1988).

51. Johnson, 55.

52. Ibid, 199.

53. Ibid, 200.

54. Hadley and Hatch, vi.

55. J. Black, R. Bowl, D. Burns, C. Critcher, G. Grant, and D. Stockford, *Social Work in Context* (London: Tavistock, 1983).

56. Ibid, 206.

57. Lord Wolfenden, *The Future of Voluntary Organisation: Report of the Committee* (London: Croom Helm, 1977).

58. Hadley and Hatch, 45.

59. Ibid, 101.

60. Ibid, 29, 146-147.

61. Ibid, 147.

62. Ibid, 163-164.

63. George and Wilding, 144.

64. Ibid.

65. Robert A. Pinker, "Social Welfare and the Education of Social Workers" in *Approaches to Welfare*, eds. Philip Bean and Stewart Mac Pherson (London: Routledge and Kegan Paul, 1983), 150-165.

66. See Johnson for a discussion of this point.

67. Adam Graycar, "Informal, Voluntary and Statutory Services: The Couples Relationship," *British Journal of Social Work* 13 (1983): 393.

68. Robert A. Pinker, "Populism and the Social Services," *Social Policy Administration*, 18:1(1984) : 92.

69. Andrew Rowe, "Roger Hadley and Stephen Hatch: Social Welfare and the Failure of the State: A Book Review," *Journal of Social Policy*, 11(1982): 556.

70. David Billis, *Welfare Bureaucracies: Their Design and Change in Response to Social Problems* (London: Heinemann Educational Books, 1984), 53.

71. Graycar's comments are a strong reminder of the dangers of uncritically romanticizing community life.

72. Neil Small, "Community Social Work in China and Britain," *Social Policy and Administration* 18:2 (1984): 155.

73. Barclay Report, xvii.

74. See the Barclay Report for its conceptualization of community-centered social work practice, 198-218.

75. Hadley and McGrath, 15-17.

76. Ibid, 252.

77. Hadley, Dale, and Sills in their 1984 publication provides a detailed evaluation of the implementation of the patch system in a local social services department in Britain.

78. Charles Perrow, *Complex Organizations* 2d ed. (Glenview, IL: Scott Foresman and Company, 1973); Rosemary Sarri and Yeheskel Hasenfeld, eds. *Human Service Organizations* (New York: Columbia University Press, 1983); Dorothy Smith, "Front Line Organizations of the State Mental Hospital," *Administrative Science Quarterly* 10 (1964): 381-399;Stewart Clegg and David Dunkerley, *Organization, Class and Control* (London: Routledge and Kegan Paul, 1980); John Meyer and W. Richard Scott, eds. *Organizational Environments: Ritual and Rationality* (Beverly Hills: Sage Publications, 1983); J. Roger Hollingsworth and Robert Hanneman, *Centralization and Power in Social Service Delivery Systems* (Boston: Kluever, Nighoff Publishing, 1984).

79. For example see, Charles B. Handy, *Understanding Organizations* (Harmondsworth: Penguin, 1978).

80. See Myron E. Weiner, *Human Services Management: Analysis and Applications* (Homewood, IL: The Dorsey Press, 1982); Michael Reed, *Redirections in Organizational Analysis* (London: Tavistock Publications, 1985).

81. Gareth Morgan, *Images of Organizations* (Beverly Hills: Sage Publications, 1986).

82. Harold Koontz and Cyril O'Donnell, *Essentials of Management* 2d ed. (New York: McGraw Hill, 1978). See Meyer and Scott or Pearce and Robinson for recent developments of the concept of environment.

83. W. Richard Scott," The Organization of Environments: Network, Cultural and Historical Elements," in *Organizational Environments: Ritual and Rationality*, eds. John Meyer and W. Richard Scott (Beverly Hills: Sage Publications, 1983a): 155-178.

84. Reed, 100.

85. Pearce and Robinson, 346.

86. Ibid, 341.

87. Ibid, 344.

88. Eugene Litwak, "Organizational Constructs and Mega-Bureaucracy", in *Human Service Organizations*, eds. Rosemary Sarri and Yeheskel Hasenfeld (New York: Columbia University Press, 1978), 123-163.

89. Gilbert Smith, *Social Work and the Sociology of Organizations* 2d ed. (London: Routledge and Kegan Paul, 1979).

90. Pearce and Robinson, 345.

91. Pearce and Robinson and Stephen P. Robbins, *Organization Theory: The Structure and Design of Organizations* (Englewood Cliffs: Prentice-Hall, 1983) give detailed examples from industry.

92. Pearce and Robinson.

93. Weiner.

94. See Billis and David Howe, *Social Workers and their Practice in Welfare Bureaucracies* (Hants, England: Gower Publishing Company, 1986).

95. Weiner, 76.

96. Including the Seebohm Report in Britain in 1978 and the Department of Social Welfare Act, 1971 in New Zealand.

97. The strength of the bureaucracy in accomplishing large scale tasks is asserted by theorists including Smith, Billis and Howe.

98. Hollingsworth and Hanneman, 17-18.

99. Michael Lipsky, *Street-Level Bureaucracy: Dilemmas of the Individual in Public Services* (New York: Russell Sage Foundation, 1980), 207.

100. Steven Wineman, *The Politics of Human Services* (Boston: South End Press, 1984).

101. See Pearce and Robinson for a discussion of the negative impact of subunit specialization and Hollingsworth and Hanneman for further explanation of the dynamics of decentralization.

102. Clegg and Dunkerley, 188.

103. Hollingsworth and Hanneman, 5.

104. Hadley and Hatch.

105. R. H. Waterman, T. J. Peters and J. R. Phillips, "Structure is Not Organization," *Business Horizon* 23:1-3 (1983): 14-26.

106. Clegg and Dunkerley, 81.

107. The distinction both Weiner and Koontz and O'Donnell draw between line and staff positions became problematic in the Department of Social Welfare's post-1986 administrative structure which created the Regional Executive Officers as staff positions.

108. Weiner, 45.

109. Administrative Review Committee, *Performance and Efficiency in the Department of Social Welfare* (Wellington: Government Printer, December, 1987).

110. See Chapter Five for an explanation of these terms as used by the New Zealand Department of Social Welfare.

111. Hollingsworth and Hanneman, 100.

112. Benjamin Barber, *Strong Democracy: Participatory Politics for a New Age* (Berkeley: University of California Press, 1984), 151.

113. The growth of participatory mechanisms initiated by the Fourth Labour Government is documented in Chapter Four.

114. Ian Shirley, "Conclusion: Critical Practice as a Model for Development," in *Development Tracks*, ed. Ian Shirley (Palmerston North, Dunmore Press, 1982), 271-289.

115. Gilbert and Specht, 213.

116. Black, et al., 5.

117. Terry Bamford, *Managing Social Work* (London: Tavistock Publications, 1982).

118. Consider Table I which contrasts the role of the professional in the Hadley and Hatch model.

119. Richard A. Weatherley, "Participatory Management in Public Welfare: What are the Prospects?" *Administration in Social Work* 7:1 (1983): 39 -50.

120. bid.

121. See Ruth Elizabeth Smalley, *Theory for Social Work Practice* (New York: Columbia University Press, 1967); Roy Bailey and M. Brake, eds. *Radical Social Work* (New York: Pantheon Books,1975); Harry Specht and Anne Vickery, eds., *Integrating Social Work Methods* (London: George Allen and Unwin, 1977); Wilbur A. Finch, Jr., "Social Workers versus Bureaucracy," *Social Work* 21:5 (1976) : 370-375; Black, et al.; Howe.

122. For example Noel Timms and Rita Timms, *Perspectives* in *Social Work* (London: Routledge and Kegan Paul, 1977); David Webb, "Themes and Continuities in Radical - Traditional Social Work," *British Journal of Social Work* 11 (1981): 143-158; Barclay Report.

123. Jeffrey Galper, *Social Work Practice: A Radical Perspective* (Englewood Cliffs: Prentice Hall, 1980).

124. Kathleen Jones, John Brown, and Jonathan Bradshaw, *Issues in Social Policy* (London: Routledge and Kegan Paul, 1978).

125. Ibid, 61.

126. See for instance, Terence J. Johnson, *Professions and Power* (New York: Macmillan Publishing Company, 1972).

127. Wilding.

128. Wilding.

129. Ernest Greenwood quoted in Mohan, 65.

130. Wilding, 5.

131. Eliot Friedson, *Professional Dominance: The Social Structure of Medical Care* (Chicago: Aldine Publishing Company, 1970); Johnson; Wilding.

132. Johnson.

133. Ibid, 77.

135. Wilding, 12.

136. Ivan Illich, Irving Kenneth Zola, John McKnight, Jonathan Caplan, and Harley Shaiken, *Disabling Professions* (London: Marion Boyars Publishing Limited, 1977).

137. Nina Toren, *Social Work: The Case of a Semi-Profession* (Beverly Hills: Sage Publications, 1972).

138. Katrina Ings, "NZASW and the Professionalisation of New Zealand Social Workers," *New Zealand Association of Social Workers Journal* 1:11(1986): 3-6.

139. Wilding, 16.

140. Ibid, 97.

141. See Bailey and Brake, Galper, and Paul Corrigan and Peter Leonard, *Social Work Practice Under Capitalism: A Marxist Approach* (London: Macmillan Press, 1978).

142. Galper, 10.

143. Noel Timms and Rita Timms, *Dictionary of Social Welfare* (London: Routledge and Kegan Paul, 1982), 156.

144. Black, et al., 200.

145. Ibid, 201.

146. Lipsky, xii.

147. Ibid, 164.

148. Ibid, 187.

149. Ibid, 179.

150. Armando Morales and Bradford W. Sheafor, *Social Work: A Profession of Many Faces* 3d ed. (Boston: Allyn and Bacon, Inc., 1983).

151. Bertha Capen Reynolds, *Learning and Teaching in the Practice of Social Work* National Association of Social Workers, Classic Edition, 1985 (New York: Russell and Russell, 1942; Ruth Middleman and Gale Goldberg, *Social Service Delivery: A Structural Approach to Social Work Practice* (New York: Columbia University Press, 1974); Beulah R. Compton and Burt Galaway, *Social Work Processes* 4th ed (Belmont: Wadsworth Publishing Co., 1989); Rex Skidmore, Milton Thackery and O. William Farley, *Introduction to Social Work* 4th ed. (Englewood Cliffs: Prentice Hall, 1988).

153. Allen Pincus and Anne Minahan, *Social Work Practice: Model and Method* (Madison: University of Wisconsin Press, 1973), 9.

154. Leonard Hunt, "Social Work and Ideology," in *Philosophy and Social Work*, eds. Noel Timms and David Watson (London: Routledge and Kegan Paul, 1978), 10.

155. Morales and Sheafer; Charles Zastrow, *The Practice of Social Work* 2d ed. (Homewood, IL: Dorsey Press, 1985).

156. Smalley, xi.

157. Middleman and Goldberg.

158. Donald E. Chambers, *Social Policy and Social Programs: A Method for the Practical Public Policy Analyst* (New York: Macmillan Publishing, 1986).

159. Bailey and Brake; Corrigan and Leonard; Galper.

160. Joel Fischer, "Is Casework Effective: A Review," *Social Work* 18 (1973): 13-14.

161. Black, et al., 222-223.

162. Smalley; Compton and Galloway.

163. For example, Howe or Pauline Hardiker and Mary Barker, eds. *Theories of Practice in Social Work* (London: Academic Press, 1981).

164. Hadley and McGrath, 8.

165. Irma Stein, *System Theory, Science and Social Work* (Metuchen, NJ: The Scarecrow Press, Inc., 1974), 34.

166. Max Siporin, *Introduction to Social Work Practice* (New York: Macmillan Publishing Company, Inc., 1975).

167. Paul H. Ephross and Michael Reisch, "The Ideology of Some Social Work Texts," *Social Service Review* 56 (1982): 275-283.

168. Siporin, vii.

169. Black et al., 231.

170. Bradford W. Sheafor, *Social Work Practice in New Zealand* (Palmerston North: Massey University, 1982).

171. Lipsky, 3.

172. Ibid, 188.

173. Gilbert and Specht, 15.

174. Pearce and Robinson.

175. Titmuss, *Social Policy*; Titmuss, *Essays*; Reisman.

176. Hadley and Hatch; Hadley and McGrath; Hadley, Cooper, Dale, and Stacy.

II

NEW ZEALAND IN THE 1980s: THE COUNTRY, THE DEPARTMENT OF SOCIAL WELFARE AND SOCIAL WORK

In the mid-1980s, New Zealand was experiencing low economic growth, high inflation rates, a rising unemployment level, a drop in export demand and a rising balance of payments deficit. "The structure of the economy was still geared . . . towards exporting bulk farm products to Britain . . . while servicing a protected domestic market at home."[1] Changes in world wide economic relations, particulary Britain's entry into the European Economic Market in 1972, placed New Zealand in the position of exploring new trade partnerships in Far East, Asia and the Pacific Rim. New Zealanders were increasingly aware that "the overall picture of New Zealand's economic performance since the 1950s [was] one of long-term deterioration"[2] and that "In the ten years up to 1983, New Zealand's national income and living standards grew by less than half the average of those in other Western countries."[3] Economic change was perceived as inevitable and the election of the Fourth Labour Government in 1984 marked the beginning of rapid and radical change in economic policies based on market liberalization with the removal or reduction import/export quotas and regulations. What this represented was a rejection of the previously tightly controlled economy and an acceptance of monetarist policies through exposing the economy to 'market forces.' Under Roger Douglas as Finance Minister, and Rogernomics as his economic package was known, the economy of New Zealand experienced a metamorphosis that not only radically changed the economic relationships of New Zealand with the rest of the world, but also changed the economic relationships among New Zealanders as well.[4]

The political scene in New Zealand was also undergoing change. The election of the Fourth Labour Government promised relief from what many perceived as an unresponsive National Government led by the strong, irascible Robert Muldoon. After their election, the Fourth Labour Government launched a massive consultation process on governmental departments and services.[5] There was a high level of activity as organizations, agencies and individuals responded to the calls for participation through written and oral submissions. A sense of optimism ensued in the New Zealand people who hoped the consultation process would result in a viable set of solutions to the problems facing the country and mitigate the growing sense of pessimism about New Zealand's future.

Socially, several of New Zealand's self-perceptions were under threat. The lack of economic growth and the policies of the previous fifteen years had contributed to a steady rise in unemployment, a fall in the standard of living relative to other western nations, a growing polarization between the rich and the poor and a realization that the 'good life' for all New Zealanders was far from a reality. In particular, the *Pakeha* (European) New Zealander's view of racial harmony was seriously challenged when Maori activists presented empirical evidence to the contrary. The data showed that the indigenous people of New Zealand, the *tangata whenua* (people of the land), were disproportionately over-represented in the lower socio-economic groups, in measures of ill-health, such as infant mortality and low life expectancy, and in the institutions of welfare and justice.[6] As a consequence, social workers practitioners and educators were increasingly under challenge to respond to Maori welfare needs. The social work community initiated practice and program responses to the challenges, including a proliferation of anti-racism workshops to address the criticisms of personal and professional racism.

THE DEPARTMENT OF SOCIAL WELFARE

The Department of Social Welfare Act, 1971 legislated the amalgamation of the Child Welfare Division of the Department of Education and the Department of Social Security to create the Department of Social Welfare. As a government department, the Department of Social Welfare was responsible to Parliament as representative of the people of New Zealand through the Minister of Social Welfare.

The Department of Social Welfare budget grew from 7.0% of the Gross Domestic Product in 1971, to 10.1% in 1980 and to 10.71% in 1985 while Social Work Services expenditure lost ground as a percentage of Departmental budget (2.2% in 1975 compared with 2.1% in 1980). By 1985, the Social Work Division had gained only slightly on its 1975 percentage by representing 2.22% of the budget.[7] For the fiscal year 1986/87, the Department spent $6,175 million, the largest single vote in the Budget, employed a staff of 6,200, allocated benefits to one and one half million citizens of New Zealand's 3.4 million people, operated 19 institutions and 170 children's homes. Less than 3% of the budget was allocated to social work services.[8]

The expenditure on Social Work Services was approximately .03% of the total expenditure for fiscal year 1986-1987. The total expenditure in Vote: Social Welfare was 11.7% of the Gross Domestic Product.[9] These figures demonstrate the small percentage of the Department of Social Welfare budget allocated to social services as compared to the budget allocation for benefits, pensions and administration.

Prior to the restructuring, the Department of Social Welfare had a traditional bureaucratic structure headed by a Director-General and three Assistant Director-Generals each responsible for one of the three following divisions: Administration, Social Work, Benefits and Pensions. The Head Office, located in the nation's capital, Wellington, had direct line authority over the Department's 73 District Offices and Area Welfare Offices and the Department's 19 Institutions.[10] (See Figure One.) By 1987, five of the 19 institutions were closed "in favour of community based care."[11] Other changes in the Department following the restructuring, and discussed in the Introduction to Chapter Five, include the establishment of a regional office structure, the abolition of the Social Security Commission and the reorganization of Head Office.

Figure Two

THE ORGANIZATIONAL CHART OF THE DEPARTMENT OF SOCIAL WELFARE: HEAD OFFICE PRIOR TO 1986

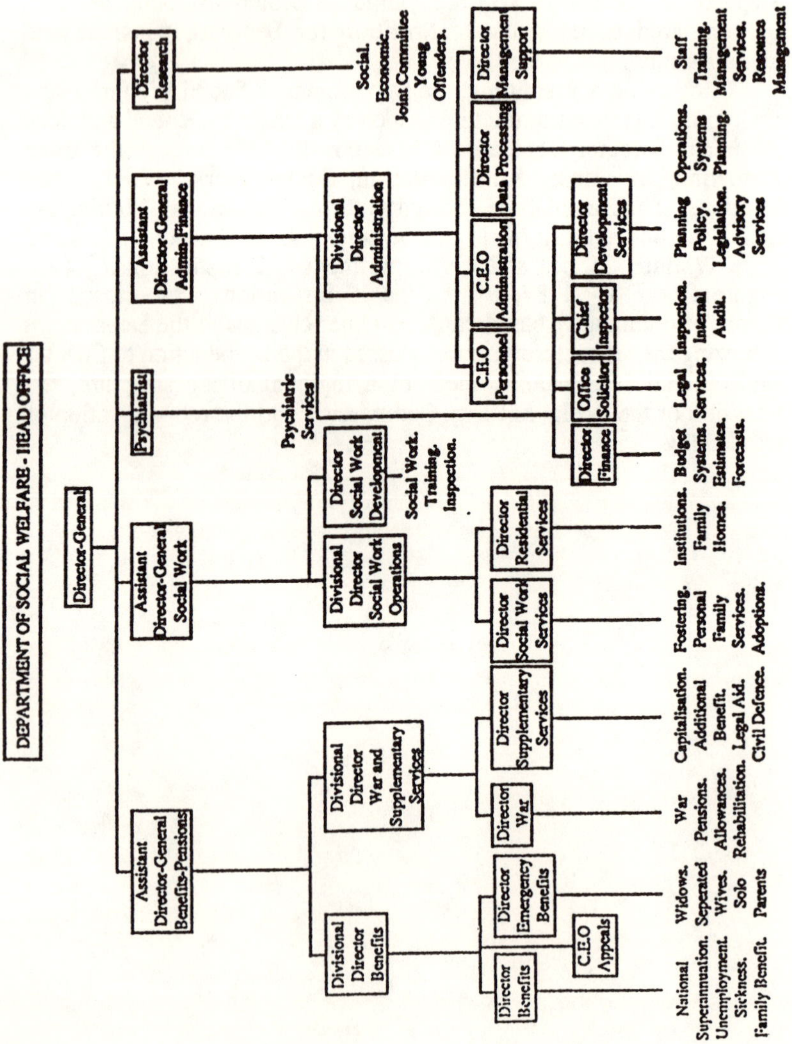

New Zealand had long been heralded as the social laboratory of the South Pacific with a comprehensive welfare system based on government provision beginning with the Old-age Pensions Act in 1898, through to the Social Security Act 1938, the Social Security Act of 1971 and the Superannuation Act of 1975.

> The advent of social security added a powerful component to the liberal-progressive model of welfare, and social security rapidly became the welfare apotheosis against which all provision was based.[12]

When the Department of Social Welfare Act, 1971, amalgamated the Social Security Department and the Child Welfare Division of the Department of Education to create the Department of Social Welfare as a centralized government agency, it was charged with the responsibility to:

> Encourage co-operation and co-ordination among organisations and individuals (including Departments of State and other agents of the Crown) engaged in social welfare activities.[13]

The Department was to accomplish these goals through a combination of direct service provision and indirect services to the voluntary sector including systems of funding, advice and administrative support. The 1972 Royal Commission on Social Security reaffirmed the responsibility of the community to give the dependent a standard of living "consistent with human dignity" relative to that enjoyed by the majority through a comprehensive system of benefits that would allow all to "feel a sense of *participation in* [sic] and *belonging to* [sic] the community" while supporting the need for co-ordination of all services contributing to the welfare of the nation.[14] The Royal Commission, therefore, reconfirmed the central role of the state in social welfare activities and established a social service delivery model based on the key role of government as funder and provider.

With the state as the main funder and provider of service, it was assumed that equality, accessibility and continuity of a quality universal service would prevail. Theoretical support for this view was found in the work of Richard Titmuss, Professor of Social Administration at the London School of Economics from 1951-1973. Titmuss articulated the application of Keynesian economic policies to social services. He clearly distrusted the 'market place' and emphasized the central role of the state in the social services.[15] Titmuss defined the role of the voluntary sector as innovator and supplemental to state provision. It was this welfare state model of social service delivery that guided social policy decisions in New Zealand up to 1986.[16]

One aim of the study was to explore possible explanations for the rejection of the existing social service delivery model based on the principles articulated by Titmuss.[17] The welfare state model, with its assumption of a high degree of collective responsibility, had dominated New Zealand social service policy for forty years. This research argues that the government adopted an alternative model, based on the principles of a 'welfare society' model as promulgated by Roger Hadley and colleagues at the University of Lancaster.[18] The model represents an application of monetarist economic policies to a social service delivery system. It is argued that the Hadley and Hatch Participatory Model of Social Service Delivery was adopted because it provided an alternative to the welfare state model of collective responsibility by emphasizing the responsibilities of the individual and the community; because it provided a theoretical rationale for reassessing welfare expenditure; and because it used the terminology of the proponents of a 'welfare society' model of service delivery voiced by New Zealand social policy analysts.[19]

The Hadley and Hatch model depends on a pluralist system of providers, focuses on a localized 'patch system' of integrated community based services, acknowledges informal care givers and prescribes a limited role for the state in direct service provision. There were strong indications at the time this research project was initiated that the Hadley model was being implemented. This research attempted to trace the influence of the Hadley and Hatch model by analyzing the social policy debates in the official publications and reports that set the stage for its implementation. Its adoption led to sweeping changes in the organizational infrastructure of social services and consequently to significant modifications in social work practice.

Under the welfare state model of service delivery, the Department had grown into a highly centralized, bureaucratized government agency. To implement the alternative model of social service delivery, radical change was required in the form of a 'restructuring' of the Department. For the purposes of analysis, the restructuring processes were grouped under four principles: regionalization, decentralization, devolution and partnership with the community. Although some features of the restructuring had been planned, piloted, or at least discussed, prior to July 1986, the restructuring process was to be altered by the commitment to biculturalism made following the release of the Report of the Ministerial Advisory Committee on a Maori Perspective for the Department of Social Welfare, known as *Puao-Te-Ata-Tu*.[20]

TERMINOLOGY

The terms 'social policy', 'social welfare policy', 'social welfare', 'social welfare services', 'social services' and 'social work' have distinct meanings. Because the boundaries between each of them are often blurred, they are sometimes used interchangeably, thereby creating confusion and inaccuracies. Social policy has multiple meanings but usually refers to all the governmental activity that impact on the quality of life in a society. Thus, it includes housing, education, environment, health, as well as, social welfare policies of income, benefits, and social services.[21] Borchardt distinguishes between social policy and public policy by defining public policy as a generic term referring to all government actions concerned with the governance of a nation: defense, public works, taxation, etc., while social policy is:

> A deliberate government sponsored programme of action designed to ensure reasonable access for all to conditions which will lead to an improved quality of life.[22]

The term 'social policy' or 'social welfare policy' as it is used in this research refers to the policies covering the six major social services provided by the state: education, employment, health, housing, income maintenance benefits and social welfare services thus reflecting the definition and usage in Departmental documents.[23]

The Resource Book prepared by the Ministerial Task Force on Social Welfare Services defined social welfare services as "services provided by the welfare state intended to improve people's social welfare-[they] can be *developmental*, *rehabilitative*, or *remedial* [sic]."[24] The Task Force noted that social welfare services refer to the full range of formally organized social welfare activities provided by local and central government agencies and by non-government agencies. The Task Force acknowledged that the boundaries between social welfare services and other social services are often indistinct, making it difficult to categorize services as a social service or as a social welfare service. There is a tendency in the literature to refer to social welfare services as simply social services without regard to the site of those services in education, health, or welfare. In this research, the term social services refers to social welfare services and utilizes the following distinctions.

> Social Services has a wider connotation and may include both direct and indirect service or resource provision that enhances quality of life: groups,

> community and social activities, i.e, domiciliary care, day care, child care, rest homes, meals on wheels, old age centres, etc. . . . Social Work has a more specific nature that depends on actions that are change focused; they may be indirect or direct but depend on a degree of personal interaction.[25]

The clarification of the terms 'social services' and 'social work' as articulated by Timms and Timms in the quote above is crucial to understanding the dilemmas, the resistance and the implications of the redesignation of division and job titles from 'social work' to 'social services' that took place in the restructuring of the Department of Social Welfare in 1986.

The process of change in government departments, services and benefits initiated by the Fourth Labour Government was labeled a 'restructuring'. The term was widely used to refer to all change processes in government and reflects a particular perspective.

> Restructuring implies that the way to carry out successful, effective organisational change [is] to alter the organization's structure.[26]

Such a perspective ignores the complex realities of organizational dynamics. Nevertheless, the restructuring process embarked on by the Department assumed this perspective and initiated the fundamental structural changes which are described in the following chapters.

Because the four principles of the restructuring (regionalization, decentralization, devolution and partnership with the community) will receive thorough examination in Chapter VI, it is necessary at this point to only briefly define the terms. Robbins[27] defines regionalization as an administrative structure that permits an organization to operate in different geographical localities without substantial changes in the hierarchical authority structure. Decentralization, usually viewed on a continuum with centralization, is a multi-dimensional concept that refers to the degree of distribution of power and authority among the actors in a social system.[28] It is important to note that regionalization and decentralization are distinct processes which can occur independently of each other. Likewise, decentralization of responsibility can occur without decentralization of power and authority.

> Referring to the transfer of political power from the central government level to a sub-national

> government . . . Hence, if a central government department were to transfer many of its functions from head office to district offices this would be a case of organisational decentralisation. If, however, the primary responsibility for those functions-in terms of programme design, funding, implementation and evaluation-were to be transferred to sub-national governments . . . [it is] devolution.[29]

Boston's definition refers to the two processes central to the understanding of devolution: power and responsibility. Boston refers to the *transfer* of political power and the *primary responsibility* for program design, funding, implementation and evaluation. It was these two features that were to become the focus of the devolution debate. Levett, Keelan and McClellan defined devolution as:

> A mechanism for allocating public money to groups providing social services in local communities. It involves an operational partnership between community and government. . . . It resulted from both a call for greater inclusion in political life by excluded or under-represented groups and a decision by government. . . . Devolution is an act of government to share decision-making on some function with affected citizens. . . . It is not a movement of decentralisation whereby decision-making is shifted from head office to district office.[30]

Devolution, as used within the Department of Social Welfare, included the notion of transfer of political power *and* of primary responsibility. Devolution was most often discussed with reference to the transfer of primary responsibility of services for Maori children and their *whanau* (extended family) to *iwi* (tribal) authorities. The issue of accountability in devolution has proved to be problematic. With a high degree of primary accountability to the Department, it was difficult to distinguish a 'devolved' program from the more traditional contractual agreements the Department had with voluntary agencies, such as Open Home Foundation or the New Zealand Society for the Intellectually Handicapped, for the provision of services to special populations. A low degree of accountability could make the program vulnerable to claims of misappropriation of public money. Such issues delayed the implementation of devolution. During the period of the research, the Community Organisation Grants Scheme (COGS) was the only devolved program within the Department of Social Welfare in operation.

The fourth principle, partnership with the community, had two major implications. First, partnership was an indication from government that the provision of social welfare services was a joint responsibility of government and the community. The meaning of the community, although vaguely defined, was generally accepted to refer to voluntary agencies, community groups and *iwi* authorities. It was an acknowledgment of the shift from the pursuit of a welfare state towards a welfare society that reflected acceptance of the New Zealand Planning Council's call for a community-based approach to social welfare service provision[31] and the New Zealand Council of Social Services promotion of the 'sharing of social responsibility' through the promotion of community self-sufficiency.[32] Second, partnership with the community included an expectation of a partnership in decision-making, as well as of provision. The government, as the review of the documentation in Chapter Four will show, embarked on an exhaustive consultative process with the community through the establishment of ministerial reviews and the Royal Commission on Social Policy.[33] As well, organizational design changes within the Department created a Social Welfare Commission with community members and community monitoring groups for each of the Department's District Offices and Institutions. These committees, while not conferred with direct decision-making power, were expected to significantly influence the operation of districts and the institutions through their direct linkage to the Social Welfare Commission.

Field social work practice is differentiated from residential social work by setting and occupy separate categories in staffing statistics within the Department. Residential social workers in the Department were based in the Department's residential institutions and homes for children and youth, while field social workers are: "Based in district and area welfare offices to carry out statutory tasks, offer personal and family services and respond to changing community needs."[34]

In 1988, of the Department's 1300 social workers, 850 were field social workers and the remaining 450 were residential social workers. In the 1970's the number of field and residential social workers was approximately equal. The 1988 ratio reflected the gradual reduction in the use of residential care which occurred and was continuing throughout the decade.

This shift in the ratio of field social workers to residential social workers reflects the Department's deinstitutionalization policy begun in the early 1980s and accelerated as part of the restructuring. The term

'Social Worker' when used in this research to designate social workers in the Department refers to field Social Workers.

SOCIAL WORK IN NEW ZEALAND

Social work in New Zealand is a relatively young occupation, without a well established professional identity. The first tertiary social work educational program was established at Victoria University in 1949 and it was the sole tertiary program in New Zealand for over twenty five years.[35] In 1964, a professional association for social workers was established by workers in the health and child welfare fields.[36] The formation of the Social Work Training Council in 1973 led to the establishment of three additional tertiary educational programs for social workers: Massey University, 1975; Auckland University, 1975; Canterbury University, 1976. As a result of the Brownlie Committee recommendation,[37] a fifth program was established at the Auckland Teachers College (now the Auckland College of Education) in 1983. The only nationwide study of social work in New Zealand was completed in 1981 and involved a sample of over 5,700 social service positions of which approximately 2,500 were paid positions.[38] It was estimated that 80% of those were in the statutory sector. Of those in paid employment, only 12% held a professional degree in social work.

The professionalization of social work during the last twenty years has been neither consistent nor unchallenged.[39] The parallel development of community work practitioners forced periodic reassessment of the role of social work vis a vis community work.[40] Proposals for professionalization through the establishment of minimum standards, membership restrictions and competency measures, has been a consistent call from health social workers in particular.[41] These proposals generated heated debates in social work ranks.[42]

The New Zealand Association of Social Workers was strongest in the mid-1970s but struggled for support and membership throughout the 1980s.[43] The Association's debates on the social work task and on professionalization are discussed as part of Chapter Four.

A study of social work practice in New Zealand completed by Sheafor, et al.[44] reconfirmed that the key tasks of social work activity among the 358 social workers surveyed were counseling and problem solving as direct practice interventions. The traditions of community work as a separate activity distinct from social work and the concentration of social workers in the statutory sectors of welfare and health may help to explain why casework has characterized social work in New Zealand during the period under study.

There were several reasons why it was decided to explore changes in social work practice within the Department of Social Welfare. First of all, the Department of Social Welfare was the largest single employer of social workers in the country[45] and several of its staff had leadership roles in the field. Secondly, since its creation, the Department had become a dominant influence in the provision of services in the statutory sector and, through its various funding schemes, in the voluntary sector as well. The Social Work Training Council, an accrediting body, had been established under the Department's auspices in 1973 and the Department, through its training institutions and various study programs, had been a major actor in the social work training infrastructure. Lastly, much of the criticism of social service provision during the 1970s and early 1980s, had been directed at the Department as the centralized, bureaucratized and mandated government department responsible for social services.[46] These criticisms were addressed in the recommendations of the reviews commissioned by the Government and the reviews initiated by the Department itself. As a result the Department embarked on a process of change that would be referred to as a 'restructuring'. It was this process of restructuring and its impact on field social work practice within the Department that this research project set out to explore.

While the primary focus was the intra-organizational relationship between the Department of Social Welfare as the statutory organization and social work, this study sets this relationship within the larger social, economic and political context. The restructuring marked a turning point in social welfare policy with the Fourth Labour Government's rejection of the existing social service delivery model based on a centralized, bureaucratized government department as the main funder and provider of service. It is argued that social work, as the major identifiable occupational category responsible for implementing government social service policy in statutory agencies, consequently underwent significant change.

It was the task of the Department's social work staff to implement the model and the principles of what was later to be referred to as 'the new way of working'.[47] The Department of Social Welfare had been supportive of the slow but steady growth of qualified social workers. It is argued that the Department played a major role in social work professionalization during the 1970s not only because it was the largest employer, but also because of the key role the Department assumed in the provision and resourcing of education and training of social workers in the statutory and voluntary sectors under the Social Welfare Act of 1971. Equally important was the establishment of the Social Work

Training Council in 1973 as an accrediting and standard setting body under the auspices of the Department.

As the Department became more professionalized, social work received increasing criticisms of elitism, non-accessibility and over-emphasis on individualized casework methods to the exclusion of preventative methodologies such as community work and community development.[48] To these criticisms was later added the charge of mono-culturalism.[49] This research analyzes the debates on social work professionalism and definitions of the social work task within the Department of Social Welfare. It draws on data collected in interviews with the Regional Executive Officers of Social Services and Alternative Care (REO's) and in field research with two social work teams. It is in the comments of the respondents that the dilemmas of practice are brought into sharp relief. The researcher was aware that some of the social workers within the Department had a commitment to many of the principles espoused as characteristics of Hadley and Hatch's Participatory Model of Social Service Delivery[50] prior to the restructuring. The question was, did the social workers perceive the new policy directives as a legitimation of good social work practices and was the adoption of the principles of 'the new way of working'[51] based on a commitment to biculturalism, actually taking place at the interface of social work services with clients? There were indications that with the apparent adoption of the alternative model, the Department's support for social work professionalization had reversed, and a deliberate strategy of deprofessionalization of social work was initiated. The research set out to explore these issues.

SUMMARY

It was against this background that this research project was formulated. These challenges demanded that social workers reassess the foundations of practice and their personal and professional attitudes toward racism, the validity of *Pakehas'* working with Maori people; and the glaring absence of Maori social workers in social service agencies, government departments and teaching institutions. They also recognized their lack of even a basic knowledge of Maori people, Maori language, customs and the demands of Maori formal protocol.[52] This time of pervasive change in social work was seen by the author as an excellent opportunity to explore the motivation, form, process and content of the changes taking place. Social workers were trying to make sense of the diverse challenges to their practice by reassessing current practice and developing models of practice to meet New Zealand's changing environment and the challenges of the Maori people.

NOTES

1. Simon Collins, "Rogernomics: The Economic Aftermath" in *The Making of Rogernomics,* ed. Brian Easton (Auckland: University Press, 1989), 188.

2. New Zealand Planning Council (NZPC), *The Economy in Transition: Restructuring to 1989* (Wellington: NZPC. 1989), 13.

3. Collins, 188.

4. Brian Easton, "The Treasury and the Origins of Economic Advice" in *The Making of Rogernomics,* ed. Brian Easton (Auckland: University Press, 1989), 68-91; New Zealand Planning Council.

5. Jonathan Boston, "Reorganizing the Machinery of Government In New Zealand: Objective and Outcomes" (Wellington: Victoria Univeristy, Policy Planning Group, Faculty of Commerce and Administration, 1990).

6. Ministerial Advisory Committee on a Maori Perspective for the Department of Social Welfare, *Puao-Te-Ata-Tu :The Day Break Report* (Wellington: Department of Social Welfare, 1986), 15.

7. Ministerial Task Force on Social Welfare Services, *Social Welfare Services,* (Wellington: Department of Social Welfare, July, 1986), 66.

8. Department of Social Welfare (DSW), *Briefing Papers for the Incoming Minister of Social Welfare* (Wellington: Department of Social Welfare, 1987a).

9. Department of Social Welfare, *Contracting for Social Services: Principles and Guidelines* (Wellington: Department of Social Welfare, July,1988c), 108.

10. Ministerial Advisory Committee.

11. DSW, *Contracting*, 15.

12. Margaret Tennant, *Paupers and Providers* (Wellington: Allen & Unwin, N.Z. Limited, 1989), 6.

13. Department of Social Welfare Act, 1971 (Wellington: Government Printer, 1971), Section 4:2:d.

14. Royal Commission on Social Security, *Social Security in New Zealand* (Wellington: Government Printer, 1972), Section 42:65.

15. Vic George and Paul Wilding, *Ideology and Social Welfare* 2d ed. (London: Routledge and Kegan Paul, 1987).

16. Brian Easton, *Social Policy and the Welfare State in New Zealand* (Auckland: George Allen and Unwin, 1980); William Oliver, "Social Policy in New Zealand: An Historical Overview," In *The April Report,* Royal Commission on Social Policy, Vol. I (Wellington: Government Printer, 1988), 3-45.

17. Richard Titmuss, *Social Policy: An Introduction,* eds. Brian Abel-Smith and Kay Titmuss (London: George Allen and Unwin

Ltd, 1974): Richard Titmuss, *Essays on 'The Welfare State'* 3d ed. (London: George Allen and Unwin Ltd, 1976).

18. Roger Hadley and Stephen Hatch, *Social Welfare and the Failure of the State: Centralized Social Services and Participatory Alternatives* (London: George Allen and Unwin, Ltd, 1981); Roger Hadley and Morag McGrath, eds., *Going Local: Neighbourhood Social Services* National Council for Voluntary Organisations, Occasional Paper 1 (London: Bedford Square Press, 1981); Roger Hadley, Peter Dale and Patrick Sills, *Decentralising Social Services* National Council of Voluntary Organisations (London: Bedford Square Press, 1984).

19. New Zealand Planning Council (NZPC), *Planning Perspectives: 1978 - 1983* (Wellington: Government Printer,1978); New Zealand Planning Council (NZPC). *The Welfare State,* (Wellington: Government Printer), 1979.

20. Ministerial Advisory Committee.

21. Neil Gilbert and Harry Specht, *Dimensions of Social Welfare Policy* 2d ed. (Englewood Cliffs, NJ: Prentice-Hall, 1986).

22. D. H. Borchadt, 'Introduction', in *Social Policy and Its Administration,* Joanne Marie and Adrianne Wise (Rushcutter's Bay, Australia: Pergamon Press, 1977), vii.

23. For example, Ministerial Task Force on Social Welfare Services, *Social Welfare Services* (Wellington: Department of Social Welfare, July, 1986).

24. Ibid, 43.

25. Noel Timms and Rita Timms, *Dictionary of Social Welfare* (London: Routledge and Kegan Paul, 1982), 182-183.

26. Roy McLennan Kerr Inkson, Stephen Dakin, Philip Dewe and Graham Elkin, *People and Enterprises: Human Behaviour in New Zealand Organisations* (Sydney: Holt, Rinehart and Winston, 1987), 298.

27. Stephen P. Robbins, *Organization Theory: The Structure and Design of Organizations* (Englewood Cliffs: Prentice-Hall, 1983).

28. J. Roger Hollingsworth and Robert Hanneman, *Centralization and Power in Social Service Delivery Systems* (Boston: Kluever, Nighoff Publishing, 1984), 7.

29. Jonathan Boston, "Democratic Theory, Devolution and Accountability" in *Devolution and Accountability,* eds. J. Martin and J. Harper (Wellington: G. P. Books, 1988), 3.

30. Allan Levett, Josie Keelan, and Velma McClellan, *Making Devolution Work: Report on the Community Organisations Grant Scheme* (Wellington: Department of Social Welfare, June, 1988), 1, 11.

31. NZPC, *The Welfare State;* NZPC, *Directions* ; Davey and Dwyer.

32. New Zealand Council of Social Services, *Establishing District Councils of Social Services* (Wellington: Department of Social Welfare, 1976).

33. Royal Commission on Social Policy, *The April Report* (Wellington: Government Printer), 1988a.

34. Department of Social Welfare, *Contracting for Social Services : Principles and Guidelines* (Wellington: Department of Social Welfare, July,1988c), 65.

35. University Grants Committee, *Social Work Review Committee: The Brownlie Report* Discussion Paper No. 6 (Wellington: Government Printing Office, 1982).

36. New Zealand Association of Social Workers, *Social Welfare at the Crossroads: Report on Social Welfare in New Zealand* (Wellington: NZASW, 1971).

37. University Grants Committee.

38. Rochford and Robb.

39. New Zealand Association of Social Workers, *Social Worker's Conference: 'Community'* (Auckland: NZASW, 1976); New Zealand Association of Social Workers, *Biennial Conference: Conference Papers* (Palmerston North: NZASW, 1978); New Zealand Association of Social Workers, *Biennial Conference: Social Justice, A Social Work Concern for the 1980s* (Wellington: NZASW, 1982).

40. Aotearoa Community Workers Association, "History of the Aotearoa Community Workers Association and Community Work Training National Proposal," *Kupu Kaimahi-A-Iwi: Newsletter of the Aotearoa Community Workers Association, Inc.* 1 (1989): 2-3.

41. For example, Ken R. Daniels, *Competent Health Social Work* (Christchurch: Department of Social Work, University of Canterbury,1989).

42. Mark Flowers, "Social Work Issues for the 1980s," In *The 1981 Social Work Lectures,* ed. Ken R. Daniels (Christchurch: Canterbury University, 1981).; Eve Hessey, "Why should social workers be professionally trained?" *New Zealand Social Work Journal* 7:3 (1982), 18-21; Eve Hessey, "Professional Training and the Probation Service," *New Zealand Social Work Journal* 9 (1984), 6-8.

43. Sarah Fraser, "President's Report," *Social Work Review: NZASW,* 1:1 (1988), 30-31.

44. Bradford W. Sheafor, Robert Teare, Mervyn W. Hancock and Thomas P. Gauthier, "Curriculum Development through Content Analysis: A New Zealand Experience," *Journal of Education in Social Work,* 20-21:3 (1985), 113-124.

45. M. W. Rochford and M. J. Robb, *People in the Social Services: A New Zealand Study* (Wellington: New Zealand Social Work Training Council 1981).

46. New Zealand Planning Council (NZPC), *Planning Perspectives: 1978 - 1983* (Wellington: Government Printer,1978); NZPC, *Directions* (Wellington: Government Printer, 1981); Judith Davey and Maire Dwyer, *Meeting Needs in the Community: A Discussion Paper on Social Services* (Wellington: NZPC, 1984).

47. DSW, *Contracting.*

48. NZASW, *Social Worker's Conference* NZASW, *Biennial Conference* (1978); NZASW, *Biennial Conference* (1982).

49. A. H. Johnston, *Report to the Minister of Social Welfare on the Current Practices and Procedures Followed in Institutions of the Department of Social Welfare in Auckland* (Wellington: Department of Social Welfare, 29 October, 1982).

50. Hadley and Hatch.

51. DSW, *Contracting.*

52. Department of Social Welfare, *Institutional Racism in the Department of Social Welfare: Tamaki-Makau-Rau, Auckland (Revised)* (Wellington: Department of Social Welfare, May, 1985b).

III

RESEARCH DESIGN: RATIONALE, METHOD AND RESPONDENTS

This chapter addresses issues of research methodology, presents the rationale for the research design, and describes the three research strategies utilized in this research study. The first strategy was a content analysis of the documents published during the period 1969-1988. These documents set out the debates on the four social policy issues which embrace the the fundamental dilemmas facing the social services in the mid-1980s: the statutory-voluntary balance in social service delivery, the appropriate model of service delivery, the level of professionalism required by the workers and optimum definition of the social work task and biculturalism. The analytical framework presented in Chapter One addressed these four themes as central to an understanding of social work practice within the New Zealand Department of Social Welfare. The second strategy employed in-depth interviews with the eleven middle-management staff responsible for social work and social services in the six newly established Regional Offices of the Department of Social Welfare. These eleven Regional Executive Officers were responsible for implementing the directives of the restructuring throughout the country. Several research techniques for gathering data from two social work teams comprised the third strategy. The objective in the design of a multi-level research methodology was to provide a means of examining the links between the theory discussed in Chapter One, the content of the social services debates as outlined in the document analysis in Chapter Four, and practice, as described by the social workers reported in Chapters Five, Six and Seven. This chapter, in addition to addressing the issues of research methodology, also offers a brief description of the two groups of social work respondents: the Regional Executive Officers (REOs) and the social work team members.

Social scientists categorize research designs as either exploratory or descriptive. The categories are not mutually exclusive.[1] The purpose of exploratory research is "to seek out new insights, ask questions, [and] assess phenomena in a different perspective"[2] with the ultimate aim of generating theory. Although exploratory research is not locked into a rigid design or ultimate outcome, e.g., hypothesis testing, it nevertheless is a planned approach with a high degree of flexibility and an emphasis on seeking contrary evidence or innovative conceptualizations. Exploratory designs are less structured than descriptive designs and are utilized in the pursuit of less developed research areas.

> They are essential whenever a researcher is breaking new ground, and they can almost always yield new insights into a topic for research.[3]

Because of the lack of representativeness, adherents of the positivist tradition in research view exploratory studies as seldom providing definitive answers to research questions and as having limited generalizability of the insights they do provide.

This study utilized an exploratory research design but did, however, address the issues of reliability and validity that confront qualitative researchers within the naturalistic paradigm.[4] Thus, it is proposed that the two research designs are best conceptualized on a continuum rather than as distinct types. The research questions of this study were to explore and identify the events leading up to the restructuring of the Department of Social Welfare in 1986; to gain an understanding of why and how it occurred with such apparent ease; to delineate the changes in the social service organizational infrastructure; and to understand the significance of those changes for social work practice within the New Zealand Department of Social Welfare. The events in New Zealand were always conceptualized as a case study with strong links to international trends and events. Although the research design for data collection was not strictly formulated, neither was it as loosely formulated as, for example, an anthropological ethnographical study.

It is in the case studies of the two social work teams that the exploratory nature of the research design is most clear. The field work with the teams was conducted with a minimum of pre-determined approaches. In case studies:

Bias might be manifest in the very cases that were selected for study, as well as the open-ended nature of the case approach, which may allow the investigator to influence the nature of the case under study.[5]

In response to such criticisms, the process of choosing the teams to be studied was conducted so as to permit a degree of representativeness and several methods of verification and feedback were built into the research design to minimize researcher bias.

QUALITATIVE AND QUANTITATIVE TECHNIQUES

The basic reason for the choice of a qualitative method was the exploratory nature of the study which relegated matters of representativeness as less important. In 1988 the social services were undergoing rapid and pervasive change and social workers, like many others, were striving to make sense of a changing world. Secondly, the changes, once set in motion, were continuing with increasing momentum and few indications of abatement. The social work community was eager for an opportunity to make sense of their work environment. Qualitative techniques, particularly in-depth interviews and participant observation, promised the best opportunity to understand the complexities of the relationship between broad based economic, political and social changes and changes in the Department and in social work practice.

> Qualitative methods . . . [are] more suitable when we seek to gain insight into the subjective meanings of complex phenomena in order to advance our conceptualizations of them and formulate hypothesis.[6]

Data was obtained from several sources to provide a holistic view through the "gradual synthesis [to enable] a grasp of relationships" that might not as readily emerge from a fragmented quantitative analyse.[7]

Because the process of restructuring was in its initial stages, ambivalence and anxiety about the form and structure of changes and their implications was at a high level. There were control processes in operation that were judged might make potential respondents resistant to participation in a research project. For example, it had been rumored that the sudden retirement of the highest ranking social worker at the request of top management of the Department occurred because of his alleged resistance to the proposed changes. This rumor had the effect of stifling critical comment from other social workers and confirmed the view of many social workers that the position of social work in the Department was particularly tenuous. In addition, it was expected by the researcher that many of the respondents would feel under threat due to the proposed changes in practice and job expectations. As well, there was a high level of uncertainty within the entire state service structure due to the passage of the State Sector Act of 1987 which altered the relationship between the government and its employees.

These factors lent additional support to the choice of a qualitative research methodology which permits the researcher to more specifically develop a rapport, if not a relationship, with respondents.

Qualitative research methodology is highly dependent on the establishment of a personal contract between the potential respondents and the researcher. A qualitative methodology, it was assumed, would help to minimize respondent resistance and elicit responses with a high degree of validity. Moreover, the key respondents were all social service personnel, the majority of whom were social workers whose main medium of communication was oral and whose primary structure for oral communication was the interview. In addition, the researcher was a social work educator. It is important to note that no selected respondents refused to be interviewed, in fact, they were surprisingly frank and candid in their remarks.

Rubin and Babbie argue that quantitative research techniques may be more appropriate:

> When we already know much, when we have a relatively high degree of control of the research situation or when we seek to verify an hypothesis or describe the characteristics of a population.[8]

Such was not the situation in this case. And, in fact, there were strong contra-indications to the potential success of quantitative techniques. The understanding sought was complex, contradictory and vulnerable to mis-interpretation. As well, considerable disquiet had been expressed by the proposed social work respondents about frequent consultations and requests for reports, data and policy submissions with no opportunity for feedback and no apparent effect on policy directives. The design of the qualitative research was interactive to ensure timely feedback through the planned verbal and written feedback and verification systems discussed below.

Rubin and Babbie argue that quantitative and qualitative methods are complementary and they advocate research designs that include characteristics of both. They acknowledge that some social workers, perhaps in response to the proliferation of quantitative studies since the application of computer technology in research, have labelled qualitative research methods as obsolete. Several leading social work researchers implore the profession to favour qualitative methods.[9] Advocates of the 'naturalist' paradigm shift in organizational research favour qualitative methods.

> Qualitative methods particularly interviewing and observation . . . can accommodate and explicate multiple, conflicting and, often unaggregatable realities, and they are sensitive to and, indeed, depend on the interaction or exchange between the researcher and the objects or respondents of the study.[10]

This research design utilized qualitative research techniques supported by the utilization of varying data collection techniques and verification systems designed to increase reliability and validity.[11]

THE DOCUMENT REVIEW

The first method of data collection was an analysis of the debates on social service policy and delivery systems as documented in the reports, reviews, publications and conference papers published between 1969 and 1988. Over 120 major documents were reviewed. These documents were published by policy advisory groups (e.g., the New Zealand Planning Council and the Social Advisory Council); by the voluntary sector (e.g., New Zealand Federation of Voluntary Welfare Organisations); by government appointed review committees and task forces (e.g., Ministerial Advisory Committee [1986], Ministerial Task Force [1986]); by the social work association (e.g., biennial conference papers of New Zealand Association of Social Workers); and by the Department itself (e.g., Review of the Social Work Division [1982], *Institutional Racism,* [1986]). Every attempt was made to examine all the documents published by the bodies, committees and organizations listed above. A system of cross-referencing led to the identification of additional relevant documents within the public sector and to documents published by the Department itself.

The documents were drawn from University Libraries, the Department of Social Welfare Library and the Government Printing Office. Cross-referencing methods were applied to the documents to identify publications under separate authorship and documents not previously examined. The effort made to locate and examine all publications referenced in the documents was successful with the exception of the Ministerial documents (discussed under a separate section below). Some of the papers from the New Zealand Association of Social Workers (NZASW) conferences were incomplete but only one document authored by the Social Advisory Council in 1973 and mentioned in Wilson[12] could not be located.

Extensive notes were taken on the contents of the documents setting out the main argument or focus, the supporting rationale and the specific recommendations advocated. Throughout the content analysis, this process was sustained as essential to minimize bias. As the document review progressed, themes began to develop but the exploratory process was maintained to "enable seeing what isn't there and looking for patterns."[13] The preliminary framework based on the research questions was an overall guide and was employed for reflection, but was not applied to the document data gathering phase. Such a strategy permits "unexpected finds [to] occur because this approach reveals otherwise undetectable patterns and gaps in the data"[14] and reinforces the need for document analysis to be systematic.[15]

THE INTERVIEW SCHEDULE

The interview schedule utilized with the Regional Executive Officers and with each member of the two social work teams was comprised of twenty structured open-ended questions organized in four sections. The first section of eight questions under the heading 'Philosophy' asked respondents to comment on the objectives of regionalization as an organizational strategy. The recommendations of *Puao-Te-Ata-Tu*[16] were specifically addressed. The second and third sets of questions under the headings 'Organisational Changes' and 'Managerial Supports' were directed at eliciting their perceptions of changes in decision-making systems and managerial styles as aspects of organizational design. The last set of three questions under the heading 'Social Work Services' was designed to gather information on performance, expectations and objectives of social work.

All respondents were sent a copy of the interview schedule prior to their interview along with an introductory letter and an appointment time. All respondents received the same interview schedule, a copy of the research proposal and request for demographic information which is discussed below.

CONFIDENTIALITY

The level of confidentiality that could be offered to the two groups of respondents was minimal because of the nature of the research design. The Regional Executive Officers (REOs) held highly visible organizational positions and were few in number. Six of the eleven REOs were responsible for 'Social Services' which included social work services. The other five REOs were responsible for 'Alternative Care' which covered residential care and the transitional or deinstitutionalization programmes for children and youth. The REOs are not individually identified but are referred to by number to distinguish one REO from another. The REOs of Social Services are not distinguished from the REOs of Alternative Care to offer as much confidentiality as possible. As well, identifying characteristics were omitted from their responses. This was not always possible, since in some cases, the removal of the characteristic would make the comment meaningless. The respondents were aware of the level of confidentiality that could be given to their interviews in the research process. They were offered the option of asking that specific comments not be used. In the two incidences when such a request was made and respected. As well, the researcher asked each REO if they wished to view the draft. Only one Regional Executive Officer asked to exercise this option and the draft was sent for review and comment.

In the case of the District Office respondents, minimum confidentiality has even clearer implications for the social work management staff and the team members are readily identifiable. Drafts of the chapters were sent to each District Office, read and commented on by both the Assistant Director: Social Services and the senior social workers as team leaders. The chapters were also made available to all the team members. Although the Assistant Directors and the team leaders made comments and corrected technical inaccuracies, they did not request any material be deleted and expressed verification, if not total agreement, with the descriptions as presented in Chapters Six and Seven.

The issues of confidentiality in qualitative research projects are always complex. However, because of New Zealand's population of just over three million, the social work community is so small as to make respondents in a project like this very easily identifiable. It is only their professional commitment to improved practice that made the project possible. Because of these constraints on confidentiality the following request was added to all copies of the research study in following the acknowledgements and in the text below.

It is expected that all readers will respect the integrity of this research study by handling the material contained herein judiciously to insure that the respondents are not harmed in any way by their willingness to participate in the pursuit of knowledge and understanding.

THE ENTRY PROCESS

It is characteristic of organizations undergoing change to be resistant to efforts to track the change process and, in particular, to individuals outside the organization doing the tracking. Bailey notes that gaining entry to organizations is difficult at the best of times because administrators often feel they have everything to loose and nothing to gain.

> Many times the study will yield few benefits for the Administration . . . The presence of an outside observer can disrupt or slow the daily routine of work activities and can damage morale if employees think that the observer is a management spy. Further, the observer can hurt the administrator's career by making allegations of waste, inefficiency, discrimination, or scandal within the organization.[17]

This is particularly relevant to the present study because, as the document analysis in the next chapter will demonstrate, the Department had been under criticism by social policy analysts and minority interest groups for several years. Additional outside scrutiny in a major research project was not viewed favourably. Initial efforts to gain permission to conduct research within the Department had met with polite inaction. The change occurred when the researcher received a nomination in a public forum of social service groups to serve on the Palmerston North District Executive Committee. The District Executive Committees (DECs) were created as District Office monitoring bodies during the restructuring as part of the Department's commitment to a 'partnership with the community' in fulfilment of the recommendations of *Puao-Te-Ata-Tu* .[18] When the researcher's nomination was confirmed with an appointment by the Minister of Social Welfare, support from and access to the Department for research purposes became possible. This entree was further supported by the researcher's educative role with many Departmental staff as students in the various university programmes and seminars sponsored by the researcher's university. An additional crucial factor in gaining access to the Department was the support for the research from the Central Office Regional Director (who was subsequently to become an Assistant Director-General Region serving on the Head Office Executive Management Team). This individual, with whom the researcher had previously had only limited professional contact, was aware of an earlier research project in the Department (on computer utilization in 1982) and commented on the ethical standards employed and adhered to in that research project. It was he who "walked it through"[19] the administrative hurdles.

> The request was not delivered through regular channels such as mail, messenger, or chain of

> command, but instead was carried personally to the administrator's desk by the contact or middleman.[20]

Bailey[21] notes the critical role a contact within the organization can perform as an advocate within the system for the researcher. In a repeat approach in February, 1988 to the Central Regional Director, full documentation of research objectives, proposed research design, demographic information sheet and interview schedule was presented.[22] The Central Regional Director took the full research request to Head Office of the Department of Social Welfare and in the July meeting of the Executive Management Team and Regional Directors, it received full endorsement. A formal letter from the Deputy Director-General to all Regional Directors in late July of 1988 noted the endorsement of top management and asked all staff for full cooperation. This approval was almost simultaneous with the confirmation of the researcher's appointment to the District Executive Committee by the Minister of Social Welfare.

THE MINISTER OF SOCIAL WELFARE

As the research progressed it became clear that a key informant would be Ann Hercus, the Minister of Social Welfare, during the initial years of the restructuring. During her stewardship as Minister of Social Welfare from October 1984 until mid-1987, several key decisions were made regarding social service delivery and social work. Library searches of both the University and National Library systems, however, revealed no authored materials. A copy of one speech, delivered to the New Zealand Association of Social Workers prior to the 1984 election in which Dame Hercus became a Minister of Parliament was located in the Department of Social Welfare Library in Wellington, New Zealand's capital city. Efforts to examine the ministerial papers and communications were unsuccessful although, as the document review in Chapter Four demonstrates, the former Minister's philosophy and directives were evident in the secondary resource material which was available. Key examples are the decision to disestablish the Social Work Training Council in 1984 and the creation of the New Zealand Council on Training and Education in the Social Services in 1986. A direct request was made to Dame Hercus in 1989, as Permanent Representative for the New Zealand Mission to the United Nations, for resource material and/or an interview. Both were denied. In her letter the former minister explained she had made a decision "not to give interviews about my previous positions as a Cabinet Minister when I retired from politics (this includes academic interviews) and this is a firm decision . . . "[23]

NEGOTIATING FOR THE INTERVIEWS WITH THE REGIONAL EXECUTIVE OFFICERS

The 1986 restructuring of the Department created six Regional Offices each with several regional executive officer positions to support the various programmes and functions of the Department.[24] Two of the Regional Executive Officer positions in each office were directly involved with the provision of social services and/or social work services. The positions of Regional Executive Officers of Alternative Care and of Social Services were *staff* not *line* positions and as such were to exemplify the new philosophy of participatory management and decentralized decision making. That is, the position holders were to advise, counsel and support District staff but not make decisions which were the perogative of either the local District or of top management.[25] The REOs, then, were key personnel in the new organizational structure since they held a pivotal position between the new policies and their implementation. As a group, the responsibilities of the REOs covered the entire nation and hence, as respondents they provided a national perspective.

The next step in gaining access to the Regional Executive Officers was to approach the Principal Social Worker in Head Office, Wellington, further confirming Schatzman and Strauss's contention that:

> Negotiation, articulation and permission seeking are parts of a process, not events to be accomplished just one time. Entry to the field is, in fact, a 'continuous process'.[26]

The Principal Social Worker's position had been newly created as a staff position, apparently in response to the dissatisfaction of social work staff at the disestablishment of the line social work position in Head Office. The position was not filled with a Departmental career social worker, but by an appointment of an experienced social work administrator from the health sector. Because of her staff position status, she could only offer her support of the proposed research project and arrange for me to meet with the REOs at their regularly scheduled meeting to request their cooperation. At that meeting, a formal presentation of the research proposal was made with the commitment to present preliminary impressions and to offer a verification session following the completion of the field work at the end of 1988. In addition, the REOs were offered the opportunity to comment on the draft of the chapter dealing with their responses. Only one of the REOs was to exercise this option. At the close of this meeting, all of the REOs agreed to take part in the research.

The assistance of the Central Regional Director was indispensable in arranging interviews with each of the REOs. Prior to the interviews, each REO was sent a personal letter, thanking them for their willingness to participate and confirming the interview appointment. This letter included a brief description of the research, a Demographic Information sheet and the structured interview schedule of twenty open-ended questions.[27] The mailing was designed to alert the respondents to the specific objectives of the research and to focus the interview by removing the necessity of obtaining factual information during interview time. This worked particularly well in that little of the interview time was spent on eliciting or confirming factual details.

The Demographic Information Sheet asked for factual data about the respondent, e.g., work history, qualifications, professional affiliation, and included a request to list significant events and reports in the restructuring process. This modest request for written data was particularly illuminating. Despite the fact that there had been a number of reports and reviews only four of the respondents listed more than one 'significant event or report'. The respondent's hesitation to provide complete written data provided further support for the qualitative research methodologies chosen. What was noteworthy was that *Puao-Te-Ata-Tu* was listed by eight of the eleven respondents as a significant report, reconfirming the perceived importance of this report in the restructuring of the Department.

Eleven of the twelve REO positions in Social Services and Alternative Care were filled during the field research period. Nine of the eleven appointments were permanent; the remaining three were filled by 'acting' appointments of varying duration. All interviews with the REOs were completed between September and November 1988 to minimize distortion due to subsequent events. Eight of the interviews took place in their Regional Offices. Two took place in mutually agreed venues, one at a half way point that required a three hour drive into the remote southern reaches of the Central North Region. The last interview utilized tele-conferencing technology. Most interviews were an hour and a half long although one was nearly three hours. One interviewee requested the tape be turned off during the discussion of an example which included a specific staff issue. Eight of the interviewees were well prepared for the interview, having completed the demographic information sheet, reviewed the interview schedule and made marginal notes on the questionnaire.

At the completion of the data collection phase, a feedback and verification session was held with the REOs at the office of the Principal Social Worker, Head Office, Wellington. This opportunity for exchange lent valuable insights and confirmation to the broad based preliminary findings. The feedback and verification session was significant to the researcher because it demanded the preparation of an oral presentation on the development of a tentative framework and preliminary findings of the research. The presentation fulfilled the commitment to a research philosophy that research should be promptly reported to the participants and they should have an opportunity to critique preliminary findings. These points are explored further in the section below on the feedback and verification sessions.

COLLATION OF INTERVIEW DATA

Brief notes were taken during the interviews on large notecards for each respondent. Following the interview, the researcher jotted down the main points the respondent made during the interview, the new information or insights provided, and noted comments that were said with high emotional content or confidence. As well, all interviews were audio taped and subsequently analysed using a multi-step process. Firstly, all taped interviews were reviewed in their entirety by the researcher who noted and categorized the sections for transcribing under the four headings used in the questionnaire itself: Philosophy, Organizational Changes, Managerial Supports and Social Work Services. In listening again to the interview, the researcher used the criteria set out by Opie to highlight selected comments based on: (a) "the intensity of the speaking voice," (b) "the contradictory moment" defined here as alerting the researcher to apparent rationalizations by the respondent in comments linked by the term 'but', (c) the emotional content or tone of the statements, and (d) "the extent to which the participant uses whole sentences, rather than the more usual recursive speech patterns."[28]

The respondents' comments were then compared with the brief notes taken during the interview and the summary prepared after the interview. Special note was taken of comments that reappeared in subsequent interviews and those comments which reflected a unique insight or perspective. After the initial draft of the interviews was prepared, the transcribed tapes were reviewed several times for further verification purposes. This procedure was repeated with the interviews of the two social work teams and the corollary interviews with the District Office respondents.

FEEDBACK AND VERIFICATION SESSIONS

Three factors motivated the commitment to the follow-up meetings with both groups of respondents--the REOs and the social work teams. First of all, the feedback and verification sessions provided the opportunity to present timely preliminary impressions to the respondents as an acknowledgement of their participation. This was deemed important in a research project of this kind since the formal summary at the completion of the project could be expected to take two to three years. Second, the feedback sessions presented an ideal time for the respondents to critique the developing analytical framework and to verify or to modify the preliminary impressions at a critical stage in the research process. The preliminary feedback provided the researcher with an opportunity to "test the validity of [the] emerging propositions."[29] Lincoln refers to this as a 'member check':

> Member check is an old sociological term that refers to the process of checking findings with members of relevant groups of those who provided the original information.[30]

Lastly, the feedback session was initiated by the researcher as part of her commitment to an non-exploitative relationship with research respondents.[31] The feedback sessions provided confirmation of the developing analytical framework and preliminary findings.

The data from the respondents was subjected to yet another validity check. As has already been noted, drafts of the relevant chapters were sent to the respondents to read and comment on the chapters prior to their completion. Several respondents did comment and correct factual inaccuracies but did not request the deletion of any material.

DATA COLLECTION WITH THE SOCIAL WORK TEAMS

The next stage of the data collection was designed to provide an in-depth examination of practice within two social work teams. The Hadley and Hatch, Hadley and McGrath, and Black and colleagues publications[32] provided models of team examination. However, their methodologies required an expenditure of time and resources outside the scope of this research study. Nevertheless, their models did provide valuable ideas and insights for consideration, many of which were incorporated, albeit on a smaller scale. For example, the strategies of reviewing District Office memos and observing social work interventions and team interaction were drawn from their research designs.

The challenge was to create a research design for this phase of the project that would both meet the objectives of the inquiry and the limits of time and resources. The combination of team and individual social worker observation, examination of team and District Office documentation and in-depth individual team member interviews seemed to provide the best mix of data collection techniques to meet research objectives. "In-depth interviewing is a logical partner with participant observation."[33] It was important to present a research design for this part of the field work that would have the best chance of eliciting full cooperation of the respondents and providing different perspectives of social work practice. Hence, the selection of the teams was purposeful.[34]

It was decided that several steps be taken in the process of identifying, selecting and negotiating with the social work teams who were attempting to implement the new policy directives. Informal discussions were held with Departmental staff, colleagues and former students about possible suitable teams. Here care had to be taken to lay the ground work for negotiation of possible teams in such a way as to minimize any potential resistance while still identifying possible suitable teams before any commitments were made. The organizational climate of the Department was so stressful that considerable effort was made to avoid any semblance of a 'rejection' by the researcher that could be interpreted negatively by either social work staff or management.

The Central Regional District Director was most helpful in describing the District Offices and suggesting teams that were actively attempting to implement the new practice directives. The difficulties were immense and the teams fulfilling the pre-established criteria were few in number despite the Region's six District Offices and approximately twenty social work teams. The changes in the Department had created a sense of turmoil for many of the teams. High rate of turnover and the hiring of Maori and Polynesian staff, under Equal Employment Opportunity commitments, meant that many teams had been or were in the process of redeployment. Frequent changes in supervisors and administrative staff meant that several offices or teams were not available for research purposes.

Finally, four teams were identified as possibilities, only two within the Central Regional District: the Palmerston North District Office team covering the city itself and the Community Development team of the Napier District Office. The other two teams were in the Central South Region: the Child Protection Team of the Lower Hutt District Office and the Generic Team of the Porirua District Office. Cooperation from the latter teams required the support of the Director of the South Central Regional Office.

Formal approaches to the District Offices were made first through the District Office Directors who had responsibility for all functions in the District (administration, benefits and pensions, and social services) and subsequently, through the Assistant Director: Social Services (who were responsible for social work services and a growing number of social service functions, e.g., licensing of community care homes). The Director of the South Central Region was already in possession of a letter from the Deputy Director General pledging Departmental support for the research project. The researcher made an in-person informal approach to the District Director and then to the Assistant Director: Social Services. In the case of the Lower Hutt District Office, the Director delegated the decision to the Assistant Director of Social Services. If the Assistant Director of Social Services approved, then a third, formal meeting was arranged with the supervising social worker and the identified team. The research process was explained, time commitment requirements discussed and a commitment was made by the researcher to present the preliminary impression and verification session following completion of the field work as was done with the REOs.

At this point the decision was made to include the Assistant Directors of Social Services as key respondents. As well, provision was made for corollary interviews with selected social work staff. The basis of the selection of corollary interviews is discussed below.

Of the four teams with whom discussions reached the third, formal meeting stage, one team was deemed unsuitable by the researcher because the team was about to be redeployed due to staff changes and a second team had to be turned down because a firm commitment had already been made for the two teams required within the research design. Once a team had agreed to participate, the researcher then met with all District Social Services staff in a regularly scheduled staff meeting to explain the purpose of the research and the research process. The cooperation of all staff was requested and the possibility that a few others might be asked for an interview was mentioned. This proved to be extremely valuable because during the on-site field work week, several staff approached the researcher to give their perceptions of the restructuring and the impact it was having on their practice. Formal interviews were held with selected staff outside the teams when it became apparent that supportive information was required based on the researcher's assessment of the unique perspective the particular respondent could provide to an understanding. The choices in each District are explained further in the Chapters Six and Seven. Only one request for an interview of a staff person outside the selected team was not completed and that was because a crisis in a child abuse case intervened and the interview could not be rescheduled. A further example of cooperation of staff outside the teams was exemplified by the willingness of staff members to come early to discuss their work or to stay late, when the scheduled interviews with the selected team precluded discussions with other staff members during regular office hours.

The field work period with both teams was a full week which was extended beyond the normal working hours to enable completion of the task. In each case a minimum of a half a day was spent with each team member in the course of their normal duties. Unscheduled decision-making meetings, formal staff meetings, home visits with clients, interdisciplinary case conferences and a *hui* (a meeting following formal Maori protocol) were all part of the week-long experiences.[35]

The first team chosen had a five year history as a 'Community Development Team' although the Napier District Office had a reputation within the Department as a community oriented District since the early 1970s. The Departmental hierarchy recognized the work of this team and used it as an example of a team already functioning in the way that represented the new philosophy of community orientation. This team was in a stable district office with relatively low turnover at the direct line practitioner level and had experienced administrative and supervisory staff. The District Office was in a small seaside town, Napier, on the east coast of the North Island and served a large geographical district with a widely dispersed population.

The second team chosen was in a District whose Assistant Director: Social Services acknowledged his support of the Hadley and Hatch 'patch system'.[36] A modified patch system with participatory management had been implemented in his District and his supervising social workers had worked with him to apply the principles to the New Zealand situation. The directives about 'the new way of working'[37] were well known to the staff of this District. Although the Assistant Director: Social Services and the Senior Supervising Social Work were long service District employees, the office was characterized by high turnover at the direct-line practitioner level. This team was located in an urban center. The city of Porirua is a densely populated, multi-cultural community which includes one of the oldest, and largest, government housing tracts in the country.

The two teams chosen presented contrasts in philosophy, structure, purpose and gender makeup. The Napier Team had a male supervisor with an equal gender split in staff and equal Maori-Pakeha membership. The Porirua team had a female supervisor with an all female Pakeha staff. The Napier team had a community development focus and was struggling to maintain that focus and function in the light of a redefinition of social work task within the Department. The Porirua team had a geographically based 'patch' philosophy but was moving to a 'generic' social work focus (working with the entire range of presenting problems and client groups) within a culturally-based team structure. However, both teams were attempting to retain and/or implement those practices and functions that were consistent with the redefined agency goals and directives.

THE FIELD WORK METHODOLOGY

Following the explanation of the research, the specifics of the team observation and interview process were discussed with each team. In addition to the scheduled formal interview utilizing the structured questionnaire, the team members were asked to show the researcher a piece of their work that they felt demonstrated the work they were doing and their efforts to incorporate 'the new way of working'[38] being implemented by the Department. As much as possible, this piece of work was to be a part of their normal working pattern rather than something arranged specifically, and should take up at least half a day. The supervising social worker or senior social worker received the same instruction with the additional task of planning the week with the staff prior to researcher's arrival. The team leaders and the teams were asked to remain flexible to permit the researcher to fully experience the work place. This permitted the researcher to participate in the routine of the office, e.g., in emergency decision-making meetings and to accompany staff on a child-abuse referral investigation. The planning task of the social work team supervisor was essential because of the distances involved. The success of this phase of the project was due in part to the high calibre of assistance the researcher received from each of the team leaders.

Each of the team members received the same packet of materials prior to commencement of the field work as was sent to the REOs: a personalized letter of request to participate with the summary of the research proposal, the structured questionnaire schedule and the Demographic Information sheet. As with the REOs, the social workers in the District demonstrated an effort to consider the objectives of the research prior to the interview (one arrived with several pages of handwritten notes) and several commented on the helpfulness of having the schedule beforehand in alerting them to the specific focus of the research. They were less likely to have completed the demographic information sheet before the interview than the REOs. All, except two, completed the Demographic Questionnaire before the end of the research period. The last two were received by mid-November, 1988.

THE NAPIER DISTRICT OFFICE AND THE COMMUNITY DEVELOPMENT TEAM

The Napier District Office had the reputation of a strong commitment to a broad based definition of the social work task. The office had a long history of social worker staff who argued for community based activities and involvements. In the mid 1970s, the Napier Office Assistant Director of Social Work prepared a paper in which he attempted to document their efforts to implement the principles of the 1971 amalgamation. The District had established a District Volunteer Scheme in the early 1970s in which volunteers worked along side Departmental staff. The volunteers were offered both training opportunities and supervision. This volunteer program continued throughout the seventies and continued as an active part of the District's services at the time of the research. An outreach program was developed in the schools by a member of the Preventative Team shortly after the amalgamation. The schools program was basically an early identification program centered around group discussion of 'issues of living'.[39] The involvement of the District Office in this program was phased out in the early 1980s when the school guidance counsellors assumed responsibility for the program. The District continued its commitment to community development activities through it support, advice and training for the established voluntary agencies and the emerging community groups.

It was this five member Community Development Team that was the main focus for data collection in Napier. Three corollary interviews were held to ensure comprehensive data collection. The Assistant Director: Social Services who had held that position since 1977, was instrumental in supporting the preventative/supportive services functions of the community development team. This administrative post took on distinctive managerial features after the restructuring with decentralization of decision making which gave the Assistant Directors responsibility but limited discretion in budget allocation. For example, the staff position allocation system was replaced with a salary allocation system that gave the Assistant Director's discretionary powers in salary increases for staff and the ability to hire part-time or contract staff which was not possible under the old system. The Senior Social Worker in charge of child protective services was seen as essential in providing relevant observations on the implementation of the 'new way of working'[40] since the community development team's focus was only one aspect of community-oriented social work. The qualified social worker recently appointed to the Alternative Care position in the District was seen as an important respondent in examining the operationalization of the community care emphasis. In addition to these formal interviews, numerous interchanges took place with other staff, some initiated by the researcher but most initiated by staff who wanted to contribute their impressions and experiences to the research.

THE PORIRUA DISTRICT OFFICE AND THE GENERIC TEAM

The Porirua Office, under its Assistant Director: Social Work, had a reputation for innovation and creativity. The Social Work Service had adopted a modified 'patch system' as its method of service delivery shortly after the visit of Roger Hadley to New Zealand in 1982 in an attempt to move away from the individualized, casework approach and to find a more effective method of dealing with the constant pressure of crisis cases. The efforts of this District Office to apply the 'patch system' were widely known and emulated in several District Offices. In 1985, the Assistant Director experimented with a model of participatory management which involved all social work staff in decision making. This experiment was abandoned after nearly a year as unworkable in an office with the constant pressure of client service and among staff with widely varying levels of expertise, experience and commitment to the project. Both of these efforts, however, continued to have an effect on the philosophy of service delivery and management of the office.

This generic team of four social workers was headed by a Supervising Senior Social Worker. Two weeks prior to the field work, a Senior Social Worker joined the team. She would assume full responsibility for the team over the following few months as the Supervising Senior Social Work assumed higher level management tasks. The composition of this particular team was a result of a District social work staff decision in 1987 to reconstitute the teams along cultural lines. i.e., Maori, Pakeha and Pacific Islanders, a process that was not yet complete. This basis for the teams represented a move from the geographically based patch system. The staff recommenended reorganizing the teams on a cultural basis to meet the needs of Porirua's multi-cultural community and to attempt to relieve the stress in staff relationships due in part to the attempts to implement the recommendations of *Puao-Te-Ata-Tu.*

Only one formal corollary interviews was held in the Porirua District Office. The Assistant Director: Social Services had held this position since late 1978. He had led the country in the application of Hadley and Hatch's patch system and was attempting to apply the best of that experience to the demands for a culturally appropriate office structure. Informal discussions were held with several members of staff including the Senior Social Workers of the Court Team, the Pacific Island Team and the Maori Team. However, the volume of informal discussions was considerably less than in the Napier Office. Two factors may account for this: the pressured work pace in this office and the tension between cultural groups in the office.

The Porirua Office because of its urban nature and its location on the third floor of the Housing Corporation presented a psychological, although not physical barrier to access. Entry to the office was restricted to one door on the north side of the six-story building leading to a small lobby and two elevators. It was however, close to both the main highways and to the bus center. If psychologically inaccessible to clients, the Porirua Office was relatively accessible to the Head Office who routinely seconded the Porirua staff to Head Office working parties. This became an issue for all staff but, in particular, for the small number of Maori and Polynesian staff who were asked to work on special projects, to participate in formal *powhiri* (ceremonial welcomes) at the Head Office and to attend *hui* (formal meetings) as Departmental Staff representatives.

Although this pressure was felt to some degree by the Maori staff at the Napier office, their distance from Head Office, over five hours by car and not much less by commercial air, reduced the possibilities for secondment(temporary deployment of staff for special assignment). The Napier Office was more accessible to clients, in the sense the Department was located in a low rise, three floor, complex of governmental building in the center of town. However, many staff, particularly the Community Development staff felt the current building with its formal lobby, its social work services on the third floor requiring elevator access and the receptionist behind a glass enclosure, was far inferior to their previous quarters which were on the first floor of a comfortable building where community workers and clients could gain ready access to the team through a back door.

LIMITATIONS OF THE METHODOLOGY

Qualitative research provides a rich and comprehensive insight into complex phenomena. It seldom offers definitive answers to research questions and is limited in its generalizability.[41] The structure of this research design attempted to minimize these methodological weaknesses by utilizing several data collection and verification strategies. The document review drew on the all publications on the debates on the issues of social service provision addressed in the study. All the Regional Executive Officers of Social Services and Alternative Care within the Department were interviewed. Their collective responsibilities covered the nation. The choice of teams in different regions and in different settings, urban and rural, provided contrasting experiences to bring a depth to the research that more similar teams or teams in the same region, would not provide. The feedback sessions with the REOs and with each of the teams provided a valuable verification of preliminary framework and findings. This was further strengthened by the opportunity taken up by the respondents to read and comment on drafts of the relevant chapters in late 1989 and early 1990.

The impact of a research process on respondents was first highlighted in the Hawthorne Studies of the 1920s.[42] This researcher gained access to the organization based on her previous involvement with the Department, on her recent appointment to a Departmental monitoring committee and on the strengths of the many professional relationships she enjoyed with Departmental staff. Nachimas and Nachimas[43] consider that no research effort can be 'non-intrusive' therefore, researchers have a responsibility to consider the impact of the research process on the respondents. The commitment to the feedback and verification sessions and to the presentation to the respondents of the drafts was in partial recognition of the potential for greater understanding that the research process could bring to the respondents in their work as professional social workers.

SUMMARY

This chapter addressed issues of methodology by discussing the two main research designs used in social science: exploratory and descriptive. Drawing on the work of research theoreticians, the two research designs are conceptualized on a continuum rather than as polarities. This research project was described as fundamentally exploratory. Exploratory studies utilize primarily qualitative techniques while descriptive studies tend to utilize quantitative techniques.

Comments on the debate between the two were explored but their complementarity was emphasized. Although qualitative techniques are used in all three strategies employed in the research design including the document review, the methodology was informed by an appreciation of the strengths and weakness of each research design. The three research strategies were constructed to provide data from multiple sources using distinct data collection techniques and several verification strategies to increase reliability and validity.

The field work was supported by detailed analysis of formal, public documentation dealing with social welfare services policy commencing just prior to the creation of the Department of Social Welfare the first eighteen months of the restructuring ending in December 1988. The findings of the document analysis is reported in Chapter Four. A structured questionnaire schedule of twenty open-ended questions was administered to all the Regional Executive Officers of Social Services and Alternative Care within the Department. These positions were key pivotal positions in the implementation of the new policy in the Districts. All the incumbents, except one, were career departmental social workers able to provide insightful commentary on changes within the Department based on through knowledge of the Department.

The second set of respondents were the two social work teams, one urban and one rural. One team had a community development focus, served a small town and a large, sparsely populated, horticultural district. The second team served a densely populated multi-cultural urban community contingent to the nation's capital. The team had recently moved from a patch system to culturally based teams. Participatory research techniques, observation, document analysis and in-depth interviews using the developed structured questionnaire were utilized as consistent with the research methodologies favoured by proponents of the naturalists' paradigm.[44] The research design, then, was constructed to provide a comprehensive examination of a complex phenomena by utilizing a variety of data collection techniques within an exploratory design framework and applying qualitative analysis. The results of the field work are reported in Chapters Five, Six and Seven.

NOTES

1. Kenneth D. Bailey, *Methods of Social Research* (New York: The Free Press, 1978); Gerald Adams and Jay D. Schvaneveldt, *Understanding Research Methods* (New York: Longman Publishing, 1985); Allen Rubin and Earl Babbie, *Research Methods for Social Work* (Belmont CA: Wadsworth Publishing Company, 1989).

2. Adams and Schvaneveldt, 103.

3. Rubin and Babbie, 86.

4. Pamela S. Hinds, Sharon Scandrett-Hibden and Leon S. McAulay, "Further Assessment of a Methods to Estimate Reliability and Validity of Qualitative Research Findings," *Journal of Advanced Nursing* 15 (1990): 430-435.

5. Adams and Schvaneveldt, 114.

6. Rubin and Babbie, 365.

7. William J. Reid and Audrey D. Smith, *Research in Social Work* (New York: Columbia University Press, 1981), 90.

8. Rubin and Babbie, 365.

9. Reid and Smith; Rubin and Babbie; Henry Wechsler, Helen Z. Reinherz, and Donald D. Dobbin, *Social Work Research* 2d ed. (New York: Human Services Press, 1981).

10. Yvonna S. Lincoln, ed., *Organizational Theory and Inquiry: The Paradigm Revolution* (Beverly Hills: Sage Publications, 1985).

11. Hinds, et al.

12. I. G. Wilson, "Napier Department of Social Work and Voluntary Work" (Napier: Department of Social Welfare, 1976).

13. Thomas F. Carney, *Content Analysis* (Winnepeg University of Manitoba, 1972).

14. Ibid., 65.

15. Karl Erik Rosengren, ed., *Advances in Content Analysis* (Beverly Hills: Sage Publications,1981).

16. Ministerial Advisory Committee on a Maori Perspective for the Department of Social Welfare, *Puao-Te-Ata-Tu: The Day Break Report* (Wellington: Department of Social Welfare, 1986).

17. Bailey, 223.

18. Ministerial Advisory Committee.

19. John M. Johnson, *Doing Field Research* (New York: The Free Press, 1975).

20. Bailey, 223.

21. Ibid.

22. See Appendix I.

23. For the complete text of this letter see Appendix III.

24. See Appendix IV for the 1986 organizational chart.

25. Department of Social Welfare, *Management Plan, 1986* (Wellington: Department of Social Welfare, 1986a); Department of Social Welfare, *Management Plan,1987* (Wellington: Department of Social Welfare, 1987c); Department of Social Welfare, *Report of the Department of Social Welfare for the Year Ending 31 March 1988* (Wellington: Government Printer, 1988b).

26. L. Schatzman and A. L. Strauss, *Field Research* (Englewood Cliffs, NJ: Prentice Hall, 1973).

27. See Appendix I.

28. Anne Opie, "Qualitative Methodology, Deconstructive Readings, Appropriation of the 'Other' and Empowerment" (Wellington: Victoria University, Department of Sociology), 7-8.

29. Schatzman and Strauss, 31.

30. Lincoln, 153.

31. H. Roberts, ed., *Doing Feminist Research* (London: Routledge and Kegan Paul, 1981).

32. Roger Hadley and Stephen Hatch, *Social Welfare and the Failure of the State: Centralized Social Services and Participatory Alternatives* (London: George Allen and Unwin, 1981); Roger Hadley and Morag McGrath, *When Social Services are Local: The Normanton Experience* National Institute Social Services Library, No. 48 (London: George Allen and Unwin, 1984); J. Black, R. Bowl, D. Burns, C. Critcher, G. Grant, and D. Stockford, *Social Work in Context* (London: Tavistock, 1983).

33. Richard A. Grinnell, ed., *Social Work Research and Evaluation,* (Itasca, Il: F. E. Peacock, Publishers, 1981), 350.

34. Michael Patton, *Qualitative Research Methods* (Beverly Hills: Sag, 1980).

35. See Appendix IV for a summary of research activities in the Napier District Office and in the Porirua District Office.

36. Hadley and Hatch.

37. Department of Social Welfare (DSW), *Contracting for Social Services: Principles and Guidelines* Wellington: Department of Social Welfare, July, 1988c) .

38. Ibid.

39. Wilson.

40. DSW, *Contracting.*

41. Rubin and Babbie.

42. Peter Drucker, *Management* (London: Pan Books, Heinemann, 1981).

43. David Nachimas and Chava Nachimas, *Research Methods in the Social Sciences* 2nd ed. (New York: St. Martin's Press, 1981).

44. Lincoln; Hinds, et al.

IV

THE NEW ZEALAND DEBATES: 1969-1988

Chapter One delineated the theoretical framework for analysing the context and implications of a move from a welfare state toward a welfare society for models of service delivery and social work practice. This chapter presents the document analysis of how this shift occurred in New Zealand during the period 1969-1988. The focus of the analysis is the Department of Social Welfare as the major statutory organization responsible for social service delivery in New Zealand. The documents which formed the basis of this analysis included the publications of the Department of Social Welfare, the New Zealand Planning Council (NZPC), the Social Advisory Council (SAC) and the New Zealand Association of Social Workers (NZASW). Additional materials were drawn from the reports of working parties and task forces established by the government; from the 1988 Report of the Royal Commission on Social Policy; and from publications of voluntary agencies and social service councils such as, the New Zealand Federation of Voluntary Welfare Organisations (NZFVWO) and the New Zealand Council of Social Services (NZCSS). Over hundred and twenty documents and numerous associated memoranda were analysed. These materials reflect the formal, public debates on the provision of social services in New Zealand.

The document analysis confirms that the amalgamation creating the New Zealand Department of Social Welfare followed a similar development in Britain subsequent to the release of the Seebohm Report in 1968. As a result of the Seebohm Report, the British Government created the Social Service Departments (SSDs) as centralized social service agencies with the responsibility of consolidating services and achieving coordination and efficiency.[1] Similarly, the objectives of the New Zealand amalgamation were aimed at increasing coordination and centralizing services; but, the features of the amalgamation had three significant differences. First, the New Zealand Department of Social Welfare did not assume responsibility for health social work services which in Britain included services to the elderly. Second, the New

Zealand Department was not based on a local authority structure as was its British counterpart. Lastly, the New Zealand Department was charged by the Department of Social Welfare Act, 1971 with responsibility for the provision of direct social services and supportive services to the voluntary sector and other government agency providers.[2]

Four themes were traced in the analysis of the documents. Graycar delineated the debates on the present and future operations of the Welfare State as "revolving around arguments about the degree of state intervention and the public/private split".[3] The public/private split was the first theme that emerged from the analysis and was considered under the heading 'Statutory-Voluntary Balance'. This debate centered on the extent of state responsibility for social services as New Zealand moved toward a welfare society. This theme is fundamental to discussions of welfare pluralism.[4] The second theme that emerged, discussed under the heading 'Service Delivery', traced commentary on the four principles that were to become the cornerstones of the 1986 restructuring: regionalization, decentralization, devolution, and partnership with the community. Management style, as the remaining aspect of organizational design discussed in the analytic framework chapter, was included under this heading. Billis[5] observed the constant attention given in social work literature to social work professionalism and definitions of the social work task. Debates on these two topics appear under the heading 'Social Work'. These three themes are obviously interrelated and interdependent as the document analysis will attempt to demonstrate.

The last theme traced was that of biculturalism. This analysis focuses on the development and impact of biculturalism on the social services during the period under study. The Department of Social Welfare embraced a commitment to the principles of the Treaty of Waitangi and bicultural practice as part of the restructuring process initiated in 1986. Although there are a few references to Maori-*Pakeha* (White Euopean) relationships in the earlier documentation, it is not until 1982 that references to cultural issues begin to appear with regularity in the documentation analysed. Because the move to biculturalism would become a significant factor in the form and content of the restructuring, analysis of biculturalism was added as a major thematic heading in the document analysis after 1982.

The purpose of the document analysis was to explore the debates on social service policy through the four themes that emerged: the statutory-voluntary balance, social service delivery issues, social work and biculturalism. It was not to present a detailed historical account of the period 1969 - 1988. The emergence and re-emergence of the themes may appear repetitious to the reader, but the repetition illustrates the growing strength and increasing acceptance of specific conceptualizations of each of the themes. A second issue for the researcher in the presentation of the document analysis was the proliferation of government reports and reviews commencing with the Labour Party assuming power in 1984. The sheer number of the reports and reviews was overwhelming. This reflected the objective of the Labour Party upon coming into office that "a considerable reorganisation of the New Zealand economy [and consequently all government activity] was necessary, and that this would involve considerable social dislocation".[6] The numerous reports and reviews comprehensively examined social service policy and practice. Many of the reports and reviews overlapped, were contradictory and had far-reaching implications for other actors in the social service delivery system. What was notable in the reports was the use of a common terminology (e.g., community, volunteers, partnership, biculturalism) without clarification of the meaning of the terms. A second notable characteristic of the documents was found in the apparent consensus on welfare pluralism, decentralization and partnership with the community as *the only viable* solution to the problems facing the social services.

For the purposes of analysis, the period 1969 to 1988 was divided into five periods as briefly outlined below in Table I. Each of the periods, though distinct, contain remnants of the past and the seeds of future developments and debates and, therfore, overlap. Despite the interrelatedness of the five periods, each has a distinct character which provided the basis for its designation. The significant documents and events for each period appear in a table following the general introduction to each of the periods as a further guide in the analysis. The documents and events are listed chronologically within each year.

Table II

THE FIVE PERIODS FOR ANALYSIS: 1969-1988

I. 1969 - 1974 The Amalgamation
There was not universal support for the creation of a central government bureaucracy with far reaching responsibilities over both the statutory and voluntary sector. Some felt the new department's responsibilities were too broad and others argued that the authorities granted were not broad enough to insure comprehensive and coordinated universal services.

II. 1975 - 1979 The Beginnings of Disquiet
During this period both the New Zealand Planning Council and the New Zealand Federation of Voluntary Welfare Organisations published documents expressing their concerns that the increasing bureaucratization and professionalization of social services was disempowering individuals and communities.

III. 1979 - 1981 The Turning Point
The influence of monetarism and Thatcherism paralleled increasingly vocal social pressures for change in the delivery of social services. Toward the end of this period the Maori community's awareness of the disproportionate numbers of Maori people in government welfare and penal institutions became a rallying point for action.

IV. 1982 - 1985 The Convergence of Events
It was during this period that political, economic, social, cultural and intraorganizational factors converged. The newly elected Fourth Labour Government commissioned several reviews of the social services, two of which led to the decision to place the Social Work Training Council in recession and to restructure the Department of Social Welfare.

V. 1986 -1988 The Implementation of the Restructuring

The Director-General of Social Welfare announced in the release of the 1986 *Management Plan* a new administrative structure and management style. The four principles of the restructuring were implemented and the Department accepted the recommendations of the Ministerial Task Force on a Maori Perspective, *Puao-Te-Ata Tu*, to demonstrate the Department's commitment to biculturalism. It is during this implementation period that the data collection was initiated and completed in mid- December 1988.

PERIOD I: 1969 - 1974 THE AMALGAMATION CREATING THE DEPARTMENT OF SOCIAL WELFARE

By the late 1960's western nations faced the need to re-examine their welfare systems over which criticisms of duplication, lack of coordination and absence of consultation had been leveled. One solution implemented was the development of centralized government agencies with responsibility for social services and a wide range of benefit programs. The 1968 Seebohm Report in Britain led to the creation of the Social Service Departments (SSDs) whose responsibilities included services to children and their families, the elderly and the intellectually handicapped.[7] This British development was to be emulated in New Zealand with the creation of the Department of Social Welfare in 1971.

Table III

SIGNIFICANT EVENTS AND DOCUMENTS
Period I: 1969-1974
THE AMALGAMATION

1969	Royal Commission on Social Security created Formation of the New Zealand Federation of Voluntary Welfare Agencies
1970	First Citizen Advice Bureaux established in Ponsonby
1971	Parliament passed the Department of Social Welfare Act
1972	Department of Social Welfare established Community Volunteers Programme launched
1973	New Zealand Social Work Training Council established
1974	Children and Young Person's Act provided for preventative and social work services for children and young persons requiring care, protection and control

THE STATUTORY - VOLUNTARY BALANCE

The trend toward amalgamation and centralization was equally evident outside the government sector, in the 1969 creation of the New Zealand Federation of Voluntary Welfare Organisations and in the establishment of the first Citizen's Advice Bureaux in Ponsonby, Auckland a year later. The objective of the Federation of Voluntary Welfare Organisations was:

> To help to end one of the weaknesses of New Zealand welfare agencies, both governmental and voluntary [which is] the lack of coordination.[8]

Membership in the Federation was limited to those voluntary organizations with a national structure and consequently, tended to be dominated by the larger, more formalized agencies, such as the New Zealand Society for the Intellectually Handicapped, the Crippled Children Society and the Young Men's Christian Association. By 1971, the Federation's members employed over 2,500 people with an annual budget of $10NZ million. Seventy-five percent of the operating budgets of the Federation's membership came from voluntary sources.[9]

The objectives of the New Zealand Association of Citizens Advice Bureaux were similar:

> To coordinate, encourage minimum standards for training, record keeping and confidentiality and provide at a national level consultation and cooperation between associations, government agencies and voluntary organisations.[10]

By the mid-1970's a National Association of Citizens' Advice Bureaux had been formed with thirty-eight offices in operation throughout the country working to encourage cooperation and coordination of services in both the statutory and non-statutory sectors.

SERVICE DELIVERY

Support for a centralized government agency charged with the responsibility for coordinating social services was voiced in New Zealand as early as the 1950s:

> During the 1950s concern was increasingly expressed at the fragmentation of social welfare services within government and in 1956, the Cabinet established an interdepartmental committee under the chairpersonship of Professor W. G. Minn, to look at ways to improve coordination and administration of government social welfare activities. The committee reporting to the Minister of Social Security in 1958 suggested the integration of social welfare services under a single government department but this did not eventuate.[11]

Jack and Robb[12] cited the establishment of a Social Welfare Advisory Board as the only outcome of the Minn Report. The subject of a comprehensive Department of Social Welfare was set aside as requiring further study by the 1962 Royal Commission. Several years later a report was prepared for the State Services Commission recommending the establishment of a centralized social work service within a department of social welfare to replace the services spread over several governmental departments. Such a department would offer economic assistance as part of a comprehensive service.

> The uniformity of provision and standard of provision . . . would actually be increased were the services to be dispensed by a Social Welfare Department.[13]

The creation of a comprehensive department of social welfare was discussed at the 1969 National Development Conference and became an election campaign issue.[14] Indeed, the National Party election manifesto for 1969 pledged amalgamation:

> Following the recommendations of the National Development Conference on the Coordination of Social Services, the National Government will give further consideration to bringing other areas of state welfare activity into the new department.[15]

Very early in the term of the National Government this recommendation was given approval in principle by Cabinet and a feasibility report was requested. The report supported the recommendation for amalgamation. Shortly afterward, legislation creating the the Department of Social Welfare with broad and sweeping responsibilities over the delivery of services and the providers of service both statutory and non-statutory, was passed into law:

> The Department shall maintain close liaison with and encourage co-operation and co-ordination among any organisations and individuals (including Departments of State and other agents of the Crown) engaged in social welfare activities.[16]

It is important to note, however, that the Act provided only for the amalgamation of child welfare and social security, not all of the social services. The New Zealand Association of Social Workers opposed the creation of the new department on the basis that it represented a "partial [response] . . . inadequate for both present and future needs . . . [and] implies further piecemeal development".[17]

SOCIAL WORK

The New Zealand Association of Social Workers (NZASW), established in 1964[18] attempted to expand its membership to meet the needs of the growing number of people in social work positions.[19] The creation of the Department of Social Welfare reclassified the Child Welfare Officers as social workers and contributed to a growing tendency to use the term 'social worker' to describe and classify social service positions in a number of agencies. This reflected similar theoretical developments in social work which were aimed at developing a model which would provide a 'common base' for social work practice.[20]

The New Zealand Association of Social Work conferences of this period[21] were characterized by heated debates over the contradictory trends of increased professionalization of social workers and the association's liberal membership criteria. NZASW membership criteriaThe membership criteria classified anyone holding a social work position as eligible for association membership. Some argued that without restricted entry the association would not be in a position to promote the profession effectively. Others responded that a restricted entry would be elitist, effectively limiting the association membership to the chosen few with academic qualifications and severely narrowing the association's base of support.[22]

The attention of NZASW during this period was not solely on increasing membership and establishing membership criteria. Considerable effort was expended in maximising the expressed support of the National Government in the establishment of an organization charged with the responsibility of education and training in social work. Despite the political stresses the Fourth Labour Government was facing with the upcoming election, the Social Work Training Council (SWTC) was established in 1973.[23] In its terms of reference, the Council was responsible for assessing the need for and the development of education and training in social work, establishing standards for social work practice and supporting social work research. The Council was created under the auspices of the Department of Social Welfare using the mandate of the Department of Social Welfare Act, 1971. This move further consolidated the Department's central role in social service delivery. The Department had been required under the law to:

> Provide for the training of such persons as the Minister may direct (whether employed in the service of Her Majesty or by any agencies of the Crown or

> by any other organisations) to undertake social welfare activities.[24]

The Social Work Training Council did not have a budget of its own nor the power to publish except under the auspices of the Department. The dependency on the Department of Social Welfare severely limited the Council's role. Allocation of funds for Council activities had to compete with the Department's multiple interests and such competition was often based on the principle of compensatory savings. For example, expenditure of funds to the Council had to be matched with savings or cuts in other programs.[25] The Social Work Training Council was dependent on Departmental administrative support, seconded staff, voluntary effort of social work educators, administrators and practitioners to service the Council's activities. Many in NZASW objected to this lack of autonomy. For example, NZASW had to make a formal written request to Department of Social Welfare (DSW) to be kept informed of the Council's recommendations and actions.[26]

The Department of Social Welfare was created, then, with the specific intention of developing a coordinated and comprehensive social service system. The state was to be the main provider *and* resourcer of social services. The voluntary sector was to fulfil a secondary role, complementary to state provided services. The trend toward centralized systems was equally evident in the statutory sector but in the voluntary and professional sectors. It was during this period the Federation of Voluntary Welfare Organisations was formed as was a national network of Citizen Advice Bureaux. The New Zealand Association of Social Workers established in the decade before, expanded its membership and cemented its foundations as it grappled with substantive professional and educational issues.

PERIOD II: 1975 - 1979 THE BEGINNINGS OF DISQUIET: THE GROWING BUREAUCRATIZATION AND PROFESSIONALIZATION OF SOCIAL WORK

The impact of a centralized government department was soon to be apparent. Child Welfare Officers resisted their transfer in a government department that was largely devoted to the distribution of monetary benefits. They felt their specialized services to children and families had been better supported in the Department of Education. The disproportionate balance between the financial benefits and personal social work services expenditures of the Department was further exacerbated by the National Superannuation Acts of 1976 and 1977. These Acts were primarily responsible for the dramatic budgetary growth of the Department of Social Welfare during the 1970's.

In a paper in 1973, a Working Party on Social Welfare argued that the objectives of the newly created Department for preventative social work utilizing community oriented approaches, were not being met in the continuing focus on child welfare services and the casework method. The Working Party urged all agencies to:

> Shift the emphasis from casework to family-oriented counsel and welfare services . . . to develop close consultation and coordination with the community . . . [and] to develop school social work programmes and a family service.[27]

Despite the objectives of the Department of Social Welfare, there was rising concern voiced as shown in the documentation analysed below, that individualized, specialized service provision was proving intractable to efforts for a more coordinated and comprehensive service delivery.

TABLE IV

SIGNIFICANT EVENTS AND DOCUMENTS
PERIOD II: 1975 - 1979
THE BEGINNINGS OF DISQUIET: THE GROWING BUREAUCRATIZATION AND PROFESSIONALIZATION OF SOCIAL WORK

1975 Superannuation Scheme introduced New Zealand Council of Social Services established by Minister of Social Welfare

1976 *New Zealand at the Turning Point*, Report of the Task Force on Economic and Social Planning, also known as 'The Holmes Report'

1977 National Superannuation Act

1978 *Sharing Social Responsibility* published by New Zealand Council of Social Services

NZASW Conference with Ivan Illich on "The Disabling Professions"

1979 *The Welfare State: Social Policy in the 1980s*, published by the New Zealand Planning Council

THE STATUTORY - VOLUNTARY BALANCE

By 1975, it was apparent that the mandate of the Department of Social Welfare to encourage cooperation and coordination among organizations and individuals engaged in social welfare activities had not occurred as an inevitable consequence of the centralization of statutory welfare activities. In 1976, the New Zealand Council of Social Service representing local district councils of social services was set up with the objective of supporting and coordinating the efforts of the district councils on a national level. The Council of Social Services encouraged the establishment of additional local district councils with wide non-traditional membership to provide linkage between local and national government.[28] The Council of Social Services received financial and administrative support through the Department of Social Welfare because of the Department's legislative mandate to encourage cooperation across the broad spectrum of service providers. The support offered by the Department to groups such as Council of Social Services had the paradoxical effect of further consolidating the central role of the Department in the development of non-statutory welfare sector. Departmental support created dependency, thus, further weakening the very sector the mandate was intended to strengthen. For example, the Council of Social Services was never able to firmly establish itself as a viable part of the social service infrastructure due, in part, to its dependence on the Department for sanction and support.

Public contribution to voluntary agencies quickly eroded, allegedly because New Zealanders viewed the state as both the primary funder and provider of social services and because the philantrophic tradition in New Zealand was never strong or well developed. In 1971, seventy five percent of the voluntary agencies operating budget came from voluntary sources.[29] By the 1975-1976 financial year, voluntary contributions had shrunk to less than 50% of operating budget expenditures prompting major concerns about the increasing dependence of voluntary agencies on governmental funding sources despite the emergence of nation wide fund-raising efforts such as the biennial Telethon event.

Another example of the growing dominance of the Department was demonstrated in the growth of children under the Department's care following its establishment:

> Despite the higher levels of prosperity in the 1950's and 1960's, foster children under the care of the state increased from 2,400 in 1950 to 4,585 in 1975. However, in the voluntary sector, children in foster care decreased from 2,400 in 1950 to 1,284 in 1975.[30]

Such figures further confirm the consolidation of services provision in the statutory sector with a subsequent weakening of the voluntary sector through loss of service volume to the state.

The New Zealand Planning Council publications during this period[31] contained mounting critical analysis of the dominance of statutory departments in all aspects of welfare and social services. These reports warned that excessive centralization and standarization of services could create alienation from authority in those receiving the service. Whereas, "a more relaxed approach to the development of local answers to local problems would be desirable for the social fabric and for the economy".[32] The NZPC's 1976 recommendations were more strongly stated in their publication two years later when they argued that greater variations could provide substantial economic and social benefits and facilitate the better use of all resources.[33]

Early in 1978, the Council of Social Services published their first major report. This body, established in November 1975 by the Minister of Social Welfare, had been instructed by the Minister to undertake a study and present recommendations concerning the appropriate role for central government, local authorities and voluntary organizations in the provision of social services. The report contended that, with the establishment of the Department of Social Welfare, the government had an agency with comprehensive responsibility for social welfare:

> To a substantial degree this meant that the state assumed responsibility for widespread social welfare services. . . . Its establishment created a much greater demand for service in social and community welfare than had been anticipated . . . with the widening of government welfare responsibilities. . . . there has been an increasing tendency for organisations and individuals to look to central government for financial support or action. . . Here is a risk that the development of major national organisations [statutory and non-statutory] could be seen as absolving local communities from their welfare responsibilities.[34]

The New Zealand Council on Social Services strongly criticized the national social welfare organizations (such as the New Zealand Federation of Voluntary Welfare Organisations) for not contributing to the overall distribution of resources according to need at the local level. Those organizations, alleged the Council had, through political influence and emotional appeal, gained significantly in national terms but could claim few accomplishment toward their stated goals. The Council noted that both the Department of Social Welfare Act, 1971 and the Children and Young Person's Act of 1974 provided for financial support of voluntary agencies engaged in the promotion of community, family and personal well being and in providing facilities and services for the community welfare of the disabled but "the implied allocation of resources has not taken place".[35] This view paralleled comments made earlier in the Holmes Report which reported general disillusionment with centrally determined services.

> The call for community involvement in social service policy formulation and in the provision of social services, is seen as a reaction against traditionally centrally determined services developed in New Zealand and the fact that such approaches have not been entirely effective in coping with the social problems facing New Zealand. It is considered important that . . . in future there be more systematic development of community solutions to social problems within a community setting.[36]

The Council of Social Services recommended the government "adopt a general policy of involving consumers and the general public *as far as practicable* [italics added] in all aspects of social service provision".[37] The caveat was based on the Council's assessment of regional and local government's limited capability to assume social welfare tasks.

> A further difficulty with the decentralisation or devolution of social service activity is the current state of local and regional government. . . . There is unlikely to be substantial development in the direction of decentralisation without the development of a more rational structure of local and regional government able to assume greater responsibility in the allocation of resources.[38]

The Planning Council concluded by arguing for a deliberate promotion of desirable trends which they contended were: (a) the strengthening of local communities and their ability to respond to their own needs, and (b) a change in emphasis from ameliorative or curative services to prevention and the promotion of general well-being. These objectives, it was argued, could be achieved by greater use of voluntary agencies, by central government moving from service provision to monitoring and promotional functions, by devolving responsibility for allocation of resources to the local level, and by channeling resources to promotion and prevention. The articulation of these 'desireable trends' would resurface with increasing regularity in the coming years as the debates on social policy directions continued.

The Planning Council repeated similar sentiments three years later when it argued that:

> Public participation in decision making and the devolution of some responsibility to the regional level are seen by many as essential techniques to bring about improved planning and delivery of services.[39]

Moreover, the Planning Council specifically noted that the design and delivery of services "should spread the burden of care and responsibility more widely within society".[40] These views, then, reiterated the sentiments expressed the previous year by the New Zealand Council of Social Services.[41]

Toward the later end of this period, the Planning Council became more adamant in its support for a "bottom up" approach to social policy decision making and provision.

> The real need, if the welfare state is to find new directions in the 1980s, is for the state to do less and at the same time assist people to do more for themselves. This will involve a shift in emphasis from the "top down" approach and the reliance on institutions, toward greater involvement and responsibility on the part of all citizens, i.e., a reinforcement of the 'bottom up' participatory approach.[42]

This advocacy was predicated on the assertions that: (a) increased spending by the state does not necessarily produce better results or meet people's expectation, (b) there are both rigidities and anomalies in the system as it developed and (c) a great many individuals support the need for alternative or additional forms of social service delivery.[43] The proliferation of unemployment committees, Women's Refuges and Rape Crisis Centres, alternative health care facilities and alternative schools during this period were cited as examples of the dissatisfaction with the system. Economic concerns were evident in the Planning Council's 1979 publication by the numerous references to tax-payers, cost effectiveness and the tax burden. This reflected the growing dominance of economic policy concerns in government and the deepening economic recession in New Zealand.

SOCIAL WORK

For social work, the two biennial conferences of their professional association held during this period were significant. An unauthored paper presented at the 1976 conference delineated six major dilemmas facing social work in New Zealand.[44] The dilemmas addressed in the conference paper are detailed here because they crystallize the major debates in social work during this period. The first three of the dilemmas focused on definitions of social work and the social work task that resulted from the assumption that the designation 'social worker' was applicable to anyone engaged in social service activities. The paper cited the existence of a small, but vocal group of community workers, who objected to being classified as social workers because they perceived their practice as distinct from social work. Many of these community workers were part of the Community Volunteer Programme. This program had taken on a clearly community development/social action approach by the mid-late 1970's.[45] Other community workers, some of whom were employees of local government involved in youth work and recreation, rejected social work with its emphasis on casework which they viewed as social control. The Association, which had grown from a child welfare and health social work base, faced the dilemma of how to meet the needs of an increasingly vocal and diverse membership while maintaining some standards in training and orientation.

The fourth dilemma addressed in the conference paper was that of the growing professionalization of social work. By the time of the 1976 conference, the efforts of many including the Social Work Training Council, to support the establishment of training opportunities had materialized. University based training programs had been established at Canterbury, Massey and Auckland Universities.[46] As well, there was growing resistance to the use of volunteers in the statutory sector as part of the social service delivery system. Those supporting professionalism saw the use of volunteers as undermining the professionalization of social work. The practice of social work, it was argued, required trained social workers. Community workers, it was asserted in this paper, saw such a move as being contrary to the principles of community development and community work which emphasized participation of community groups and individuals in service provision. Community workers' viewed the move toward professionalization as distancing workers from clients and disempowering clients by increasing their dependency on experts for problem resolution.

The last two dilemmas addressed in the conference paper were the developments in generic social work theory and the cultural dilemma. This last dilemma addressed the unease many *Pakeha* social workers reported in attempting to work effectively with the growing number of Maori and Polynesian clients. The absence of Maori and Polynesian social workers in the Association ranks was noted. This was not the first time that issues of culture had been raised at a Social Work Conference[47] but it did reflect a developing sophistication with the complexities of cultural issues by acknowledging that there might be added considerations in cross-cultural social work then the ones currently being addressed.

Unfortunately, the conference papers from the 1978 Biennial Conference held at Massey University were incomplete. However, this does not deny the significance of this conference in the debates about social work professionalism and the social work task. The keynote address was given by Ivan Illich who presented material from his jointly authored 1977 publication on *The Disabling Professions*. Illich's views were well received by the anti-professional lobby in the social work and community work ranks. Rather than a challenge to guard against the excesses evident in traditional professions, the Illich critique was regarded as confirmation that through increasing professionalization, social work was in danger of becoming an elitist monopoly guilty of all the worst excesses of the privileged, established professions. The Illich critique added a further dimension to the work of the radical social work theorists[48] who contend that the casework focus of social work relegated the social work task to a social professionalization criticism of developments in control function in society.

This second period (1975 - 1979), then, witnessed heated debates about social service delivery models and social work. Two major bodies argued increasingly adamantly in their publications for a shift from a service delivery model which was centrally resourced and provided to a model that would both recognize and assist local community development and service provision. The Planning Council and the Council of Social Services were not unaware of the potential difficulties in the approach they were advocating, but both councils emphasized the advantages of a preventative, community based approach over a curative, professionally provided centralized social service delivery system. The professionalization of social work experienced great strides through the development of university based training programs and in the growth of association membership. At the same time, these developments were heavily criticized by supporters of radical social work theory and by the critics of professionalization of social work. It is in the documents of this period that the seeds of the restructuring are clearly evident. The features of an alternative delivery system discussed during this period would become incorporated in the principles of the 1986 restructuring.

PERIOD III: 1979 - 1982 THE TURNING POINT

Analysis of the documents of this period reflected the expectation of imminent political and social change. No longer was change at issue, for change was seen as inevitable. It was only the timing, the form and content of the changes that was yet to be determined. Social service debates during this period were dominated by events in Auckland. This city, with a population of nearly one-third of New Zealand's population, was beset with the problems of rapid urbanization, disproportionate unemployment in the Maori and Pacific Island communities, a strengthening of the Maori activist movement (e.g., Bastion Point and Maori Land Rights demonstrations) and signs of increasing racial strife between *Pakeha* and Maori and between Maori and Pacific Islanders.

Two developments in Auckland set the scene for the beginning of this period. The first was the decision in 1978 to implement a plan "for decentralizing the Department's operations in the Auckland area"[49] with the goal of dealing more efficiently with this concentration of the Department of Social Welfare services. Administration of the Auckland area had become problematic because of its sheer size, the proliferation of district offices and its geographical distance from Head Office, Wellington. The creation of the Auckland Region in 1980 was regionalization in its pure form because it was administrative only--it involved few delegations of authority.[50] It did however, provide the opportunity for the Department to debate, experiment and evaluate selected issues of regionalization as a precursor to the deliberations and decisions that were to take place later.

The second development was the decision by the Human Rights Commission under Section 5 (1)(3) of the Human Rights Commission Act of 1977 to receive and resolve the complaints laid before the Commission by the Auckland Committee on Racism and Discrimination (ACORD). This decision was made on the 6th of April 1979 and the enquiry was set to commence in Auckland, 11 February to 13 February, 1980. There was, however, two years lasped before the report was sent to the Minister of Justice on 30 August 1982.[51] ACORD made complaints about the treatment of young Maori in the six Department of Social Welfare institutions for young people in and around the Auckland area. The significance of the ACORD Report was not only in its attention to the treatment of Maori youth in the institutions, in particular about the alleged indiscriminate use of the isolation in the secure units, but in drawing attention to the alarmingly disproportionate numbers of Maori in the nation's institutions of youth justice and welfare. This reality became a central issue in Maoridom's claim to assume responsibility and control for their own people.[52] The heading of 'Biculturalism' was added to the document thematic analysis from this period forward to reflect its significance as a major concern for the Department of Social Welfare.

Table V

SIGNIFICANT EVENTS AND DOCUMENTS
Period III: 1979 - 1982
THE TURNING POINT

1979	Human Rights Commission accepts the complaints laid by the Auckland Committee on Racism and Discrimination
1980	Auckland Region created
1981	*Directions*, the New Zealand Planning Council report advocating a shift of responsibility for social programmes to non-government providers
1982	Ann Hercus, Keynote Speaker at the NASW Conference "applauding the virtues of a mixed economy with a diversity of institutions and many power centres"
	Human Rights Commission Report on the Department of Social Welfare treatment of young Maori released
	University Grants Committee, Review Committee (The Brownlie Report), *Social Work Education in New Zealand Universities*
	Report of Committee to Report to the Minister of Social Welfare on the Current

Practices and Procedures Followed in Institutions in Auckland: The Johnston Report

Community Development Unit established in Head Office

Roger Hadley described his model of community oriented practice to Head Office staff and District Directors

---

THE STATUTORY - VOLUNTARY BALANCE

The arguments for an alternative to state dominated, centralized services was gaining widespread support with the New Zealand Planning Council's further clarification and strengthening of their preference for community based services. By the time *Directions* [53] was published, the Planning Council was clearly advocating a shift of responsibility for social programs to non-governmental providers. The Planning Council argued for community participation, better coordination, a preventative approach to the delivery of social services, a devolution of governmental responsibility, decentralization and support for self-help groups and community initiatives. These were the very characteristics delineated as the essential features of a welfare society.

Three developments provided additional support for the model the New Zealand Planning Council was promulgating. The first was widespread endorsement for Thatcherism and British-style monetarist policies. Brian Easton, the New Zealand economist, noting the changes occurring in New Zealand's political and business centres, argued:

> The welfare state evolved in New Zealand as a consequence of the unregulated private market's failure to attain social goals in social welfare . . . In particular, there is no certainty that in a private market economy, the distribution of goods and services to individuals will be socially acceptable.[54]

He concluded his thesis with a warning that some would later argue went unheeded:

> What the people of New Zealand want could be subverted by others in the name of the dominance of the economy. . . . The Welfare State has been a community response to historical change. To go against this historical thrust would be to abandon New Zealand as a community.[55]

Monetarist economic theory, with its emphasis on the free market and individual responsibility, began to dominate the thinking of the political and business communities. The 'historical thrust' Easton refered to provided little resistence. Concerns about cost effectiveness, advanced management techniques, inputs and outcomes became prevalent as views about the continued viability of the welfare state dominated the political and economic scene.

The second major influence was the development of a model for community social work in Britain as articulated by Roger Hadley and colleagues[56] and described in Chapter One. To recapitulate, Hadley with Hatch argued for redressing the imbalance between state and non-statutory provision of social services. The argument was based on a conceptualization of social work in close interaction with a circumscribed geographical community or 'patch' in which the social work task is broadly defined to encompass the full range of services from financial and psychological supports to comprehensive and specialized services utilizing both informal and formal networks. The two cornerstones of the model, participation and the use of volunteers, had received attention in a New Zealand Federation of Voluntary Welfare Organizations publication[57] although based on an earlier conceptualization of the model. The Federation's publication acknowledged the Minister of Social Welfare's support for the 'patch system' and noted that under successive National Party governments, the growth of financial support to voluntary agencies from vote Social Welfare had grown from $4,837,000 in 1975/6 financial year to $15,984,382 in the 1980/1981 financial year.[58] The Federation cited the special financial programs for the New Zealand Society for the Intellectually Handicapped and Plunket Society. These funding arrangements further established these voluntary organizations as quasi-government agencies dependent on high levels of government funding and exemplified the growing trend by government to use the voluntary sector as a significant provider of social services for identified groups.

Support for the Hadley and Hatch model was further promulgated by a highly respected social worker upon his return from a year in Britain as the recipient of the Nuffield Scholarship. In mid-1982, Ketko published his report, *Social Work Developments in England,*

1981/1982. Ketko was a top ranking career social worker in Head Office with a responsibility for social work policy. His report, which was mainly descriptive, reflected a dissatisfaction with the dominance of centralized, bureacratized social service provision and advocated the adoption of a community-centered approach to social service delivery. His preference for the community-centered approach of Hadley and Hatch was based on two critical features:

> 1. The strengthening of informally and formally organized voluntary support systems so that the need to turn to the statutory sector is reduced
>
> 2. The establishment of programmes to increase the effectiveness of direct intervention by the social services when this remains necessary through seeking earlier identification of those at risk and by deploying a larger proportion of personnel in front-line positions with the ability to provide help.[59]

Such an approach, Ketko argued, would increase the capacity of communities to assume and/or extend their caring capacities by governmental funding and resourcing programs designed to support community efforts. The approach would rely heavily on early identification and intervention by informal care-givers with minimum training and expertise but backed up by a small cadre of specialists. Ketko's support was a decisive factor in the promulgation of the ideas of Hadley and Hatch. It is assumed that Ketko was instrumental in arranging for Hadley's presentation to Head Office Staff and District Directors at their annual conference in 1982.

The growing influence of the community-centered approach was evident in the Department's report of the *Review of the Social Work Division*.[60] This review had been set up as a joint exercise between the Department of Social Welfare and the State Services Commission. It was the brief of the Review Team to respond to concerns about recruitment for managerial and training positions in Head Office and to address the appropriateness of social work staffing at the middle management levels in District Offices. The Review Team, however, assumed a much wider brief. The Review recommended a statement of values, principles and commitments encompassing all areas of its work be formulated by the Department and that "urgency be given to developing goals and objectives for the Social Work Division".[61] These recommendations seemed to imply a lack of direction, an implicit criticism of the social work service and a demand for leadership from the Department.

It is imperative to note that the *Review of the Social Work Division* made no specific reference to the ethnic issues addressed in the Johnston Report on Maori youth in Department institutions published earlier that year.[62] The Review did address the issues of the Auckland Region by rejecting the concept of regionalization as a viable management structure. The Review recommended that a regional director's role be one of leadership, not authority, and recommended delegations of authority be passed directly to District Offices.

> We consider it is time that the Department made a conscious policy move towards a more decentralised system of management and that an early step in implementing this is to review the social work delegations with a view to retaining the absolute minimum of decision making within Head Office. The Working Party is divided on the extent to which major casework decisions relating especially to children in care, should be delegated to Directors specifically.[63]

Further recommendations of the *Review of the Social Work Division* included the establishment of a Senior Practitioner Grade in an effort to reward and retain practitioners at the front-line and the development of a comprehensive training program for practice and supervision including a Certificate of Proficiency to be offered internally by the Department. The Review quoted the Social Work Training Council statistics[64] which showed that only 17% of all social workers had a qualification appropriate to their task and only 3% of the Department's front-line workers held a social work qualification. Despite the discussion on the needs of training and the specific types of training that were required, there was no mention made of training needs in cultural sensitivity or bicultural practice. The recommendation for a departmental certificate may have been a reaction against the strong support in the Brownlie Report[65] for university based social work training programs and the growing frustration with the apparent inability of the Social Work Training Council to develop social work training opportunities for youth and community workers.[66] The Review recommended that departmental policy recognize social welfare volunteers as part of the Department's services. There was considerable variation from district to district in the use and support of volunteers and considerable variation over time within a particular district, as well.[67] The recommendations of the Review acknowledged the marginality of volunteers in the Department and recommended the volunteer programs be regarded as an integral feature of the Department's activities.

In addition, the Review expressed scepticism with community development activities as a statutory responsibility and drew once again from the British experience.

> In the present state of limited resources [the Review] tends to agree with Professor Pinker's minority view [in the Barclay Report, 1981] that a statutory social work service must be selective in its approach to community work and that . . . it has neither the capacity, the resources nor the mandate to go looking for needs in the community at large'.[68]

The scepticism with statutory based community development activities clearly evident in the Review, ran contrary to the expressed support of a community-centered social work approach which permeated other departmental documents and the 1982 establishment of a Community Development Unit based in Head Office. The purpose of the Community Development Unit was "to assist field and residential social work services to respond effectively to new and changing community needs and expectations".[69] The recommendations of the *Review of the Social Work Division* [70] proposing the delegation of social work decision making to the District Offices and supporting a community social work model utilizing volunteers, voluntary agencies and informal networks would feature in the restructuring of 1986. Few of its other recommendations were implemented.

SOCIAL WORK

The University Grants Committee, the body responsible for oversight and funding of tertiary education in New Zealand, instructed a review of social work training opportunities be undertaken. The Brownlie Report which was published in May of 1982 noted that of the 2,500 surveyed full-time paid employees in social work, only 14.3% held a social work qualification although the percentage was substantially higher (32.5%) for those in supervisory or administrative positions.[71] social workers number of trainedThe Brownlie Report strongly argued for the university as the appropriate site for social work training while acknowledging the issues of access and equity. Recognition of the needs for training and education for social workers in the Auckland Region was noted as was the political reality which precluded any effort to resurrect a social work program at the University of Auckland following its demise in 1981. The Brownlie Report urged the establishment of a social work training program in the Auckland Teachers College, as a tertiary institution with the capability and willingness to support a program tailored to meet the needs of the large multi-racial population of Auckland. The Brownlie Report supported social work professionalization and urged expanding access through initiatives in certificate and extramural programs.

The debates of the 1982 New Zealand Association of Social Workers Conference, entitled "Social Justice: A Social Work Concern for the 80s," acknowledged that the features of the welfare state were undergoing a metaphorphosis. Ann Hercus, Minister of Social Welfare gave the keynote address at the Conference in which she set out her assumptions about the welfare state and social policy:

> I applaud the virtues of a mixed economy. I want an economy which is market based . . . because the alternative (monolithic state control) would destroy our pluralistic democracy. . . I want an open, pluralist, participatory democracy, with a *diversity* [sic] of institutions, *many* [sic] power centres. But I can see that even the value of majority rule cannot be accepted as an absolute principle; it has to be restricted by the principle of inalienable rights of individuals, which no majority verdict may abrogate. . . Social justice in a democracy must involve the synthesis of those two great values-the rights of the individual and the rights of the community.[72]

Ranganui Walker, a noted Maori leader and academic, contended in his reply to the keynote speech that a pluralistic democracy did not exist in New Zealand's centralized, bureaucratic governmental system:

> The linkages between freedom and individualism on the one hand and equality and collectivism on the other are complex and often involve competing and equally valid rights . . . [the keynote speaker] advocates a pluralistic democracy with many power centres . . . we have in the last decade drifted into the power of the superstate which threatens to subjugate us all. . . . You, as social workers . . . have a responsibility to assist in the development of

> community groups as alternative power centres to moderate the influence of the superstate.[73]

An attack on the supremacy of economic theory in determining the goals of New Zealand was the focus of the second response to the keynote address given by Alf Kirk of the Federation of Labour. Rather than the development of many power centers his view of the last decade of New Zealand was further "concentration of power in the hands of a few . . . a growing gap between the rich and the poor".[74] Kirk's criticism extended to social workers in their professional role.

> The point that is important to bear in mind is that many of the poor and the oppressed in our society are victims of the options taken by professionals; can social workers, committed to 'professionalism,' really be an authentic voice for social justice to those people?[75]

The challenges presented at this conference further deepened the developing crisis of confidence in New Zealand's social work community. This crisis became more acute and pervasive as the radical social work literature proliferated, as the split between social workers and community workers grew, and as the Maori demands for Maori social workers for Maori clients became more vocal.

BICULTURALISM

The Department of Social Welfare initiated its own review of the *Current Practices and Procedures Followed in Institutions of the Department of Social Welfare in Auckland* in response to the Human Rights Commission Report. This report by Johnston, which was prepared in six weeks and issued on the 29th of October, 1982, acknowledged:

> Many, if not all, the practices and procedures which formed the basis of the representations by ACORD have been eradicated and the Department has embarked on a program of innovative change.[76]

The recommendations in the Johnston Report emphasized the need for pre-entry, in-service and advanced training at every level of staffing and noted that the Department's scheme for training for newly appointed residential social workers had never been implemented.

While recommending measures to prevent institutionalization of Maori youth, the Johnston Report addressed the monoculturalism of institutions under the heading of 'Cultural Practice':

> With the large proportion of Maori and Polynesian young people in the Homes, the Committee of Enquiry was interested to learn to what extent it was possible for them to become involved in the expression of their own culture and to what extent cultural values were evident on shaping the general policy of the institutions.[77]

Johnston raised the question but did not report if cultural values were integrated into institutional policy or make clear recommendations. Although Johnston's discussion of cultural issues consumed only three pages of the sixty-three page report, the comments are significant because it was the first time that a report from the Department specifically addressed issues of monoculturalism.

The Johnston Report strongly recommended that "every effort should be made to find alternative care within the community".[78] The Report strongly supported policies that would stem the tide of Maori youth into welfare and penal institutions.

> That policy will demand much of the local Maori communities. But if those communities are willing, in one way or another, according to their own traditions, to provide the necessary shelter and nurture for Tu-Tangata, then they may rightly expect financial resources put at their disposal for such a purpose.[79]

This quote referred to the request by Maori people 'to care for our own' and clearly stated the expectation of a subsequent transfer of resources from the state for that purpose. Transfer of resources for community provided social services would come to characterize Government-Maori relations in the following years.[80] The Johnston Report pointed to two programs as examples of efforts to utilize and develop community efforts to prevent young people coming into care. The first was the Community Care Unit of the Department in South Auckland that utilized social workers with extensive knowledge of and commitment to the identified local community. The second was a West Auckland cooperative scheme involving the Departments of Social

Welfare, Maori Affairs, Justice, the local schools and Police Youth Aid Officers.

> A highly important adjunct to this scheme is the acceptance of responsibility by the local Maori Community for dealing with offenders in a manner springing out of the Maori culture and centred upon the Hoani Waititi Marae. The Marae has at its disposal a whole network of community groups scattered throughout the area available for involvement in this community responsibility for its own people.[81]

The joint efforts exemplified in these two examples were indicative of a growing awareness of the interrelationships of social problems and of the imperative to assume the holistic approach as integral to the Maori world view.

It is essential to note that the debates concerning community involvement and decentralization during this period had several unique characteristics. Community involvement had a vague and generalized meaning. While implying participation of a wider representation, community involvement was not couched in terms of representations of gender, race, or users of the service as was to be the case later in the 1980's. Decentralization had a classic definition of delegation of authority and responsibility down the hierarchy, in this case to lower levels in the government departments or a decentralization from central to local government but did not include notions of power sharing with Maori or disadvantaged groups. Devolution was used interchangeably with decentralization although at times it referred to transfers of responsibility for various tasks between government departments, from one level of government to another, i.e., from national to regional or local government, or from government departments to non-statutory agencies. Focused consideration of racial or cultural issues, for example on the role of *iwi* authorities, had not yet emerged.

PERIOD IV: 1983 - 1985
THE CONVERGENCE OF EVENTS LEADING TO THE RESTRUCTURING

There were four clearly identifiable sources gaining momentum for dramatic social policy change during this period. In the political arena, the National Government was facing serious threat to political supremacy which it would lose in the election of 1984. Policy analysts were vocally decrying the bureaucratization and professionalization of social services. Maori activists were clamouring to assume responsibility for their people disproportionately represented in welfare and penal institutions. Social workers, community workers and social policy makers were continuing to debate the virtues of alternative social service delivery systems.

This turmoil was reflected in the accelerated pace with which working parties and reviews were initiated, extensive community consultations were arranged, submissions on various proposals were elicited, and reports were disseminated during the years immediately preceeding the restructuring. Biculturalism, as a major factor to be considered in the planning and delivery of social services, gained significant political power during this period.

Table VI

SIGNIFICANT EVENTS AND DOCUMENTS
Period IV: 1983 - 1985
THE CONVERGENCE OF EVENTS

1983	Maori Advisory Unit established in Auckland
	State Services Commission booklet on "Public Service in Multi-Cultural Society" recommended that (1) there be equal employment representation in relation to ethnic populations and (2) government departments maintain records of staff ethnic composition
	Maatua Whangai, a program established as a joint effort of Department of Justice, Maori Affairs, and Social Welfare
1984	*Meeting Needs in the Community* published by the New Zealand Planning Council
	Maori Economic Development Summit Conference

	Economic Summit acknowledged three sectors (government, business and voluntary) as equal partners in the quest to build a more prosperous, and harmonious society." The metaphor of a three-legged stool was used to portray the relationship with all three legs essential to maintain balance
1985	*Institutional Racism in the Department of Social Welfare*
	Maori Advisory Unit Report
	Labour Department announced Community Organisation Grants Scheme

---

The first two years of this period were dominated by increasingly caustic political debates on social and economic policies and by the 1984 snap election which brought about the fall of the National Government, the "Think Big" capital investment development projects and Prime Minister Robert Muldoon. The Labour Party Caucus chose David Lange as Prime Minister and Roger Douglas as Finance Minister as leaders committed more to a rejection of the past than with a vision of the future. Easton argued that Labour visualized a restructuring option which:

> Involved liberalisation, with the removal of external and internal protection. . . . There is no indication in the Labour Opposition debates of the monetarist macroeconomic strategy that was finally adopted . . . Rather, the restructurers were led, step by step, down the monetarist commercialist path, probably for much of the time not fully aware where that path was leading.[82]

Pervasive social and economic changes were promulgated through the numerous working parties and review committees commissioned shortly after the Labour Government assumed power.

Issues of biculturalism and the major public consultation efforts of the government in several areas of government activity dominated 1985 and 1986. In the social services a complex consultation process was established for a benefit and tax review and for public submissions on the proposed changes to the Children and Young Person's Act of 1974. What was significant about these consultations was that the process utilized was based on the government coming to the people to accept formal and informal submissions, in written or oral form, in public meetings and on *marae* (tribal grounds). The Maori voice was increasingly more vocal, more organized and more focused. The submissions of the Maori community on the proposed changes to the Children and Young Person's Act clearly stated their desire to take responsibility for their own and their insistence that if a Maori child were taken into care the process of that care must respect Taha Maori.[83]

THE STATUTORY - VOLUNTARY BALANCE

The briefing papers to the incoming Minister of Social Welfare in 1984 emphasized the pressures on the Department due to the sharp rise in unemployment and in particular, the stress in the social work division due to the increased levels of family dysfunction and family violence referrals. Departmental social work staff were under considerable strain from:

> The demands for them to become more involved in and supportive of community initiatives while at the same time coping with a growing workload of statutory duties . . . despite attempts at community care and the Maatua Whangai programme, admission figures in institutions have reached new highs this year.[84]

The Briefing Papers, however, contended that "in recent years, the Department has sought to scale down its costly institutional programme"[85] in favour of community care. The Briefing Papers encouraged increased Departmental support for community based initiatives.

The Minister of Social Welfare in her conference address of the Annual Meeting of the Social Advisory Council reconfirmed support for continued existence of the Social Advisory Council.[86] This was interpreted by the Council as approval for its efforts in supporting the networking tasks of the District Councils of Social Services at the local level. The purpose of the District Councils was to encourage coordination and cooperation among local community groups and voluntary interests. A conference recommendation proposed a Federation of the thirty seven district councils as essential to carry out their task.

Additional support for the voluntary sector was heard from two sources within the Department of Social Welfare. Helen Wyn of the Department's Social Programme Evaluation Unit authored a paper on the Department's voluntary funding schemes and concluded that:

> Presently, virtually everything has to be approved through Head Office . . . [the need for] ministerial approval for most funding decisions tends to be labour intensive and slow. This [is] seen as inconsistent with the desire to gain from the innovation and flexibility of the voluntary sector.[87]

Wyn called for a streamlining of the voluntary funding process and noted that voluntary agencies tend to be more responsive to community needs and provide a more cost-efficient service than government. Her colleagues, Carson and Hennessey (1984) in their interim report on the allocation of social work resources, argued that their research demonstrated that the existing workload formula only included intervention cases that have already come to notice. Within the formula there was no mechanism for accounting for preventative or alternative social work activities such as community work or coordination with volunteers and voluntary organizations or groups. Their data demonstrated that:

> In the 1975 caseload formula weights 75.6% of time was to be allocated to casework compared to now 67% . . . due to the changing nature of departmental casework.[88]

In addition, basic grade social workers had increased their allocation of time for coordination with voluntary organizations from 15% in 1983 to 18.4% in 1984. Such an increase, Carson and Hennnesey postulated, reflected a willingness to engage in more community oriented activities. However, strict use of the workload formula could mean social workers would be disadvantaged in evaluation and promotion rounds despite current policy directives. Carson and Hennessey[89] recommended that the workload formula be changed to allocate a minimum of 18% of basic grade time social work time to non-casework community oriented activities.

Outside the Department, Planning Council in their publication, *Meeting Needs in the Community*,[90] called for community-based alternatives with a "devolution of government responsibility and decentralisation of services".[91] The publication offered a critical analysis on the role of the state in the provision of social services delineating the potential weaknesses of provision in the voluntary sector. Davey and Dwyer offered a description of existing community based programs in the Departments of Health, Social Welfare, Maori Affairs and Justice as examples of the support and potential of community based programs. *Meeting Needs in the Community* asserted that a community oriented approach was supported nationally by the New Zealand Council of Social Services and internationally by the Organisation for Economic Co-Operation and Development. In the introduction to this publication, Planning Council Chairman expressed the view of the Council as supporting:

> The ideal of a 'welfare society' replacing the 'welfare state.' Internationally, the OECD [is] prominent in advocating such a shift.[92]

Moreover, it was significant that this same agency had in an earlier review of the New Zealand economy explicitly advocated such a shift.[93]

It was the view of Davey and Dwyer that "indications are that the encouragement of 'community' rather that 'state' services is becoming clearer as a policy objective".[94] They supported the conclusions of the Barclay Report on the roles and tasks of British social workers[95] advocating governmental support of family based informal caring networks. Such support was seen to reduce the potenitalities of family care system breakdown and the subsequent need for formal services. Davey and Dwyer, in their recommendations for community-based services, warned that:

> (a) All sectors have a role to play in meeting needs and that the government cannot be reduced to a residual role in service delivery
>
> (b) Despite the attractiveness of flexible, market-based services, their growth may perpetuate inequalities of access
>
> (c) It cannot be assumed that an increased role of the voluntary sector in service provision will, on its on, lead to better, more effective or more participatory services, and
>
> (d) If emphasis is laid on encouraging families and non- governmental groups to provide increasing

> amounts of care, thus reducing dependence on central government, then this suggests that the state's role is residual or a *provider of last resort*.

Davey and Dwyer cautioned that, "Some suggest the thrust for community-based services is motivated by a desire to reduce government responsibility for providing care" because "despite widespread support for the idea of 'community services,' the funds available do not appear to have increased in real terms".[96]

Although there were indications that the government was giving signals of a shift to heavier reliance on the voluntary sector, the message was ambivalent. In mid-1985, the Minister of Labour announced his intention to phase-out the Voluntary Organisation Training Programme (VOTP). This scheme provided support for staff salaries in voluntary organizations. Many voluntary organizations were solely dependent on VOTP monies for staff salaries. The outcry was so strong that by December, 1985, a new scheme of support to the voluntary sector was proposed: the Community Organisation Grant Scheme (COGS). The establishment money of $20 million was to come from existing grants in the Departments of Labour and Social Welfare. Whether or not it truly reflected existing levels of allocation was impossible to determine but many felt it was substantially lower than the VOTP budget. The scheme was innovative in its administrative structure and was to become the prime example of devolution in practice.[97]

COGS had a two tier funding system. An allocation of $11.5 million was to be distributed to national organizations such as Rape Crisis Centres and Te Kohanga Reo. The latter program, meaning literly, 'language nests,' provided for the teaching of Maori language and culture to children under five years old. The remaining allocation to be distributed through a system of COGS allocation committees for 'essential social services' as determined by locally based committees responding to local needs. A national structure was created with eleven field workers whose responsibility was to support the local committees with two national coordinators assuming overall responsibility and with direct accountability to the Minister of Social Welfare.[98] The administrative structure, however, was for advice and support only. The allocation of resources was the responsibility of the committees who were charged with the responsibility of protecting their allocation carefully by resisting any pressure to conform to government expectations for allocations.[99] The COGS program was the first and, virtually the only, truly devolved program in the Department before 1988 and, hence, was used repeatedly by the government as a prime example of government policy and of the ability of the community to take responsibility for its own needs. It critical to note that the COGS program, despite its community emphasis, continued its reliance on the state as the sole funder.

SERVICE DELIVERY

In proposing a shift to decentralized services and a heavier reliance on voluntary groups to provide service, Davey and Dwyer warned that although such policy objectives include increased flexibility, participation of consumers, and responsiveness to diversity, shifting the base of a service is not sufficient to ensure the participation of, let alone accountability to, clients or to the wider community. They noted that such a shift in New Zealand would be complicated by two factors. Firstly, they argued, there were indications of definite limits to the ability and the willingness of families and volunteers to provide more care. This was partly because New Zealand has an historical dependency on the state for social provision as a "comprehensive welfare state where centralisation and universality are emphasized, and the needs of individuals, families and households are defined for them by government."[100]

Secondly, effective decentralization and devolution is dependent on a strong local governmental infrastructure to promote community development and services. Such an infrastructure was not evident in New Zealand. Davey and Dwyer concurred with an earlier observation of the Planning Council:

> In the area of social services, as in other aspects of national development, there is unlikely to be substantial development in the direction of decentralisation without the development of a stronger and more rational structure of local and regional government able to assume greater responsibility in the allocation of resources.[101]

Moves to develop a stronger local government were under discussion during this period and the debates about that process, for example on revenue sharing alternatives, would come to play a dominant role in the political arena in the following years.[102]

One of the major arguments in favor of decentralization and devolution was the demand for meaningful partnership with the community, broadly conceptualized during this period as contribution to social service planning. Large bureaucracies were seen as alienating and unresponsive to local needs. The research of Davey and Dwyer led them to the significance of two aspects of participation which do not necessarily occur simultaneously: participation in decision making and participation in provision. They noted that "the greater the amount of participation, the more complex and time-consuming the process of decision-making tends to be".[103] Yet,

> Consumer involvement should be encouraged for ideological reasons, as a recognition of people's right to participate and to be in control of their own living and as an antidote to dependency.[104]

While acknowledging that instances of both types of participation are part of New Zealand's social fabric, participation was not assessed as equal or equitable when examining the realities of representativeness on decision making bodies:

> More participation and self-help require greater input from clients, however, the lower income, less educated groups generally have less time and fewer influential contacts to ensure their particular needs are met. The possibility of greater inequality with more 'community based' services is very real.[105]

SOCIAL WORK

Davey and Dwyer viewed professionalism and participation as mutually exclusive. Social service professionals in health, justice and social welfare:

> Work on applying expert knowledge on the analysis and treatment of an individuals problem and see themselves as able to make the best decision.[106]

The emphasis on the employment of educated professionals not only led to higher socio-economic status for these groups but had accentuated the class differences between professions and clients. Davey and Dwyer asserted that anti-welfarism and anti-professionalism was evident in the exponential growth of alternative health care facilities, advocacy groups and self-help groups of the previous decade.

The newly appointed Minister of Social Welfare, aware of these contrary views, embarked on a program of change by initiating a series of ministerial reviews of existing structures and program. Among the initial reviews commissioned was a review of the Social Work Training Council.[107] When the Minister appointed a Ministerial Review Committee, she simultaneously requested that the Social Work Training Council prepare its own review of its activities. The self evaluation provided the Training Council with an opportunity to summarize its accomplishments during its twelve year history, to comment on its inability to develop an extensive 'mosaic of educational opportunities,' and to acknowledge the voluntary contributions of its members over the years. The Training Council noted its lack of funds, its dependency on Departmental staff secondments (temporary appointments) and the inadequacy of Department administrative support as major constraints in its achieving the objectives set out in its terms of reference. Despite these constraints, the Social Work Training Council had been supportive of the establishment of four university-based social work programs; had established program standards and completed a round of accreditation of the university based programs; had brought New Zealand social work into the international social work network; and had completed a number of research projects, the most notable of which was the Rochford and Robb[108] nationwide survey of social service personnel.[109]

The Ministerial Review Committee was extremely critical of the Training Council's emphasis on university based programs and attacked the Training Council for its preoccupation with professional education at the expense of pre-entry and specialized training programs for youth and community workers.[110] The Ministerial Review Committee called for the replacement of the Social Work Training Council with an Aotearoa Training Council that would emphasize the bicultural needs of New Zealand society and the training needs of voluntary workers.

The Ministerial Review Committee Report stimulated fierce debate for its perceived anti-professional bias and its explicit emphasis on biculturalism. Both Reports were submitted to the Minister in June 1985. The Minister placed the Social Work Training Council in remission while she considered an alternative. This decision dealt a devastating blow to the social work professional community already under strong criticism for its inability to meet the social problems plaguing New Zealand society. It effectively curtailed the university accreditation processes and the Certificate of Qualification in Social Work for individual social workers and threatened the significant formal link with the international social work community.[111]

It would be nearly two years before the Council on Education and Training in the Social Services (CETSS) would be officially established in late 1986[112] and nearly four years before the new Council leadership officially presented the work of the CETSS to a major social worker's forum. In July of 1989, CETSS presented a major proposal for program accreditation and validation to the New Zealand Social Workers Conference held in Palmerston North.

BICULTURALISM

The joint efforts of government departments to deal with the issue of disproportionate Maori youth in government institutions led to the creation of the Maatua Whangai program in 1983. The *Hui Whakatauira*, held in 1981, had urged the Department of Maori Affairs to promote a program to address this issue.[113] The Departments of Maori Affairs and Social Welfare urged cooperation with the Department of Justice for a comprehensive approach. The objective of the program was to stem the tide of Maori youth into government institutions through the development of *whanau* (extended family) support systems and *whanau* placements. The program was funded by the three departments for an initial period, although the administrative responsibility was held by the Department of Social Welfare. The eight Maatua Whangai positions were funded in selected Department of Social Welfare District Offices

The same year the Maori Advisory Unit was established in the Auckland Regional Office charged with the responsiblity to advise the Department of policies, changes and needs relating to Maori people with "a view to making changes and taking action" on all matters regarding Maori people including the staffing, recruitment and function of the department and to consult with "the Maori community".[114] The establishment of the Maori Advisory Unit was significant because it signalled the beginning of the Department's explicit commitment to Maori people; a commitment that was later subsumed under a commitment to biculturalism.

Ian Douglas noted the changes taking place in *Pakeha*-Maori relations in New Zealand society in the mid-1980's:

> As late as the 1960's government policy towards the Maori people was very much predicated on the perceived need to fuse the two races; not just economically and socially, but physically. . . .[We have] begun to perceive a different vision of a radically mixed society based not on absorption of one race by the other, but on a relationship of mutual respect, enabling each race to make its distinctive contribution to a community which would be the richer for upholding such distinctiveness.[115]

The growing support for biculturalism demanded re-evaluation of *Pakeha*-Maori relationships in every sphere of life. In 1985, the Department of Social Welfare was confronted with two internal reports that questioned the validity of its service provision. The first was the publication of the *Institutional Racism in the Department of Social Welfare: Tamaki-Makau-Rau*.[116] This report had been officially in process for nearly two years, with a draft presented to the Maori community in November 1984 and the revised edition circulated in May of 1985. The report was prepared by nine women social workers in the Auckland Regional Office who used the mandate of the State Services Commission's recommendation that "Government Departments gather data on the ethnic composition of their staff" to legitimize their research. They shared a concern:

> About racism in Aotearoa [New Zealand] and in our Department. . . . The Department practices institutional racism. . . . We have a responsibility to work for change within our organisation. . . . This group is committed to a bicultural society. . . .We believe that Maori people as the indigenous people of Aotearoa have a right to power and resources.[117]

Institutional Racism offered a comprehensive set of recommendations to the Department. It called for the establishment of an anti-racism training program monitored by Maori people as part of a request to the Maori people of Tamaki-Makau-Rau (Auckland) to develop their bicultural vision for the Department. It rejected the recommendation of the State Services Commission for proportional staff representation on a national basis. Instead, *Institutional Racism* recommended an ethnic composition of staffing in each work unit that reflected the consumer group being served. It cited the low number of Maori staff within the Department and called for an active Affirmative Action Programme for Maori people based on accurate personnel data, training, and support systems. For such systems to be effective, the Report recommended job advertisements be bilingual and changes be made to the State Services Commission criteria for 'merit selection' that would recognize biculturalism as equal in value to work experience, personal qualities and educational qualifications.[118]

These recommendations were based on data that showed an inverse relationship between *Pakeha*/Maori staff to consumers and dominance of decision-making positions in the Department by *Pakeha* staff. *Institutional Racism in the Department of Social Welfare*[119] asserted that the services provided by the Department were fundamentally racist in nature and concluded:

> The Department must become bicultural. To do this it [the Department of Social Welfare] must return power and resources to Maori people so that they may be equal participants in policy and decision making.[120]

The recommendations of the *Institutional Racism* were echoed in the Maori Advisory Unit Report[121] issued shortly afterwards. The Maori Advisory Unit had been established in 1984 in response to the recommendations of the Human Rights Commission and the Johnston Report about the Department's policies in residential care. The Unit was commissioned by the Director-General to comment on the Department's capacity to meet the needs of the Maori people in relation to service delivery. The Unit viewed its task as bringing a bicultural perspective to the Department. In their report, the Unit supported biculturalism "as the only process towards a truly multi-cultural society".[122] The Unit's Report noted the feeling of powerlessness in the bureaucracy and urged a process to 'humanize' the institution:

> Humanity must be practised internally before it can be implemented through services offered to the public. Low wages in the clerical system, high staff turnover in parts of the Department's operations, a feeling of powerlessness and an inability, or lack of encouragement to contribute ideas or feedback on Departmental policies and procedures which are perceived as unjust or unrealistic, rank high as part of the response we received from our korero [talks] with Department employees.[123]

This feeling of powerlessness was particularly acute with Maori staff who felt they had to "leave their Maoriness at home. . . . Being a Maori should be considered an asset, not a hindrance to one's work and opportunities within the Department".[124]

The Maori Advisory Unit Report dealt with the meaning and central importance of *whanau* in Maori society and its implications for Departmental policy and practice in benefit and service provision. The Report lamented:

> The practice of placing Maori children in *Pakeha* foster homes has been shown to be inappropriate but still occurs. This situation is being addressed in the Maatua Whangai concept, but unfortunately instead of being allowed to grow and develop is generally floundering because it has been slotted into the presently existing structure as 'Maori fostering'.[125]

The stated primary objective was the development of a *whanau* which would "cater for all Maori children".[126] The Report asserted that the continued institutionalization of Maori children and the nonrespect of Taha Maori and *whanau* in welfare institutions was racist.

The Maori Advisory Unit Report concluded by restating its commitment: (1) To the concept of Maatua Whangai as an alternative model of welfare, (2) To the role of community development in ensuring that the responsibility for providing care returns to the *whanau*, the hapu and *iwi*, (3) To decentralization of power and resources to *whanau* and community linked groups, and (4) To the participation of community members in the recruitment and selection of staff supported by adequate training programs.

Instituional Racism and The Maori Advisory Unit Report were discussed at the Assistant Directors of Social Work Conference in October, 1985. That Conference resolved to "to develop a viable, community-based social work service that is responsive, accountable, bicultural and sustainable".[127] The Assistant Directors asserted that four principles were integral to the interpretation of the Department's mission: (1) Welfare: being able to establish and sustain, social and cultural identity, (2) Biculturalism: including the recognition of the rights of the Tangata Whenua, (3) Community based services, and (4) Minimum effective intervention, provided in the least intrusive form and at the lowest intensity necessary.

This period, then, saw the convergence of the themes advocating a shift away from state provision towards the provision of service in the voluntary and informal sectors. Decentralization and devolution were seen as two mechanisms that could offer an alternative to centralized, bureaucratized services. The strength of the Maori community in demanding a voice and a role in the care of Maori youth was equalled only by an apparent willingness of the Department to respond to minority requests. There was, as well, some cynicism expressed that the 'buzz' words such as, participation, community, biculturalism and the numerous calls for consultations in the reviews and reports were a smoke screen for a systematic dismantling of the welfare state, a cynisicism that was later to be verified.

PERIOD V: 1986 - 1988

THE IMPLEMENTATION OF THE RESTRUCTURING

By the beginning of 1986 the pace of change was further accelerated by the Fourth Labour Government's announcement of plans for several additional reviews in the coming year. Government departments under review initiated extensive internal organizational, management, personnel and service delivery changes in response to draft previews of task force or review committee recommendations in an attempt to maintain organizational integrity and credibility. The stresses associated with sweeping change were apparent throughout the government service. The widespread adoption of corporate terminology, business management practices and short-term financially based evaluation systems meant that government departments which had been operating under a long-term service ethic were now attempting to embrace a results oriented strategy in the struggle for organizational survival. The terminology was in marked contrast to the liberal language of previous years. It is also important to note the high degree of similarity in the recommendations of the various reports and reviews which indicated a consensus on the solutions, real or assumed, to the issues and problems under consideration.

Table VII

SIGNIFICANT EVENTS AND DOCUMENTS

Period V: 1986 - 1988

THE IMPLEMENTATION OF THE RESTRUCTURING

1986 Working Party Report: *The Organisation of Social Work Services at the District Level*

Management Plan, Department of Social Work

Social Advisory Council, *Partnership: The Delivery of Social and Community Services*

Ministerial Advisory Committee on a Maori Perspective, *Puao-Te-Ata-Tu: The Daybreak Report*

Ministerial Task Force publication, *Social Welfare Services: A Resource Book*

Driver and Robinson, *Voluntary Social Services*, New Zealand Planning Council

DSW funding to Community Volunteers cease

"New Direction in Management: Communication, Formal Systems for Briefing and Consulting,"

1987 Social Security Act Amendment established the Social Welfare Commission

Department of Social Welfare: *Corporate Management Plan*

The budget announces review of defence, education, housing and social welfare adding to reviews in health and tertiary education already underway

Social Welfare Services: The Way Ahead
Council on Education and Training in the Social Services established, reporting to Departments of Education and Social Welfare.

National Community Workers Association formed with $15,000 grant from Department of Internal Affairs

Minister of Social Welfare, Michael Cullen rules out privatization of welfare services in address to AMP Society's senior managers:

"My government accepts that it has a fundamental responsibility to provide for the welfare needs of all New Zealanders, and there is no intention to reduce the range of services and responsibilities currently undertaken by the Department of Social Welfare" (in 12 October 1987 memo to all staff from J. Yuill, Acting Director General)

Performance and Efficiency in the Department of Social Welfare: Report of the Administrative Review Committee

1988 State Sector Act provided "greater opportunity to reward good performance and strengthen management teams"

Sharing Control: A Policy Study of Responsiveness and Devolution in the Statutory Social Services, State Services Commission

Management Plan, 1988, Department of Social Welfare

Equal Employment Opportunities, Management Plan

Royal Commission on Social Policy, *The April Report*

Future Directions for Social Work, Department of Social Welfare

---

In early 1986, the Minister of Social Welfare established a Task Force on Social Welfare Services. This Task Force prepared a document, *Social Welfare Services: A Resource Book*, which was circulated in July. The Task Force called for public submissions in a consultation process to be completed by 30 September of the same year. In the foreword to the Task Force's discussion document, the Minister of Social Welfare stated:

> I have received many requests for a total review of social welfare services. . . . This government is committed to public consultation *before* [italics added] embarking on reforms.[128]

Yet, both the *Management Plan, 1986* [129] and the report of the Ministerial Advisory Committee on a Maori Perspective for the Department of Social Welfare, *Puao-Te-Ata-Tu*[130] had been released in the past two months. *Puao-Te-Ata-Tu,* released on the 8th of July 1986, recommended sweeping changes in policy, structure and practice within the Department. This report, which became central to the restructuring strategies of the Department, was almost immediately referred to exclusively by its Maori title to symbolize the Department's commitment to biculturalism. Many of its recommendations had already been initiated as part of the Management Plan released by the Department a few weeks prior to the release of *Puao-Te-Ata-Tu.* Hence, the consultation process initiated by the Ministerial Task Force on Social Welfare Services had been pre-empted by the major policy, structure and practice changes announced in the *Management Plan* and recommended by *Puao-Te-Ata-Tu.*

The implementation of the 1986 Departmental *Management Plan , 1986* and *Puao-Te-Ata-Tu* created multiple stresses for all levels of staff as they attempted to cope with the operationalizing the recommendations. Extensive personnel changes were implemented in Head Office including the reorganization into program directorates with extensive staff redeployment and redundancies. The pressures on the Department were compounded by a change in departmental minister in mid-1987 and the announcement of an Administrative Review Committee set up by Cabinet in July 1987 to report directly to the Ministers of Social Welfare, Finance and State Services by the end of the year. The brief of the Administrative Review Committee was to recommend changes in management systems and "changes in the means of delivery of department services which would improve efficiency".[131]

The first months of 1988 were filled with speculations on the recommendations to be made by the Royal Commission on Social Policy set up the year before. Controversy reigned when the Minister asked for the Royal Commissio's report, originally scheduled to for September, to be submitted in April. Some argued that the Report was meaningless because major policies affecting social policy had already been set in place. The credibility of the Government and its stated policy of consultation was under serious question and its actions would add to the serious rift in the Fourth Labour Party ranks over Roger Douglas's monetarist economic policies.[132]

Royal Commission on Social Policy was a massive undertaking which utilized the community consultation process developed and refined during the numerous previous reviews and task forces commissioned by the Fourth Labour Government. The five commissioners sat for eighteen months aided by full time and seconded staff from central and local government. The five volume report, though comprehensive and comprised of major discussion and detailed research papers drawing on the extensive statistical data available, suffered by the Minister's demand for an early report. Without sufficient time to debate and crystalize a clear, critical framework of recommendations, *The April Report*, as it came to be known, was a muddle of conflicting ideas and belaboured discussion that reflected the ambivalence and diversity of New Zealand society. The Royal Commission did, however, clearly support the primary responsibility of the state in social service delivery and funding.[133]

THE STATUTORY-VOLUNTARY BALANCE

A departmental Working Party Report on the *Organisation of Social Work Services at the District Level*, offered that in their opinion that:

> The Department does not necessarily have to take a provision of service role in every instance as at times it may be more appropriate to take a facilitative role enabling community groups, non-statutory organisations, etc., to provide the service, *with the Department providing the necessary resources* [italics added].[134]

The Ministerial Task Force on Social Welfare Services prepared the *Resource Book* to facilitate their public consultation process on the complex issues of the role of the state in service provision. The Task Force invited comment on "desirable relationships between different sectors providing welfare services".[135]

The Task Force asserted that there was no longer a consensus that central government should provide social services directly but foresaw a role for central government in overall national planning and coordination of services; in research, monitoring and evaluation; and in establishing regulations, standards, legal remedies and procedures.

> While further shifting of funds and decision-making power may be desirable, it can have disadvantages.

> Local prejudices may deny some people the social welfare services they need; there is a lack of personnel with planning and research skills at local levels; there is no agreement about what size populations should be served or what the boundaries of local areas should be.[136]

The Planning Council, however, continued its strong support for the shift of responsibility toward individual and community responsibility in its recommendations for:

> A collective approach at the community level with the state not as a provider but as a supporter and funder of services. The emphasis differs from a welfare approach in advocating shared responsibility for caring.[137]

However, Davey, writing under the auspices of the Planning Council, went on to argue that the Planning Council's position did not suggest a wholesale shifting of service provision to the voluntary sector. Instead, she insisted that the Planning Council supported a differential approach that would assess the appropriateness of the type of delivery system or administrative structure, dependent on the desired outcome. A differential approach would produce the maximize efficiency and effectiveness within the principles of social service practice. This was a clearly a cautionary note issued by the Planning Council in response to rising expectations for voluntary sector provision.

The state would also be responsible for setting minimum standards and a minimum level acceptable in service provision. Davey argued that: "There is evidence of some movement towards this goal over recent years"[138] and that the resistance to the shift came from the paternalistic and self-perpetuating approach of most government services.

> While the advantages of the shift may be small gains to a lot of people, the losses are concentrated and felt by influential and articulate groups. The attitudes of professionals who have a vested interest in welfarism and fear a lowering of standards produce significant barriers, e.g. mental health professionals who oppose the use of funds for 'drop in' centres and preventative

> programmes, teachers who fear radical changes in curriculum.[139]

The major role of the state, Davey contended, was in the setting of objectives for social policy. This involved ensuring adequate income through some system of income distribution, the promotion of national growth through macro-economic policies and the provision of a 'safety net' for income support. Social objectives could be met through a differential approach that included sharing costs of service between the state, the community and the user.

> It can no longer be assumed, however, that central government will itself provide the full range of services, or that it will fully fund them even if other agencies deliver them. . . . This will mean using the resources of central government, local government, the voluntary sector, geographical communities and communities of interest, the commercial sector, households, families and individuals.[140]

This argument demonstrated strong support of welfare pluralism and Hadley and Hatch's Participatory Model.[141] Consider that for the fiscal year 1986/87, the Department was allocated the largest single vote in the Budget, and distributed benefits to one and one half million citizens of New Zealand's 3.4 million people. Yet, less than 3% of the total of $6,175 million was allocated to social work services.[142] Of that $110 million expenditure on social services, $60 million was allocated to community agencies.[143] This meant that $1 of every $3 in the social services/social work budget was distributed through non-statutory groups and organisations. Although this is indicative of a strong commitment to the voluntary sector, the contribution of the voluntary sector to service provision has been insufficiently chartered and acknowledged in New Zealand.[144]

The incumbent Department of Social Welfare Deputy Director-General: Policy and Services during this period, presented a paper in which he argued that despite the criticisms of government department's alleged internal rigidity, lack of responsiveness to client demands and the allegations that the private sector can do better, the state has a role to play "when the state is acting to redistribute income or protect individual and community rights".[145]

While at the beginning of 1987 Davey[146] was arguing that it could no longer be assumed the state would provide full range of services, The

Ministerial Task Force in its July publication, *Social Welfare Services: The Way Ahead*, asserted:

> There appears to be no widespread consensus at present on the appropriate degree of collective responsibility. . . . [the Task Force view is] that a high degree of collective responsibility is appropriate. . . . We believe that government should undertake a pro-active role in directing social policy toward the ends of equity and the pursuit of well-being for all its citizens.[147]

Despite this view, the Task Force asserted that a mixed system of welfare provision was "a long-established part of our heritage" and urged central government's continuance as "funder, provider, planner and regulator of services".[148] The Task Force visualized the direct provision role of the state would be limited to statutory and social control functions.

> We recommend that the government sector continue to play a substantial role in service delivery . . . in the direct supply of service for social control purposes . . . and in providing what we described as essential services.[149]

Although, the Task Force defined essential services rather broadly, the term, essential services, was interpreted as referring to child protective services and youth justice as the primary focus for Departmental direct service provision.

The Task Force reaffirmed the role of non-statutory providers, specifying that the voluntary sector had a significant role in complementary or supplementary services, such as in self-realization services, personal counselling, personal development of individuals, groups, *iwi*, or communities, but certainly did not whole-heartedly endorse the community-care or even the community based services to the extent expressed in the Planning Council documents. The Task Force expressed concern about the possible abuse of informal care giving:

> Informal care should be an option only when it is voluntarily entered into, when informal caregivers are comprehensively supported and where some of the costs of giving care are offset.[150]

This Task Force, then, was clearly apprehensive of the wholesale transfer of service provision and care responsibilities to voluntary agencies and informal care givers while cautiously supportive of welfare pluralism.

The February publication of the Planning Council restated the Planning Council's support for a shift to community-based services with an even stronger support for community-care and informal caring systems:

> Studies in New Zealand show that kinship systems are still strong and probably more flexible than state programmes. They are also more appropriate in the supply of emotional and cultural support. The largest amount of caring and personal services is still carried out informally by families and kin, often with little back up or relief from social service agencies.[151]

Davey once again stressed the growth in locally-based and community care programs such as rape crisis centres, women's refuges, and Maori training and employment initiatives, as reflective of the ability and desire of communities to define their own needs and plan their own services. In the 1986/87 fiscal year the forty-seven refuges affiliated to the National Collective of Independent Women's Refuges formed in 1979/80, received $1.8 million from the Department.[152]

Although the government seemed to be shifting the balance for the burden of direct services provision to the voluntary sector, the government sent a paradoxical signal in its announcement of its intention to remove the tax deduction of contributions to charities and to tax income from the trust funds and investments made by voluntary agencies. This proposal drew a sharp outcry from a sector already pressured by reductions in income and increased requests for service. Max Abbot in his Editorial to the Mental Health Foundations publication[153] argued that such a move would be the death of the struggling voluntary sector. The government delayed action on the proposal but the legacy of the threat contributed to the cynicism of the voluntary sector about the motives of the government with regard to the funding and provision of social services. While the Royal Commission offered strong support for the central role of the state in the provision of social services, it clearly acknowledged the contribution and the continuing role of the voluntary sector in the provision of services.[154]

SERVICE DELIVERY

The Ministerial Task Force on Social Welfare Services noted that there were many other consumer concerns such as, the inflexibility of government services and funding, the availability of casework services to the exclusion of group and community work, currently being being addressed by other task forces such as those on income maintenance, health benefits and accident compensation. "Considerable effort is being made to ensure coordination and *consistency* [italics added] of approach between the task forces".[155] The effect of such efforts to ensure coordination and consistency may have stifled critical debate on proposed solutions to the issues facing the social services.

The coordination efforts were evident in the interlocking task force and review committee memberships and the similarity of recommendations. For example, in the Department's the first such formal management plan issued for the fiscal year 1986-1987, the Director-General stated that in his attempt to meet the organizational goal of the Department he had been :

> Grappling with two sets of problems: (l) how to create a structure for the organisation that will make major improvement to the delivery of service possible and, (2) how to develop the Department as an organisation.[156]

The decisions he took were to regionalize the Department based on the guiding principle of bringing the decision making closer to clients and staff. This was to be accomplished by delegations of authority to District Offices for maximum autonomy and a program of consultation with staff on organizational details. The second set of decisions, grouped under the heading of 'Organisational Development' and utilizing business management terminology, indicated the adoption of management performance criteria, the creation of a *corporate* (italics added) identity, a formal system of briefing and consulting and a renewed commitment to training.[157] These initiatives closely parallel the recommendations of the Ministerial Advisory Committee on a Maori Perspective, *Puao-Te-Ata-Tu,*[158] which was released just weeks later, in June, and on which the Director-General of Social Welfare sat as a member.

The May 1986 the Departmental report, *The Organisation of Social Work Services at the District Level*, recommended that programs and activities of the Department be community-based and established in partnership with the client and client group. The same month, the

Social Advisory Council, under the auspices of the Department of Social Welfare, published their report on *Partnership: The Delivery of Social and Community Services*, which attempted a balanced assessment of the strengths and weaknesses of community-based services.

> It has often been argued that the provision of services through non-statutory organisations is both cheaper and more effective than through Government departments. . . It is far from obvious that these generalisations are justified. Dedication, innovation and flexibility are evident in many statutory agencies, as are restriction on financial resources, dependence on the quality of personnel available, and unevenness of provision from one locality to another. Nor are all non-statutory agencies free of bureaucracy or of inflexible commitment to established ways.[159]

The Social Advisory Council concluded its report by acknowledging that "the welfare state is simply not able by itself to provide all the social and community services " for the people of New Zealand and urged recognition of the contribution of the non-statutory sector and the development of a "more equitable and productive partnership in the delivery of social and community services".[160] This theme of unequal partnership was further developed in the research carried out under contract to the Planning Council by Driver and Robinson (1986). Their report suggested that:

> Voluntary agencies and informal groups usually take on the difficult developmental, preventative and non-institutional social service activities while being denied the on-going funding and other forms of assistance that are necessary for this to be done effectively. It seems that 'cost saving' has often replaced 'cost effectiveness' in government's relationship with the voluntary sector and this has been counter-productive in providing a genuine alternative to institutional social services.[161]

Driver and Robinson recommended that field staff move to a supportive and advisory role and establish consumer involvement with the community group as a criteria for funding. Nevertheless, it is noteworthy that this recommendation assumed *the continued responsibility of government for funding of social services.* This is a key point, for in all of the discussions regarding decentralized, community based services, it was assumed that central government would continue its historic role as the funder of social services. For example, in the foreword to the Driver and Robinson report, Gary Hawke, as Chairman of the Planning Council, stated the Planning Council's support for decentralized social services "*matched by appropriate funding and support systems*" [italics added]. The Council had asked the authors of the report to study "the ways in which resources from taxpayers are made available to voluntary and community groups" without commenting on the fundamental question of the extent of government funding which he contended was an issue for public debate on social policy. The Chairman, however, reiterated the Council's support for an alternative model of social service delivery.

> The traditional welfare state model of services designed, funded and delivered by central government departments is only one of these ways. Particularly in a society undergoing considerable change and increasing its cultural and regional diversity, there is clearly a useful role for a more flexible and decentralized approach through local groups.[162]

Driver and Robinson reviewed several decentralized and/or devolved funding schemes in existence (the Community Organisation Grants Scheme being the only one in the Department of Social Welfare) and noted that governmental departments have been responsive to calls for decentralized funding and community participation. They noted, however, that the proliferation of these schemes without interdepartmental cooperation may have negative secondary effects.

> Already there are signs of consultation 'overload' and the prospect of setting up and servicing a variety of local advisory and funding allocation committees, each relating to a different department, is unlikely to be welcomed. . . .The most crucial factor in any consultation is that it be *honest* [sic]...Many groups felt that policy directions had been decided in advance. . . . Real consultation must begin with a question requiring a response, not with a decision requiring confirmation.[163]

Puao-Te-Ata-Tu[164] would have a pervasive impact on service delivery in the Department. *Puao-Te-Ata-Tu* recommended major organizational changes within the Department of Social Welfare to provide a direct mechanism for the community in general, and Maori people in particular, to participate in policy making. These goals were reflected in the key recommendations of the report which became the criteria for evaluating and implementing subsequent changes in the Department.

Puao-Te-Ata-Tu recommended abolishing the Social Security Commission and replacing it with a Social Welfare Commission whose membership would be composed of four principal officers of the Department, two people nominated by the Minister of Maori Affairs after consultation with tribal authorities, and two people nominated by the Minister of Women's Affairs. The Commission was to have a broad based advisory and consultative role. Secondly, it recommended the establishment of locally based District Executive Committees (DECs) and Institutional Management Committees (IMCs) comprised of community nominated members appointed by the Minister. The responsibilities of these community committees would be to assess community welfare projects and to monitor and review the Department's services. These local committees would report directly to the Social Welfare Commission.[165] Yet these recommendations had been proposed in the *Management Plan, 1986* and the implementation of decentralization and regionalization initiated *prior* to the release of *Puao-Te-Ata-Tu.*

Davey, in her report published under the auspices of the Planning Council, argued that decentralization would not necessarily guarantee better democracy or better services. While noting that several government departmental initiatives could be examples of decentralization:

> Real change must involve devolution, which is defined as the transfer of powers and resources from one agency to another. It goes further than delegation and envisages a real shift of power and a considerable increase of autonomy at lower or outlying levels.[166]

Davey pointed to the moves to devolve functions to the *iwi* authorities as a positive step toward this goal.

The Ministerial Task Force on Social Welfare Services advocated the retention of national funding where the monitoring and control of resources was important for reasons of equity and efficiency.

> However, even where national programmes are required, most of them need to be administered locally (delegated) so as to take advantage of local knowledge and be more accountable to the community.[167]

The Task Force did endorse a two-tier funding system by the Department with the first tier to national programs providing essential services. Second tier funding was a block allocation to districts on a modified population basis. The disbursement of second tier funds was dependent on local decision making for local needs. Second tier funding would be for programs, not agencies, and was to be aimed at encouraging maximum flexibility and responsiveness to local needs. The Task Force comment that effective devolution would be dependent on "a knowledgeable, skilled, interested and committed community"[168] seemed to imply uncertainty of its existence. Driver and Robinson[169] in their review of voluntary funding raised similar questions about the capability of the community to meet the expected demands.

Meanwhile, the Administrative Review Committee argued for the "greater provision of services in the community with the Department acting mainly as funder or regulator".[170] The Administrative Review Committee endorsed the two tier approach of the Ministerial Task Force but called for a sharper demarcation of functions. As well, the Administrative Review Committee:

> Clearly distinguished the separate roles of funder and provider [which] avoids the conflict of interest and the rigidities and confusions that occur when the two are combined.[171]

The Department would be responsible for funding both providers and consumers; for evaluation, monitoring and setting of standards; for coordination of services/planning, policy planning; and for direct services such as child protection and court related work. Direct service responsibilities would fall to the state only under specific conditions.

> Only where improved financial costing methods recommended in this report show that direct provision would clearly be more cost effective than contracting to the non-governmental sector. The Department would also need to retain direct service provision where there are no community providers available.[172]

Subsequently, the Permanent Heads of Social Service Departments (Internal Affairs, Social Welfare, Labour, Women's Affairs Justice, Maori Affairs, Education, Health, and National Library) requested the State Services Commission establish a task group to examine the issues of devolution under the mandate of Recommendation 13 (c)of *Puao-Te-Ata-Tu.*[173] The Task Group on Devolution, established in May 1987 and presented its report in February 1988, concluded that:

> Power sharing through devolution is only one of a number of means of better meeting client's needs and it should *not* [italics added] be automatically considered to be the preferred way of achieving this aim.[174]

The Task Group expressed the opinion that the emphasis on money in power sharing negotiations was proving a distraction from the more substantive policy issues. "The process of sharing power with clients . . . might actually *increase* (sic) social disadvantage" of minority interests and the Task Group noted a growing disenchantment with implementing policies without direct community input. Furthermore, the Task Group explored the multiple motives underlying support of devolution and cautioned that devolution could be an 'easy way out' for unresponsive organizations. They cautioned that devolution could be used as a cost-saving device, as a means to discredit participation in service delivery, or as a way of government saving overheads by using volunteer community labour rather than salaried government staff.[175]

The Royal Commission's view concurred with that of the Task Group on Devolution and offered a clarification of the concept by warning that devolution is too often used:

> To refer to the transfer of responsibility for social services to the community, rather than to community participation in decision making about social policies.[176]

The Royal Commission expressed concern that those groups that reflected communities of interest rather than geographical communities would be disadvantaged in local decision making because their numbers in any one locality might be insufficient to insure representation in local decision making.

The Administrative Review Committee viewed the replacement of the Social Work Division and the Benefits and Pensions Division by the Programme and Services Divisions as reflecting a "consumer orientation".[177] The Administrative Review Committee supported the implementation of the recommendations of *Puao-Te-Ata-Tu* in the creation of the Social Welfare Commission, the District Executive Committees, the Institutional Management Committees and regionalization as attempts to provide mechanisms for the participation of the community in the department's policy and service delivery. The Administrative Review Committee, however, argued against dual accountability:

> While we agree that there are a number of areas where individual employees and the Department as a whole have important obligations to consumers, we do not feel they they can or should be directed by or accountable to consumers.[178]

Instead, the Administrative Review Committee argued for a clear distinction between *accountability within the organization* and *responsiveness to consumers* to avoid the conflict of interest and reduced efficiency that results from dual accountability systems.[179] It urged the adoption of participatory management throughout the Department to replace what the Administrative Review Committee refered to as an administrative management model prevalent in the government service.[180] They recommended a team approach with maximization of the delegation of authority already to enhance effectiveness at every level of the Department. Such changes would require attention to improve the level of managerial skills and support participation through training and recruitment initiatives.

The Task Group on Devolution conceptualized participation with the community in terms of responsiveness. The term 'responsiveness' was used throughout the Department's documents of this period as distinct from 'accountability'. The Task Force cited the OECD's public management concept of 'responsiveness' which defined the concept as possessing four key dimensions: (a) comprehensibility of policies and programs to clients, (b) access of clients to services that meet their needs, (c) relevance of policies and programs to clients, and (d) the ability of clients to participate in the design, delivery and evaluation of programs.[181]

In order for the responsiveness of the existing social services to be increased, the Task Group suggested four specific actions. The Task Group recommended the enhancement of information and advocacy services targeted at disadvantaged clients. Secondly, it suggested the establishment of 'user groups' at the local level whose role would be to monitor and report on local and national social service program delivery and recommended the development of agency networking mechanisms with local level data sharing. Lastly, the Task Group suggested the introduction of a "responsiveness development programmes" across government.[182]

When the Department of Social Welfare's Director-General wrote the *Management Plan, 1988*, he signed it for the first time as 'Chief Executive'. This action reflected his status change under the State Sector Act of 1988 indicating that he no longer enjoyed the full protections of a state servant but had entered into a contractual agreement with the government as employer. In the 1988 Management Plan, he accepted the directives of the Administrative Review Committee by reiterating:

> The Department of Social Welfare is *accountable* [sic] to its Minister for the efficient performance of its Mission . . . [and is to] be *responsive* [sic] to its clients.[183]

The task facing the Department was how to be both accountable and responsive when the two objectives met in inevitable conflict. The Task Group on Devolution drew on the concepts of representative and participatory systems of democracy advanced by Hadley and Hatch to urge a shift toward more participatory forms of policy making.

SOCIAL WORK

The Department's Working Party on the *Organisation of Social Work at the District Level* had issued their report in May of 1986. The Working Party acknowledged awareness of the proposed regional structure, the intended policy move toward maximum delegation of authority to the districts and the intention to develop a planning capacity that distinguished between resourcing and provision. The report however, pointed out that:

> The unannounced arrival of CM [Circular Memo] 1986/82 on Regional Office Staffing at the end of this exercise created confusion. . . . There was insufficient explanation to make sense out of the lines of accountability.[184]

To add to the unsettled feeling among the social work staff:

> It is perhaps relevant to note that while many recommendations identified in the Review of the Social Work Division in December, 1982 have been met, the underlying issues relating to clarity of purpose and direction remain and have been intensified in the intervening years. Staff are feeling increasingly undervalued.[185]

The Working Party described itself as welcoming the proposed changes in the role of Head Office from Operations to Policy Development. This move was seen as a strategy to mitigate the high level of stress on the District Office level decision making process by increasing District autonomy through removing Head Office's direct involvement in District Office functions.

It was the opinion of the Working Party[186] that social work resources were being progressively redirected toward preventative work using community development processes. This trend was reversed in the withdrawal of funding for community development activities in the budget directives issued in 1988. The Working Party cautioned, however, that organizational structure and procedures inhibit community development activities[187] because that type of work was not accounted for in workload allocations. Also, the results of community development activities were difficult to assess in the quantitative terms characteristic of the newly adopted management evaluation systems. Driver and Robinson contended their extensive community consultation revealed a remarkably high level of agreement for a more community oriented and supportive role for statutory agencies:

> What was surprising was the degree to which departmental staff agreed with the criticism. . . . Nonetheless, there was a feeling of uncertainty as to whether involvement in the local community was approved by Head Office and a fear of raising community expectations too high. The lack of funds and other resources and the statutory responsibility for assessing programmes and policing standards has limited the move toward a supportive role.[188]

These observations add confirmation to the findings of Black, et al.[189] on the dominance of individual casework and the resistance to implementing other social work intervention strategies in statutory agencies.

The recommendations of the Administrative Review Committee included sweeping reforms for Departmental social workers through an extensive reorientation of resources to a community services model. The Committee recommended a service delivery model which would be:

> Staffed with people who have the appropriate skills, rather than the large social work operation that exists at present . . . rather than the present predominance of casework skills, a shift [in] skill areas will be required.[190]

Such a shift would require social workers to acquire (a) liaison skills with *Pakeha* agencies, the Maori community and *iwi* authorities, (b) service and program planning and development expertise and (c) experience in contract development and administration of funding. The combination of the recommendations of the Ministerial Task Force and the Administrative Review Committee had the effect of further deepening the crisis of confidence in statutory social workers, who had since 1982 been under serious criticism from the Maori community for their monocultural practice and their emphasis on individualized casework.

The Principal Social Worker, in an attempt to provide leadership and restore a sense of direction and purpose with the social workers in the Department, presented a discussion booklet to the Assistant Directors of Social Work Conference in August, 1988. In the introduction to the document, she acknowledged that:

> The practice of social work is undergoing a radical change. Acceptance of the principles of *Puao-Te-Ata-Tu* implies that every familiar role and activity needs to be re-examined in light of a partnership of decision making and resource sharing with the community, and in particular with Maori *whanau*, *hapu* and *iwi*.[191]

The Principal Social Worker presented a clear challenge to her department to acknowledge that the task of fixing perceived shortcomings in social work was a dual responsibility.

> Social Worker's strive for excellence in their practice, but they depend on managers to provide adequate supervision, training and resource allocation and good social work practice can be effective only when it is

> supported by good management and informed by clear policy.[192]

The Principal Social Worker noted that many changes had occurred in social work practice including the development of culturally sensitive practice models, the establishment of Maori and Pacific Island teams, the involvement of local *iwi* in recruitment and selection of staff, and the development of strong links with the Maori community through Maatua Whangai.

> The increasing pattern in service delivery is to promote and fund preventative community-based services. Department policy on funding of local service is for decisions to be made locally, with guidelines set nationally to ensure comprehensiveness and equitable provision. . . . The Department's social workers will need new skills in coordinating the development of local resources and . . . . in setting and maintaining standards in training, practice and accountability.[193]

During this period the social work profession was rendered virtually powerless by the Ministerial decision to place the Social Work Training Council in remission in 1985 and then to replace it with a new council which took years to establish. Certification of individual social workers and accrediting of training programs were left in a state of limbo. As well, the New Zealand Association of Social Workers was struggling with demands that it respond to the calls for the development of a bicultural code of practice. The years 1984 -1988 were years of struggle for the Association, with few funds, no full-time administrative staff seconded from the Department, and a diminishing membership accelerated by the loss of two identifiable groups: community workers and Maori social workers. The community workers formed their own association in 1987. With funds provided by the Department of Internal Affairs, the Community Workers Association held a national community workers *hui* and established localized modular training programs.[194]

There was predictably, growing support for a Maori Caucus within the Association of Social Workers. Although initially formed within the Association, the Maori Caucus formally left the Association in late 1987. The Maori Caucus retained a loose affiliation with the New Zealand Association of Social Workers.[195] The Association did continue to provide the Journal, newsletters and leadership to the general membership during this period. The Association was to experience a resurgence of membership and strength in 1989 with the licensing proposals of the Council for Education and Training in the Social Services; with their own initiative of a Certificate in Competency; and with the renewed interest in clinical practice in the voluntary and the developing private sectors. But 1988 was a depressing year for the association with minimal investment in its activities by its members and a very uncertain future.

BICULTURALISM

The Department of Social Welfare's *Management Plan, 1986,* in its Mission Statement made the commitment to:

> Maintain a department which is efficient and flexible in operation, ethical and sensitive to the needs of clientele and staff, and which provides services which are culturally appropriate.[196]

The particular needs of Maori people were recognized not only as a goal in service delivery but as part of the overall plan for the Department. Biculturalism, however, as a specific goal within the Department was not explicitly endorsed in the 1986 Management Plan.

The Working Party on *The Organisation of Social Work Services at the District Level* rendered the opinion, in their report issued in May, 1986, that "the principle of bicultural practice has been adopted" by the Department's social workers and recommended that the Department's top management officially adopt the principle of cultural appropriateness of service. The Working Party also recommended that a Maori Advisory Unit be established in each regional office "to enhance the cultural sensitivity in staff and provide a Maori perspective on policy, programmes and procedures".[197]

The Ministerial Advisory Committee on a Maori Perspective for the Department of Social Welfare had been established by the Minister of Social Welfare in July, 1985 with the expectation that it would use the community consultation process and report within six months. In fact, the report, *Puao-Te-Ata-Tu* was not to be published until June, 1986 after the Working Party Report on "The Organisation of Social Work Services"[198] and after the DSW, *Management Plan, 1986* was released. The Ministerial Advisory Committee had seven members including John Grant, then the Director-General of Social Welfare. Between 17 August 1985 and 7 April 1986, the committee held a total of sixty-nine meetings, thirty-nine of which were on marae or in community venues. One-thousand-twenty-four verbal submissions were heard and 267 written submissions received.[199]

In their report, the Ministerial Advisory Committee stated their view that although they were reporting on the Department of Social Welfare, their comments were equally valid for all government departments.

> A main thrust of our report is therefore to do with co-ordination of resources among departments and the transfer of authority over the use of those resources to the consumer.[200]

The appendix to the *Puao-Te-Ata-Tu* offered brief background comments which mirror the primary Maori concerns of the day which were: the disproportionate number of Maori in welfare institutions and the courts, the highly centralised bureaucracy insensitive to the needs of its clients, the institutional racism of the Department, the low socio-economic status of Maori in the community and the central importance of Biculturalism, as the policy direction for race relations in New Zealand . Biculturalism was defined within Departmental functions as "the sharing of responsibility and authority for decisions with appropriate Maori people".[201]

The recommendations of *Puao-Te-Ata-Tu* were consistent with the recommendations made earlier in *Institutional Racism.*[202] Moreover, the recommendations reflected strong support for the principles of decentralization, devolution and greater participation by the community in policy and provision of social services. These were the principles repeatedly voiced earlier by the Planning Council 1979 and 1981 and by voluntary groups in the consultations with Davey and Dwyer and Driver and Robinson.[203] The first recommendation of *Puao-Te-Ata-Tu* was for the endorsement by the Government of the social policy objective to:

> Attack all forms of cultural racism . . . by providing leadership . . . [and] incorporating, the values, cultures and beliefs of the Maori people in all policies developed for the future of New Zealand.[204]

The second recommendation addressed the allocation of the necessary resources and power and authority over their use. Other recommendations requested changes in recruitment, staffing, and training which would provide affirmative action policies for Maori people and implement the principles of biculturalism within the

Department and the structural changes to the Department discussed earlier. Implementation of the recommendations of the Ministerial Advisory Committee's report, *Puao-Te-Ata-Tu* became the criteria against which all actions within the Department were to be measured.

SUMMARY

This analysis of the public and departmental documents set out the debates, concerns and issues that characterized the social service policy discussions in New Zealand from 1986 -1988. The Department of Social Welfare was created out of the optimism associated with a welfare state model of social service delivery that emphasized the benefits of centralized control for efficiency and equality. A centralized government department with widely ranging responsibilities and extensive funding programs promised a higher level of coordination, co-operation, comprehensiveness, accessibility and continuity then was evident in the splintered, uncoordinated pattern of services that characterized the social welfare field prior to the creation of the the Department of Social Welfare in 1971. The growth of social work professionalism, evident particularly in the establishment of tertiary education for social work and in the commitment of the Department to training and development paralleled the growth of the Department as a centralized government bureaucracy.

The documentation illustrated the dominance of the Department of Social Welfare in both the statutory and voluntary sectors through its funding policies, its assumption of responsibility for service provision, its central role in training and education through its role with the Social Work Training Council and hence, because of its pervasive power, its influence on social work practice.

This analysis demonstrated the diversity of views and the ambivalence toward the government policy of shifting the burden of service provision to the non-statutory sector, a policy that was fundamental to the 1986 restructuring. During the early 1980's, and particularly during the early years of the Fourth Labour Government, there was a sense of inevitability about the shift, as the documents of the period demonstrated. In the documents of 1987-1988, there are a few cautions issued and several clear challenges made to the government to move more slowly. Cautions were issued by professionals, the community, voluntary agencies and Maori people. However, government strategy had changed and the infrastructure already set in place to accomplish the shift in balance between statutory-voluntary service provision. It is important to note that in all of the debates on the statutory-voluntary balance, there was always the assumption of central government primarily responsibility for funding. There was considerable debate about how that funding should be allocated but little discussion of the fundamental question of government responsibility for the provision of resources was evident in the documents. Notable exceptions were the comments of the Chairman of the New Zealand Planning Council in his Foreword to the Driver and Robinson 1987 publication and of Davey in her 1987 report. Within economic circles, the debate focused on the means of limiting, curtailing or containing the costs of the welfare state. Yet, the basic assumption of continued central governmental responsibility was retained, at least up until 1988.

The most influential force during the last two periods of analysis, was the rise of biculturalism and the commitment to bicultural social work practice. The decisions to implement the recommendations of *Puao-Te-Ata-Tu* resulted in sweeping structural changes within the Department and subsequently in social work practice.

The next three chapters contain data obtained in the second and third levels of analysis. They report the perceptions of the Regional Executive Officers and of the social work team members in the Napier and Poriru District Offices on the impact of the restructuring of social work practice within the Department's field social work service. These chapters provide the links between the the theory and the debates on the statutory-voluntary balance, service delivery, social work and biculturalism by linking both with the practice of field social work within the Department. They demonstrate the interrelationship of strategy, organizational design and performance.

NOTES

1. David Howe, *Social Workers and their Practice in Welfare Bureaucracies* (Hants, England: Gower Publishing Company, 1986), 2.

2. Department of Social Welfare Act, 1971 (Wellington: Government Printer, 1971), Section 4:2:d.

3. Adam Graycar, "Informal, Voluntary and Statutory Services: The Couples Relationship," *British Journal of Social Work* 13 (1983) : 380.

4. See for example, Martin Rein and Lee Rainwater, eds., *Public/Private Interplay in Social Protection: A Comparative Study* (London: M.E. Sharpe, Inc, 1986).

5. David Billis, *Welfare Bureaucracies: Their Design and Change in Response to Social Problems* (London: Heinemann Educational Books, 1984).

6. Hugh Oliver, "The Labour Caucus and Economic Policy Formation, 1981-1984," in *The Making of Rogernomics*, ed. Brian Easton (Auckland: University Press, 1989), 11.

7. J. Black, R. Bowl, D. Burns, C. Critcher, G. Grant, and D. Stockford, *Social Work in Context* (London: Tavistock, 1983); Howe.

8. New Zealand Association of Social Workers, *The Third Biennial Conference: Challenge of the 1970s*, (Hamilton: NZASW, 1970), unnumbered.

9. William Oliver, "Social Policy in New Zealand: An Historical Overview," in *The April Report*, Royal Commission on Social Policy, Vol. 1, (Wellington: Government Printer, 1988), 41.

10. New Zealand Association of Citizens Advice Bureaux, *Handbook on the Administration of a Citizens Advice Bureaux*, (Wellington: NZACAB, 1977), 36.

11. Ministerial Task Force on Social Welfare Services, *Social Welfare Services* (Wellington: Department of Social Welfare, July, 1986), 8.

12. P. Avery Jack and J. H. Robb, "Social Welfare Policies: Development and Patterns since 1945," in ed. A. D. Trlin, *Social Welfare and New Zealand Society* (Wellington: Methuen Publications, N. Z., 1977).

13. C. Bagnall, *A Department of Social Welfare for New Zealand* (Wellington: Government Printer, 1968), 57.

14. Jack and Robb.

15. Department of Social Welfare (DSW), *A Report on the Establishment of a New Department by the Amalgamation of the Social Security Department and the Child Welfare Division of the*

Department of Education (Wellington: Government Printer, May, 1970), 2.

16. Department of Social Welfare Act, 1971, Section 4:2:d (1971).

17. New Zealand Association of Social Workers (NZASW), *Social Welfare at the Crossroads: Report on Social Welfare in New Zealand* (Wellington: NZASW, 1971), 1.

18. Ibid.

19. NZASW, *The Papers Presented at the NZASW Biennial Conference* (Christchurch: NZASW, 1972).

20. Allen Pincus and Anne Minahan, *Social Work Practice: Model and Method* (Madison: University of Wisconsin Press, 1973); Max Siporin, *Introduction to Social Work Practice* (New York: Macmillan Publishing Company, Inc., 1975); Armando Morales and Bradford W. Sheafor, *Social Work: A Profession of Many Faces* 3rd ed. (Boston: Allyn and Bacon, Inc., 1983).

21. NZASW, *Social Welfare at the Crossroads*; NZASW, *Conference Papers: Report to the Fifth Biennial Conference and Convention* (Wellington: NZASW, 1974).

22. NZASW, *The Third Biennial Conference: Challenge of the 1970s* (Hamilton: NZASW, 1970); NZASW, *Papers Presented at NZASW Biennial Conference* (Christchurch: NZASW, 1972).

23. Social Work Training Council (SWTC), *Partnership: The Delivery of Social and Community Services* (Wellington: Government Printer, May, 1986); Jane Brook, *The Demise of the Social Work Training Council* (Unpublished Master's thesis, Palmerston North, New Zealand: Massey University, 1988).

24. Department of Social Welfare Act, 1971, Section 4:2:C.

25. Brook, 80.

26. NZASW, *Conference Papers* (1974).

27. DSW, *Working Party on Social Welfare* (Wellington: DSW, 1973) quoted in I.G. Wilson, "Napier Department of Social Work and Voluntary Work" (Napier: Department of Social Welfare, 1976), unnumbered.

28. New Zealand Planning Council (NZPC), *New Zealand at the Turning Point: Report of the Task Force on Economic and Social Planning*, [The Holmes Report] (Wellington: Government Printer, 1976).

29. Oliver, 41.

30. Janette Papesch and Noel Stevens, *Foster Care in Christchurch* (Christchurch: University of Canterbury, 1985), 6.

31. NZPC, *New Zealand at the Turning Point*; NZPC, *Planning Perspectives:1978-1983* (Wellington: Government Printer,

1978); NZPC, *The Welfare State* (Wellington: Government Printer, 1979).

32. NZPC, *New Zealand at the Turning Point*, 156.

33. NZPC, *Planning Perspectives.*

34. NZCSS, *Sharing Social Responsibility*, p. 6, 21.

35. Ibid., 7.

36. NZPC, *Establishing District Councils*, 110.

37. NZCSS, *Sharing Social Responsibility*, 45-46.

38. NZPC, *New Zealand at the Turning Point*, 112.

39. NZPC, *The Welfare State*, 28.

40. Ibid., 29.

41. NZCSS, *Sharing Social Responsibility.*

42. NZPC, *The Welfare State*, 28.

43. Ibid.

44. NZASW, *Social Worker's Conference: "Community"* (Auckland: NZASW, 1976).

45. Terry Kilmister, *Community Volunteers: A History* (Wellington: The Roy McKenzie Foundation, 1987).

46. The Auckland University program was subsequently disestablished in 1981.

47. For example see NZASW, *The Third Biennial Conference* and NZASW, *Papers Presented* 1972).

48. For example, Roy Bailey and M. Brake, eds., *Radical Social Work* (New York: Pantheon Books, 1975).

49. DSW, *Briefing Notes for the Incoming Minister of Social Welfare* (Wellington: Department of Social Welfare, July 22, 1984), 98:15.

50. Stephen P. Robbins, *Organization Theory: The Structure and Design of Organizations* (Englewood Cliffs, N. J.: Prentice-Hall, Inc., 1983).

51. A. H. Johnston, *Report to the Minister of Social Welfare on the Current Practices and Procedures Followed in Institutions of the Department of Social Welfare in Auckland* (Wellington: Department of Social Welfare, October 29, 1982).

52. M. Nairn and O. Sutherland, "Auckland Committee on Racism and Discrimination Submission of C & Y P A, No. 378" in the *1985 Public Submissions on the Review of the Children's and Young Person's Act of 1974* (Wellington: Department of Social Welfare, 1985).

53. NZPC, *Directions* (Wellington: Government Printer, 1981).

54. Brian Easton, *Social Policy and the Welfare State in New Zealand* (Auckland: George Allen and Unwin, 1980), 7.

55. Ibid., 177.

56. Roger Hadley, Mike Cooper, Peter Dale, and Graham Stacy, *A Community Worker's Handbook* (Bungay, Suffolk: Richard Clay, Ltd., 1987); Roger Hadley, Peter Dale and Patrick Sills, *Decentralising Social Services* National Council of Voluntary Organisations (London: Bedford Square Press, 1984); Roger Hadley and Stephen Hatch, *Social Welfare and the Failure of the State: Centralized Social Services and Participatory Alternatives* (London: George Allen and Unwin, 1981); Roger Hadley and Morag McGrath eds., *Going Local: Neighbourhood Social Services* National Council for Voluntary Organisations, Occasional Paper I (London: Bedford Square Press, 1981); Roger Hadley and Morag McGrath, *When Social Services are Local: The Normanton Experience* National Institute Social Services Library, No. 48 (London: George Allen and Unwin, 1984).

57. New Zealand Federation of Voluntary Welfare Organisations (NZFVWO), *Managing Your Voluntary Agency in the 1980s: A Resource Kit* (Wellington: NZFVWO, 1981).

58. Ibid., 8.

59. Raoul Ketko, *Social Work Developments in England 1981/1982: The Nuffield Report* (Wellington: Department of Socual Welfare, July, 1982).

60. DSW, *Review of the Social Work Division: Report of a Working Party* (Wellington: Department of Social Welfare, December, 1982).

61. Ibid., 123.

62. Johnston.

63. DSW, *Review of Social Work Division*, 38.

64. M. W. Rochford and J. J. Robb, *People in the Social Services: A New Zealand Study* (Wellington: New Zealand Social Work Training Council, 1981).

65. University Grants Committee, *Social Work: Review Committee:The Brownlie Report* (Wellington: Government Printing Office, 1982).

66. Brook.

67. DSW, *Review of the Department of Social Welfare Volunteer Programme* (Wellington: Department of Social Welfare, 1986c).

68. DSW, *Review of the Social Work Division*, 56.

69. DSW, *Briefing Notes*, 45; See Chapter Six for a discussion of how the establishment of the Community Development Team was viewed in the Napier District.

70. DSW, *Review of the Social Work Division: Report of a Working Party* (Wellington: Department of Social Welfare, December 1982).

71. University Grants Committee.

72. NZASW, *Papers Presented* (1982), 10-12.

73. Ibid., 24.

74. Ibid., 26.

75. Ibid., 28.

76. Johnston, 123.

77. Ibid., 50.

78. Ibid., 42. The term 'alternative care' would later be used in the restructuring to designate the programs aimed at developing community care arrangements for pre-adolescent youth.

79. Ibid., 52.

80. Nairn and Sutherland.

81. Johnston, 49.

82. Brian Easton, Introduction to *The Making of Rogernomics* ed. Brian Easton (Auckland: University Press, 1989), 8.

83. Nairn and Sutherland.

84. DSW, *Briefing Notes*, 147.

85. Ibid., 84.

86. Social Advisory Council (SAC), *Report of a Conference for Representatives of District Councils of Social Service* (Wellington: Government Printer, August, 1984b).

87. Helen Wyn, *Government Funding of Voluntary Welfare Agencies: A Review of Funding by the Department of Social Welfare* Social Programme Evaluation Unit (Wellington: Department of Social Welfare, 1984).

88. Richard Carson and Richard Hennessey, *A Framework for the Allocation of Social Work Resources: Interim Report* (Wellington: Department of Social Welfare, Social Programme Evaluation Unit, 1984), 32.

89. Ibid.

90. Judith A. Davey and Maire Dwyer, *Meeting Needs in the Community: A Discussion Paper on Social Services* (Wellington: New Zealand Planning Council, 1984).

91. Ibid., 1.

92. Ibid., vii.

93. NZPC, *The Welfare State.*

94. Davey and Dwyer, 37.

95. Barclay Report, *Social Workers: Their Role and Tasks* (London: Bedford Square Press, 1982).

96. Davey and Dwyer, 38.

97. Allen Levett, Josie Keelan, and Velma McClellan, *Making Devolution Work: Report on the Community Organisations Grant Scheme* (Wellington: Department of Social Welfare, June, 1988).

98. Sue Driver and David Robinson, *Voluntary Social Services: A Review of Funding* (Wellington: New Zealand Planning Council, 1986).

99. Levett, Keelen, and McClellan.

100. Davey and Dwyer, 46-47.

101. NZPC, *New Zealand at the Turning Point*, 112.

102. See Johnathan Boston, "Democratic Theory, Devolution and Accountability" in *Devolution and Accountability*, eds. J. Martin and J. Harper (Wellington: G. P. Books, July 1988), 46-71.

103. Davey and Dwyer, 10.

104. Ibid., 58.

105. Ibid., 51.

106. Ibid., 11.

107. Ministerial Review Committee, *Report on the Social Work Training Council* (Wellington: Department of Social Welfare, 1985).

108. Rochford and Robb.

109. Social Work Training Council (SWTC), *Report of the New Zealand Social Work Training Council: A Report Prepared at the Request of the Minister of Social Welfare* (Wellington: SWTC, 1985).

110. Ministerial Review Committee.

111. Brook.

112. Council for Education and Training in Social Services (CETSS), *Education and Training in the Social Services: Interim Report* (Wellington: CETSS, 1988).

113. Maori Economic Development Summit Conference, *A Briefing on Maori Economic Affairs* (Palmerston North: The Dunmore Press, 1984).

114. DSW, *Maori Advisory Unit Report* (Wellington: Department of Social Welfare, 1985d).

115. Ian G. Douglas, *New Zealand in Change: Policies and Attitudes* (Wellington: Hutcheson, Bowman and Steward, Ltd., 1985), 105.

116. DSW, *Institutional Racism in the Department of Social Welfare:Tamaki-Makau-Rau, Auckland (Revised)* (Wellington: DSW, May 1985b).

117. Ibid., 1-2.

118. Ibid.

119. DSW, *Institutional Racism.*

120. Ibid., 38.
121. DSW, *Maori Advisory Unit Report.*
122. Ibid., 5.
123. Ibid., 12.
124. Ibid., 12-13.
125. Ibid., 14.
126. Ibid., 15.
127. DSW, *The Organisation of Social Work Services*, 25.
128. Ministerial Task Force, iv.
129. DSW, *The Management Plan, 1986* (Wellington: Department of Social Welfare, 1986b).
130. Ministerial Advisory Committee on a Maori Perspective for the Department of Social Welfare, *Puao-Te-Ata-Tu: The Day Break Report* (Wellington: Department of Social Welfare, 1986).
131. Administrative Review Committee, *Performance and Efficiency in the Department of Social Welfare* (Wellington: Government Printer, 1987), v.
132. Brian Easton, "The Unmaking of Roger Douglas" in *The Making of Rogernomics*, ed. Brian Easton (Auckland: University Press, 1989).
133. Royal Commission on Social Policy, "The Funding of Social Provision" in *The April Report,* Royal Commission on Social Policy, Vol. II (1988a) 659.
134. DSW, *Organisation of Social Work Services*, 10.
135. Ministerial Task Force, 34:7:1.
136. Ibid., 26:6:18.
137. Judith A. Davey, *Social Policy Options* (Wellington: New Zealand Planning Council, 1987), 42.
138. Ibid., 40.
139. Ibid., 43.
140. Davey, 53.
141. Hadley and Hatch.
142. DSW, *Briefing Papers for the Incoming Minister of Social Welfare* (Wellington: Department of Social Welfare, 1987a).
143. Administrative Review Committee, 52.
144. Oliver; Margaret Tennant, *Paupers and Providers* (Wellington: Allen and Unwin, N.Z., Ltd., 1989).
145. Rob Laking, "Social Policy and the Future of Bureaucracy" in *Responding to the Revolution: Careers, Culture and Casualties*, eds. Jeannette Johnston and Adrienne von Tunzelmann (Wellington: Government Printer, 1987), 138.
146. Davey.

147. Ministerial Task Force, *Social Welfare Services: The Way Ahead* (Wellington: DSW, July 1987), 4.

148. Ibid., 40:6:4.

149. Ibid, 47:6:6.

150. Ibid., 47:6:27.

151. Davey, 21.

152. DSW, *Briefing Papers* (1987a).

153. Max Abbott, "Death of the Voluntary Sector" [Editorial]. *Mental Health News* 1988, February/March:3-5.

154. Royal Commission on Social Policy, "The Funding of Social Provision," in *The April Report*, Royal Commission on Social Policy, Vol. II (1988), 659.

155. Ministerial Task Force, *Social Welfare Services* (1986), 3:1:12.

156. DSW, *Management Plan, 1986* (Wellington: Department of Social Welfare, 1986a), 1.

157. Ibid.

158. Ministerial Advisory Committee.

159. Social Advisory Council, *Partnership: The Delivery of Social and Community Services* (Wellington: Government Printing Office, May 1986), 10.

160. Ibid., 89.

161. Driver and Robinson, 55.

162. Ibid., Foreward.

163. Ibid., 27, 53.

164. Ministerial Advisory Committee.

165. For a summary of the recommendations of *Puao-Te-Ata-Tu* see Appendix VII.

166. Davey, 48-49.

167. Ministerial Task Force, *Social Welfare Services* (1987), 36:5:25.

168. Ibid., 53:7:9.

169. Driver and Robinson.

170. Administrative Review Committee, 9:9:1.

171. Ibid., 55:9:2:8.

172. Ibid., 54:9:2:6.

173. Ministerial Advisory Committee.

174. Task Group on Devolution, *Sharing Control: A Policy Study of Responsiveness and Devolution in the Statutory Social Services* State Service Commission (Wellington: Government Printer, February 1988), 4.

175. Ibid.

176. Royal Commission on Social Policy, Vol. II, 844.

177. DSW, *Management Plan, 1987* (Wellington: Department of Social Welfare, 1987c).

178. Administrative Review Committee, 10:3:7.

179. Ibid.

180. The Administrative Review Committee definition of the administrative management model is discussed in Chapter Five.

181. Task Force on Devolution, 6.

182. Ibid., 7.

183. DSW, *Future Directions for Social Work* (Wellington: Department of Social Welfare, July 1988d), 8.

184. DSW, *Organisation of Social Work Services*, 6.

185. Ibid., 2.

186. Ibid.

187. This phenomena was noted by Black and his colleagues.

188. Driver and Robinson, 42.

189. Black, et al.

190. Administrative Review Committee, 65:9:9:2.

191. DSW, *Contracting for Social Services: Principles and Guidelines* (Wellington: Department of Social Welfare, July 1988c), 1.

192. Ibid., 1.

193. Ibid., Appendix B:2, 8-9.

194. Aotearoa Community Workers Association, "History of the Aotearoa Community Workers Association and Community Work Training National Proposal" *kupu Kaimahi-A-Iwi: Newsletter of the Aotearoa Community Workers Association, Inc.*, 1989, Issue I:2-3.

195. NZASW, *News and Views* (Wellington: NZASW, December, 1986b).

196. NZASW, *News and Views* (Wellington: NZASW, July 1986a).

197. DSW, *Organisation of Social Work Services*, 17.

198. Ibid.

199. Ministerial Advisory Committee, Appendix: 40.

200. Ibid., 24:79.

201. Ibid., 19:50.

202. DSW, *Institutional Racism.*

203. Davey and Dwyer; Driver and Robinson.

204. Ministerial Advisory Committee, 9.

V

THE REGIONAL EXECUTIVE OFFICERS' PERSPECTIVE

This chapter reports the results of the interviews with the eleven Regional Executive Officers (REOs) of Social Services and Alternative Care. It was the responsibility of these administrative positions to facilitate the principles of the restructuring: regionalization, decentralization, devolution and partnership with the community. Hence, their role was crucial in the implementation of the new policies within the Department. The chapter begins with a description of the Department that places the REO positions in context by comparing the aspects of the organizational design of the Department prior to the 1986 restructuring with the organizational design announced in the *Management Plan, 1986*.[1] Before reporting the results of the interviews, several terms used by the respondents are defined as used in the departmental documents, the issues that confronted the REOs in their relationship with the Districts are discussed, and the demographic characteristics of the REOs are summarized.

Prior to the restructuring in 1986, the formal design of the Department of Social Welfare closely approximated an ideal bureaucracy.[2] The Department was a tall hierarchy with three major divisions: Benefits and Pensions, Social Work, and Administration. There was a clear chain of command. Authority was vested in the Director-General and vertically delegated through the Assistant Directors-General to Head Office staff and subsequently to the District Directors and Institutional Principals. The District Offices were similarly designed using the tripartite system. Over the fifteen years of the Department's operations, a comprehensive and detailed set of rules, regulations and procedures had been developed for carrying out the Department's activities. For example, the Social Work Division had a two-volume set of rules and regulations, each over a hundred pages long with an appendum for regulation and procedural changes. There were job descriptions delineating the rights and responsibilities of each position and staff were hired and promoted on the basis of their qualifications and ability to handle the job. Staff interests were promoted through formal relationships with the State Services Commission and the Public Service Association which represented all government employees. As was reported in Chapter Four, the Department was accused by its critics of displaying the negative characteristics of a bureaucracy including undue rigidity in the application of rules and regulations, alienation from its client group, unresponsiveness to local needs and the assumption of the right and responsibility to make decisions for their client group which, the critics argued, further intensified feelings of powerlessness in the individuals and communities served by the Department.[3] The restructuring announced in the *Management Plan, 1986*[4] indicated the Director-General's decision to make extensive changes in the Department's organizational design. Several major design changes were set into place. The Department was to be regionalized and authority was delegated "to match responsibility so that District Offices can have the necessary autonomy".[5] A Directorate-General committee structure (referred to as the Executive Management Group or EMG) was set into place with a membership of the Director-General, the two newly created Deputy Directors-Generals and the four Assistant Deputy Directors-General. In 1987, the program directorates were introduced as a refinement of the structure which effectively eliminated a discrete social work identity in the Head Office formal structure.[6] In 1988, the membership of EMG was expanded to include the six Regional Directors, who were reclassified as Assistant Director-Generals (Regions). At the Regional level, a Regional Management Team (RMT) structure was established consisting of at least the Regional Directors, District Directors and Institutional Principals whose responsibility was to manage the region. The composition of the RMTs varied between Regions and over time within the Regions themselves.

As well, the Social Security Commission was replaced by a Social Welfare Commission mandated with responsibility for co-ordinating "the implementation of policy and management issues across all divisions of the Department".[7] These moves significantly expanded the top management staff compostion in the Department at top management levels: Head Office and Regions.

The Regional Executive Officer (REO) positions were established as part of the Regional Office structure. These positions were designed to offer support, advice and consultative services to the districts. The REO positions were *staff* positions and therefore were not to carry line or administrative authority. It was the stated intent that the REOs would further the objectives of the decentralization by offering services to the districts to assist them to assume maximum autonomy in the operations of Departmental functions. Because regionalization and decentralization occurred simultaneously, the role of the REOs was unclear. Role ambiguity led to misunderstandings, conflict and inappropriate task expectations by Head Office, the Districts and the REOs themselves.[8]

The role ambiguity of the Regional Offices was depicted in the organizational chart included in the first formal *Management Plan, 1986.*[9] In the 1986 organizational chart, the District Director was directly linked to the Regional Director and subsequently to the Deputy Director-General and the Director-General, implying a line of administrative responsibility from the Districts to the Regional Office and up through the hierarchy. Such a relationship seemed to contradict the announced decentralization to the Districts by implying another layer of management between the Districts and Head Office. This relationship was clarified somewhat in the organizational chart appearing in the Management Plan of 1987, if only because the chart does not imply direct accountability from the District to the Region in the way it was drawn. An implied direct authority relationship between the District Directors and the Assistant Director-General (Regions) in the organisational chart appeared in the *Management Plan, 1988.*[10] Despite the directives to the contrary, in practice, the Regions were perceived by many direct line staff as another link in the chain of command. The REOs often 'advised' the Districts on policy guidelines or operations in such a way as the Districts felt they were more accurately being 'directed.' Head Office was perceived as pressuring REOs if their districts were not 'coming on board' with new policy.[11]

The data gathering phase of this research was initiated just two years after the restructuring was formally announced in this large, previously highly formalized, stable bureaucratic structure. As already discussed, the Department had functioned for fifteen years with basically the same organizational structure despite tremendous growth in staff, function and budget. Hence, all staff were required to unlearn old assumptions and administrative behaviours and to learn a new set of developing and changing managerial relationships. Clarification of roles and the establishment of working relationships were still in its initial stages at the time of the research.

New terminology permeated the management plans and directives issued in the restructuring and in the Administrative Review of the Department completed in 1987. These new terms had distinct meanings within the Department. The Director-General in *Management Plan, 1986* indicated his desire to "create a sense of *corporate identity*" [italics added][12] through a process of making Departmental administrators *managers* and accountable for:

> Achieving tasks, building teams . . . promoting the interests of the organisation . . . [and developing] a spirit of co-operation and a sense of common purpose.[13]

The Administrative Review Committee described the Department as having 'an administrative style of management'. Such a style, the Committee contended was characterized by 'administration of instruction', top-down communication, emphasis on inputs not outcomes and a "reactive mode of operation" that directed resources to "demands and problems as they arise".[14] The Administrative Review Committee supported the briefing and consultation system announced by the Director-General in the *Management Plan, 1986* and outlined in the circular memorandum of 29 October 1986 as exemplifying the 'participatory management' style they recommended.[15] Such a style, the Administrative Review Committee contended, would encourage good management of resources, make managers more accountable, would more completely utilize the knowledge of staff members, and would permit a system of rewarding performance not previously possible under the existing employee relationships. These concepts and terminology, more associated with the profit-oriented business world, reflected the extent of intrusion by those assumptions and principles into the restructuring of the social services.

With the restructuring, the Director-General advised the participatory style of management was to be adopted throughout the Department within a 'corporate structure' that would make staff in administrative positions 'managers' with control and discretion over resources within their jurisdiction.[16] District level staff were to assume responsibility for management and decision-making functions within the broad policy guidelines established by Head Office. It was to be the role of the Regions and the Regional Executive Officers to facilitate the change. However, it must be appreciated that most of the Regional Executive Officers were career state servants with long working histories under the 'administrative management style' described by the Administrative Review Committee.[17] Their successful performance under that system had been rewarded by advancement. It was ironic that it was these same managers who were now being asked to facilitate the change to a participatory and corporate management system. However, it could be argued that the management culture of the Social Services Division was predisposed to, and in varying degrees practiced, a participatory style of management. The Social Services Division had a professional staff orientation and provided non-routine services, the division's social work value base supported a participatory, cooperative approach to decision making.

There is a second aspect of the relationship between the Districts and their Regional Offices that was important in the analysing of the comments of the Regional Executive Officers. Since 1984, The Department of Social Welfare, in common with other state funded agencies had experienced several budget cuts. These cuts included a hiring freeze, a slow down in capital resource allocation, and demands for increased reporting and financial accountability. However, the allocation of staff and capital necessary for the creation of the Regional Offices and the establishment of addition regional office positions, was accomplished outside the established budgetary justification process swiftly and without resistence or apparent concern about the extent of the resource and salary demands. Many District Office staff felt that Head Office expenditure did not substantially decrease in the restructuring process. They assumed therefore, that Regional Office had been created at the expense of the Districts, whose operating budgets *did* reduce during the period in both real and inflationary terms.[18] In addition, some staff suggested that not only did Head Office expenditure not reduce as a result of the restructuring but in fact the salary allocation *increased* in the period 1986-1988, placing a further restriction on District Office operating budget. Nevertheless, there was no doubt that the Regional Executive Officers felt little security in their positions. One REO clearly stated "that it's very hard now to come in with a significant variation of opinion".

The staff complement of the Regional Offices was a continuing issue of debate in the Districts. Regional Office positions were more often added then deleted during the period but considerable movement was evident in the addition of the Equal Employment Opportunities Officers in 1988 and in the establishment, and then subsequent disestablishment, of training positions within the regional structure. Toward the end of the research period in late 1988, the training function was further decentralized to the individual Districts. The staff size of each Regional Office varied but the projected maximum size of fifteen positions including the clerical support staff was far exceeded in the regional offices.[19]

Initially, the research design included interviews with only the REOs of Social Services. The REOs of Social Services were clearly linked to the District's Social Service Divisions and the provision of field social work services. All had come up through the ranks of field social work. However, as the REOs of Alternative Care were appointed, it became clear that their inclusion as research subjects was imperative to provide essential information on social work practice within the

Department. The Alternative Care positions were linked to residential services. These positions were created to co-ordinate efforts aimed at providing community and *iwi*- based services to adolescents. Six of the Department's nineteen institutions were scheduled for closure between September 1987 and March 1988 as were ten of the Department's 170 family homes. Substantial reductions were to be made in available placements in residential institutions for adolescents.[20] The Alternative Care workers were expected to coordinate their efforts closely with District level social workers to facilitate the deinstitutionalization effort.

CHARACTERISTICS OF THE RESPONDENTS

Each region was to have an REO of Social Services and an REO of Alternative Care. At the time of the research, eleven of the twelve REO positions were filled, nine with permanent appointments. Some of the REOs viewed the Alternative Care positions as time-limited because of the position's focus on deinstitutionalization. They predicted that once the deinstitutionalization process was completed and community based services in place, the REOs of Social Service could provide the necessary services to the Districts for both Social Services and Alternative Care.

Eight of the Regional Executive Officers were men, six of whom had entered the Department early in their careers and had spent a minimum of fifteen years with the Department. One REO had begun his career as a teacher before coming to the Department in the late 1970's as a trainer and, hence had only ten years in the Department. The remaining male REO had the least senority having come into the Department in 1983 through the Maori Advisory Unit in the Auckland Region. This Unit had been set up in response to the concerns about the disproportionate number of Maori children in care.[21] The three women Regional Executive Officers were all REOs of Social Services, had a minimum of 13 years senority in the Department, had begun their careers as direct line practitioner positions and worked their way up through the hierarchy.

Eight of the REOs had a Certificate of Qualification in Social Work based on either a Diploma or a Masters in Social Work. Four of them were promoted to their first supervisory position after completing their qualification in social work. Only one held current membership in the New Zealand Association of Social Workers although four described their professional affiliation as Social Worker or Residential Social Worker. Of the remaining responses to the question of professional affiliation, five described themselves as Social Service

Administrator/Manager, one as a Transitional Change Agent and one did not answer the question.[22] Because the REO positions had been created as part of the restructuring, the respondents were relatively new to the positions, although seven of the eleven had held top level district office positions prior to their appointment as REOs. Three appointments to the REO positions were made between November 1986 and January 1987 with two more by mid-year 1987. At the end of 1987, another two permanent appointments were made, followed by two more by April 1988. The two acting appointments had been made in mid-1988 in an attempt to ensure the offices in those regions could function.

It is against these introductory comments and the demographic characteristics of the REOs that the analysis of the interviews with the Regional Executive Officers was considered. The structured interview of twenty open ended questions asked the REOs for comment on their perspectives of the objectives of the regionalization, why it occurred when it did and how regionalization reflected the recommendations of *Puao-Te-Ata-Tu*[23] and the move toward community, community development, devolution and 'community-oriented social work'. These issues were addressed in the eight questions that appeared under the heading 'Philosophy'. Three questions were included under each of the headings 'Organizational Changes', 'Managerial Supports' and 'Social Work Services'.[24] A non-directive style of interviewing was assumed by the researcher during the interviews to facilitate exploration and permit the respondent to present their perspectives and understandings as completely as possible.[25]

SERVICE DELIVERY

Regionalization

Several of the REOs cautioned against overemphasis on regionalization of the Department. They viewed regionalization as part of an overall restructuring strategy to apply corporate management principles, particularly greater financial accountability, to the Department.

> The Director-General saw the potential in a regional structure for effectiveness and the efficiency Treasury was arguing for. Because [Treasury] wanted to go in that direction and if the Department could be a front runner . . . then [the Director-General figured] we might be better off going for it (REO:6).

Regionalization was described as Treasury-driven since staff from Treasury had been seconded to the Department to assist in the planning (REO:6, 7, 8). As two REOs expressed it:

> I've always interpreted regionalisation as perhaps the most significant strategy to ensure the survival of the organisation. It followed a period of great pressure [from] continuing public criticism of the institution, internal criticism relating to racism and sexism . . . [The Director General] was facing the prospect of the organisation becoming unmanageable . . . Regionalisation was a very astute and successful move to regain control of the organisation (REO:8).

Notably only one REO specifically mentioned the role of Ann Hercus, as the Minister of Social Welfare during the period immediately preceding the restructuring:

> If it had not been for Ann Hercus, the fact that she was also Minister of Women's Affairs, we definitely would not have had the development and eventual outcome of *Puao-Te-Ata-Tu*. I believe that it was very much driven by her and the women's movement. . . . Her involvement can be linked to the way the Maori movement has developed within our Department (REO:2).

The REOs felt that social work had increasingly been overshadowed by the exponential growth in size and function of the benefits and pensions division. This was particularly true since 1975 when unemployment continued to rise and the Department assumed a new benefit program as a consequence of the passage of the Superannuation Act.

> There is a major philosophical difference between the two major cultures in the Department . . . the culture of income maintenance and benefits, and the culture of social work and social justice (REO:6).

They expressed concern that the relabelling of the the Social Work Division to the Social Services Division was indicative of a further decrease in the influence of professional social work within the Department.

A degree of cynicism was expressed about the effect of regionalization on service delivery. Ten of the eleven REOs felt that regionalization was a costly exercise initiated during a period of financial constraint and more an attempt to regain administrative control of the organization than to decentralize authority and increase responsiveness to clients.

> The idea of the regions was to be there to support the Districts so they could do their job. That's how I understood it. But what happened . . . is we're supporting Head Office and the big Executive Management Group, the super powers. Because I am finding now they are wanting more and more information in order that they can do their monitoring (REO:7).

So despite the stated intent of regionalization to provide more autonomy to the Districts with support of the Regional Office, the REOs felt their jobs were increasingly focused on servicing Head Office. This sentiment was shared by District staff as the analysis of the interviews with the social work teams reported in Chapters Six and Seven will concur. Two of the REOs contended that regionalization "hasn't brought about any clear change in the role of the Head Office," and "certainly has not brought a reduction in its size" (REO:8, 5). At the same time, REOs acknowledged the positive effect of efforts to clarify the role of Head Office as policy making, the Regional Office as monitoring and supporting, and the District Office as operations. "Practice has not yet caught up with policy, but it is beginning to shift" (REO:10).

Decentralization

The two Auckland REOs felt the decision to create the Auckland Regional Office in 1980 provided an opportunity for the Department to experiment with decentralization and to evaluate its potential. Establishment of the Auckland Region involved minimum delegations of authority and was not intended to mitigate the central role of Head Office. However, with the existence of the Auckland Region, the REOs felt that Maori activists were more able to demand a role in developing local policies governing care of Maori children in the Auckland Region. They cited as evidence the Department's responses to the ACORD complaint laid before the Human Rights Commission in 1979, the Johnston Report in 1982 and the creation of the Maori Advisory Unit in the Auckland Region in 1983.[26]

The decision to regionalize and decentralize the Department in 1986 provided an opportunity to meet the needs of the organization for a more efficient management system while appearing to be "meeting the demands of the Maori community for local decision making" (REO:6).

The central core of the demands on the Department in the Auckland Region as a result of the investigations and reviews of custodial and secure care in Department institutions was on deinstitutionalizing pre-adolescent care. Referring specifically to the policy on deinstitutionalizing pre-adolescent institutional care, an REO argued:

> Now, history tells me that a racist institution does not listen to ethnic groups that quickly . . . It was because it was part and parcel of their own policy . . . I don't believe that Maori people can claim that they were the only ones who were thinking this way anyway [of the benefits of restructuring and deinstitutionalization]. . . . I believe that Pakehas had already through their research really believed that the institutions weren't working. . . . They were very expensive (REO:1).

REO:1 contended that the high cost of residential care was incurred because of national under-utilization of the Department's institutions and group homes while another REO contended that it was the overcrowding, the misuse of secure care and the over-representation of Maori children in care in Auckland institutions highlighted in the ACORD submissions[27] that forced the Department to respond to Maori demands for deinstitutionalization and community based care (REO:9).

Two REOs saw decentralization as an outcome of regionalization and demands by Maori people to 'care for their own.' REO:1 further argued that the Maatua Whangai program was initially not driven from a Maori perspective but was an attempt to get "brown faced foster parents." REO:1 indicated that the Maatua Whangai program had come subsequently to embrace a more Maori philosophy than was evident in it's initial development.

There was recognition that the delegations of authority to districts had "succeeded in making some problems manageable" (REO:8). The RMTs whose responsibility it was to manage the region were:

> Small enough to develop trust and understanding between themselves so that the anomalies don't become big issues, so that things are not attributed to conspiracy and all the things that you tend to get when it was Districts playing off each other against Head Office (REO:8).

Three REOs emphasized the potential under the restructuring for each region to set its own direction and to devolve to community groups in response to community needs (REO:2,5,9) but two expressed concern that overall policy guidelines so limited regional autonomy as to make it substantially meaningless.

> Some of the people in Head Office are not keen to decentralise. . . . We are now free to go our own direction (sic) in responding to regional needs, as long as it follows the government policy, *that is the catch* [italics added] (REO:9).

> It has been extremely difficult for some people in Head Office to give away the sort of decision making power they previously had (REO:10).

Their comments reflect the apparent paradox of the decentralization process in the desire of the Head Office to effectively retain organizational control.

Devolution

The REOs pointed out that the Department had a long history of devolved services to non-governmental agencies such as Presbyterian Support Services and the New Zealand Society for the Intellectually Handicapped. The issues of accountability and monitoring of those services had been raised several times but:

> What regionalisation has done is provide the Districts with the option of doing similar things in the local community . . . [and] with a more holistic approach then we've done in the past (REO:6).

However, most of the REOs contended that:

> There are [tasks] that can be done by the community itself or some community group. And if it can be then that's the best place for it . . . but there are some things you can't give away because the law wouldn't allow us to. But there are certain things which really never can be given away to the community. . . . [The services] need to be independent such as child protection (REO:6).

For some, the issue of devolution of services to the community did not accurately reflect the services provided by the Department:

> Eighty percent of the time of social workers is spent doing twenty percent of the work [statutory social work tasks] and that's the work we can't really step away from . . . All the tasks . . . that we could give away quite readily we don't do much of anyway, such as inspecting and registering children's homes (REO:6).

The REOs of Alternative Care were critical of the proposed decentralization of community services funding, one describing it as "chaotic" (REO:2). All were hopeful that the decision to decentralize the funding initially to the regions planned for late 1988 or early 1989 would have the positive effect of encouraging community based programs. Under this proposal it would be the responsibility of the REOs to oversee this first step in the decentralization process from the District Offices to local community groups and *iwi* authorities.

Partnership With The Community

In their description of social work practice within the Department, it was the opinion of several of the REOs that social workers had always worked closely with the community in the provision of services, particularly in rural areas:

> If you were going to have to drive eighty or one-hundred miles to deal with a case . . . you had to have some other structure to assist you. . . . So you got to know people in the community . . . the local cop, the headmaster of the high school, the ministers. . . . So rural workers have always had a community component in their work and a lot of social workers

> realized you just can't help a family in isolation (REO:6).

The view that working with the community and family networks had always been a part of social work in the Department was voiced by all the REOs except one. The majority viewed practice as preceding policy and noted districts with community work/development teams, active volunteer programs, and a number community oriented programs. They cited the neighborhood support centers, *whanau* schemes and the redefinitions of the residential social worker role to include family work as examples of practice that pre-dated policies urging community involvement (REO:4, 6, 7, 9). The problem they noted was the lack of any effective method of recording the community development activities so that top management was either unaware of the work or chose to ignore it. Even now, they argued, when community work/development is actioned as a policy directive, "stats don't show the effort that went into actually stopping kids coming into care" (REO:9). Concern was expressed that the decreasing number of children in care being recorded around the country would be interpreted by top management as indicating that the need for social workers was less since a primary factor in creating and maintaining social work positions had been the number of children in care.

> The number of children in care has reduced drastically but the time and effort in achieving that is not recognized, is not taken into account. . . . The statisticians in Treasury see that in 1985 we had 5,000 children in care and in 1987 we have 3,000. . . . So they'll figure we don't need so many social workers. . . . What they don't recognize is the time and effort that goes into keeping those children out of care (REO:9).

The emphasis on community, coupled with the push toward district autonomy, was seen as forcing Districts to look to their communities as their reference group, since they are accountable to them in ways they have not been in the past. "Districts [are] very close to their community groups" (REO:7).

> There is a real hope that districts would be in a better position to collaborate with other groups, cooperate and get feed back from their communities and be more

> responsive to clients. That's what we mean by community orientation (REO:8).

There was some variance of opinion, however. A few of the REOs considered that the Department was tending toward specialization in child protection and youth work while others saw the community orientation as:

> Interpreted in some places as a broadening of the client base . . . that community development and communities could make a claim on the Department and its resources. . . . But I do not think that it was ever the intention of the most senior management [that the Department would pursue an active community development programme] . . . despite the establishment of a Community Development Unit in Head Office (REO:8).

The REO:10 questioned the role of the Department in what she termed a 'community approach':

> I have trouble with the community approach in terms of whether it is this Department's job in these rather stringent times . . . It may be totally appropriate for us to support, for example, the Help Foundation to work in the area of child abuse. . . . [The question is] what should be the parameters of that involvement (REO:10).

However, she was not supportive of a major shift of service provision to the community since, she argued, the community has never really shown a willingness to take care of its own:

> The community alienates those it doesn't like or approve. Now how in God's name are we going to say they [the community] will take care of their own . . . If the state doesn't assume [responsibility] what is going to happen to battered women, to sexually abused girls and boys, to those with AIDS? (REO:10).

She acknowledged that the efforts to establish closer relationships with the community were important because delegation of community services funding to the districts was imminent. This meant that local groups and agencies would be negotiating, contracting and seeking assistance from their local district for services that were previously provided and administered through Head Office.

Management Style

One REO argued that a change in management style was necessitated by the growth in size and function in the Department which made continuation of the centralized administrative management system unsustainable. "The management styles being used [by departmental administrative staff] were those that were applicable to a much smaller organisation. . . . [Those styles] were dependent on informal control" (REO:8).

It was clear from the comments of the REOs that they felt the regionalization and decentralization, particularly when considered along with the policy of participatory management, had potentially positive outcomes. The restructuring has "allowed us...to involve district operational managers in managing the region the way they could never manage the country"(REO:8). But there were negative outcomes noted, as well:

> Since the Regional Director has become the Assistant-Director General: Region [in July of 1988] and part of the Executive Management Group, he is in Head Office two to three days a week, We now have to consider a regional office director! (REO:11).

Consideration of the establishment of yet another top level regional office position was an additional source of tension between the regional offices and the districts who saw the proposed salary expenditure as excessive and was later to be a central factor in District initiated reviews of the regional structure.[28] Four of the REOs contended that those in executive positions in social work had always operated as managers rather than administrators because of the unpredictable nature of the social work task and the values upon which the social work is based. They did acknowledge that social work managers had not previously done the long-term planning that was now required as part of their job description (REO:2, 6, 7, 8). One of the REOs was more cynical about participatory management when considered in relationship to Head Office management:

> Participatory means tapping a few people on the shoulder and getting them to work out this issue which is not too different from the old method of working parties (REO:7).

Another REO was even more critical of the style of management in the Regional Office saying she was more likely to hear of developments in her area of responsibility from other regions since her Assistant Director-General had stopped circulating copies of the documents and minutes from Head Office meetings for 'cost cutting' reasons. She questioned her ability to 'participate' if she was not well informed.

SOCIAL WORK

In the 1986 restructuring, the newly appointed Deputy Director-Generals were made responsible for resource management, and services and policy which included income security and social work services. By 1987, Head Office had been organized into two 'directorates' of Policy Development and Programmes and Services.

> Then suddenly you could see that social workers were disappearing from Head Office and when you saw the matrix there was no case for social work. . . . It was pepper-potted all through the different programmes. . . . People were cut off from their reference group (REO:7).

The move to smaller offices, such as the growing proliferation of Area Welfare Offices as sub-components of District Offices, while moving services closer to the people and making them more accessible was seen as:

> Weakening the Social Services Division because it is harder to get a critical mass of expertise under those conditions. So the interests and trends within the Social Services Division are at odds with the general trends in the Department (REO:8).

One REO predicted a "withering of the identification with the social work profession as an identifiable professional group" within the Department (REO:3).

The reasons for the attack on social work in the Department were seen to be complex:

> The precise role of social work in the current service delivery of the Department, in fact even in policy, is not well understood by the drivers of the change. . . . Neither [the Director-General] who came up through the ranks of Benefits and Pensions nor [the Deputy Director-General] who was seconded from Treasury have ever had time for social workers. . . . Their ideas come straight out of the Chicago School of Management, all you hear is programmes and money and restructuring and redundancies and PSA meetings and packages (REO:8).

The role of the social work administrator was seen to have changed from one of professional leadership to one of financial management, "which means for many of them they do not want their jobs anymore" (REO:8). The task of professional leadership was delegated further down the hierarchy to the first-line supervisors.

The impact of the anti-racism activity and training in the Department was loss of confidence of many Pakeha social workers whose sense of "legitimacy of what they're doing was thoroughly shaken" (REO:10) and a sense of "immobilization in prioritizing the multitude of perspectives all claiming validity and a few claiming priority status" (REO:8). Several REOs noted that the move to biculturalism and Equal Employment Opportunity policies meant that many Maori people were hired into social work positions without a social work orientation, without social work training or education and without a commitment to social work tasks. Changes in the orientation and in-service training provisions within the Department meant that these staff came into the districts unprepared to assume their role as social work staff and often remained unskilled because the training responsibility was delegated to the first-line supervisors who were already fully committed.

> The hidden hope of most of the managers . . . is that we will some day get through this experience of being the Department of Social Welfare. This is not a properly set up organisation, it is neither one thing or another. It doesn't provide an integrated social welfare service because there are so many functions outside our orbit . . . It has forced child and family services in with the income maintenance services in an unnatural and overmanaged way (REO:8).

The major dilemmas the REOs expressed revolved around the tasks of field social work in a statutory organization and of the Department in social service provision. All the REOs commented on the Assistant Directors of Social Service Conference held in August 1988 as clearly signalling the intention of the Department to retain few direct service responsibilities and devolve and/or contract out everything possible to 'the community'.

> We would pick up only the major responsibilities for child protection and youth . . . and almost all other responsibilities could be devolved out. That was certainly the thrust of the Hamilton Conference (REO:2).

It was at the Hamilton Conference that the publication, *Future Directions for Social Work*,[29] prepared by the Principal Social Worker and her Head Office staff was discussed.

One of the REOs commented that the tasks of social work had expanded since the Department was formed in 1971. He contrasted it with the directives for social work tasks in 1988 which are to prevent children coming into care, to maintain children with their own parents first, then within their *whanau*/extended family and with the provision of resources to enable that goal *before* statutory action is taken.

> Once the Department of Social Welfare had been established, [social workers] picked up other work [in addition to child welfare] because of the broader operation of the benefit section. . . . There was a dissonance in that social work was being used to assess eligibility for income rather than to assist people . . . We widened our service so that virtually anybody who knocked on our door with a human problem, we were bound to respond . . . but the bulk of our work was still in that child welfare area, now some are proposing child welfare again be our specialty. . . . The method was by and large to remove the children, put them in a different environment, generally an environment which excluded the natural family, and then to return them after a sort of basic standardised period of time in the hope that something had happened. Not a lot of work was done with the family. . . . What it did was to

> alienate them from their families and they often wanted to drift back. By the late 1970s, we began to change that and look for an inclusive type of situation where we also would work with the parents (REO:6).

The predominance of a casework model that did not emphasize work with the community except on a case-by-case basis was acknowledged by most of the REOs. They argued the prevalence of casework was more a reflection of the demand for crisis intervention, a reflection of the expectation that social workers should and would respond to all requests for service, a consequence of the high rate of statutory child protection referrals in proportion to trained staff and a result of understaffing and rapid turnover.

> The case work model really means that the social worker has got to deal with every individual that approaches and the goal of the Department in the Act is very broad. They [social workers] can't deal with social problems in a broad area because they are so tied up with dealing with individual approaches. . . . There is no time to address commonalities and draw those private problems into public issues (REO:9).

The continued gap between the ideals of community based approaches and social work as practiced was confirmed by the REOs despite the fact that several districts had implemented a modified patch system approach. These innovations in service delivery did not become institutionalized partly because of the factors outlined above, but in particular, because of the sheer volume of statutory work which demanded immediate individualized casework intervention.

Restructuring was seen as having a paradoxical effect on community development and community work:

> Patch is going. It was very fashionable with community development. . . . Everybody wanted to do it and the offices were structured [into geographical patches]. This idea about using your community resources and that [it] could only be done by doing a patch [is] all gone by the way side now. The term is gone and now [we are] into specialisation (REO:7).

One REO noted many social workers were resistant to abandoning the patch approach because the patch system implied a wide definition of the social work task demanding the full range of interventions to meet the social problems in a particular geographical area. Another REO did not lament its passing because she felt the patch system was ill-suited to the New Zealand context where*whanau* were not geographically based nor were agencies, decisions, or helping networks. Seven of the REOs saw the Department moving toward specialities with community work and development activities devolved outside the Department to community workers, voluntary groups and *iwi* authorities. There were considerable differences in the opinions of the REOs on the question of the social work task within the Department, although all the REOs viewed the primary task of statutory social work as child protection and services to youth. This was one of the directions clearly being indicated for statutory social work by departmental directives and the document from the Principal Social Worker.[30] Ten of the eleven REOs saw a role for the Department in community development and community work. Some felt that departmental social workers would need to be involved "because the community did not have the resources" (REO:7). Others felt that the Department was already actively involved in community development activities demonstrating the role was part of statutory social work and should remain so (REO:6, 9). A few REOs pointed to the soon to be decentralized community services function in funding and assisting community groups as *the* role for statutory social workers in community development (REO:10).

REO:1 voiced the opinion that the trend towards specialization in District offices would mean that:

> Every case, every Maori case, will become an abuse case so that the specialists teams will now deal with them rather than those workers assigned to family or *whanau* community work (REO:1).

This would occur, he contended, because of the deference awarded to specialist teams with their highly trained workers. This REO saw specialization developing at the expense of community work or development teams.

The REOs made it clear that fundamental changes had taken place in the practice of social work with the clear directives emitting from implementation of the principles of the restructuring and the recommendations of *Puao-Te-Ata-Tu.* [31]

> We see now that social workers working closely with the *whanau* is having a flow on effect to other

> children in the *whanau* . . . They don't come into care . . . but it is not just with Maori families, for the principles of family decision making are being applied to Pakeha families as well with just as positive an effect (REO:11).

BICULTURALISM

The impact of biculturalism was seen by the REOs as pervasive. All agreed that social workers, in fact all workers, in the Department had to consider their actions in light of *Puao-Te-Ata-Tu*[32] recommendations. The REOs emphasized the influence of the Maatua Whangai programme and the Report on Institutional Racism[33] as raising awareness among all workers in the Department but with social workers in particular.

> Social workers have been really positive and are trying to work out ways [to implement bicultural practice]. But the hesitation comes in the 'how to' . . . when it comes to *whanau* decision making . . . that brings up the most concern because of ensuring the safety of the child (REO:7).

The REOs acknowledged cultural differences regarding the primacy of the child over the primacy of the family/*whanau* while clearly recognizing the conflicts inherent in attempting to apply cultural guidelines within the existing legislation.

> It is very easy to incorporate the statement [of a commitment to biculturalism] in all sorts of written material, to employ more brown faces, but to expect everybody to continue to operate in the same way . . . or to almost hope things might change when you're not quite sure what the changes might be (REO:10).

The REOs acknowledged that the new hiring practices and affirmative action policies had brought many untrained workers in as field social workers without providing them adequate orientation to the Department and appropriate skill development training. Consequently, whether it was because they did not know how to go about the tasks or because they did not feel the tasks were culturally appropriate, many of the newly hired workers were resistant to performing their statutory responsibilities. One REO felt that since many Maori staff were hired with the support of the *whanau* and/or at the recommendation of an *iwi* authority, they felt more accountable to their *whanau* then to the Department. "They are not actually putting their efforts into DSW work and that is creating real problems" (REO:9).

SUMMARY

The views of the REOs reflect the pivotal position they held between top management (Head Office) and social work practice in the District Offices. Their responses indicate that they were very sensitive to Head Office directives, even when those directives were vague, open to wide interpretation, or in some cases, contradictory. The REOs were aware on a personal level of their vulnerability. The loss of a powerful social work advocate in Head Office was noted repeatedly.

However, the REOs were more than career bureaucrats, nine of the eleven clearly identify themselves as professional social workers. Their commitment to social work ethics was evident in their continuing attempts to analyze developments in the Department and to evaluate the rationale for the various policy directives in terms of 'good social work practice' and 'benefits to clients.'

Regionalization, despite the REOs cynicism about its being motivated by a concern to regain control of the organization, was perceived as offering the potential of making the organization more manageable and more responsive to both staff and clients. Decentralization of 'delegations of authority' had made a difference in their view but the delegations came down with so many guidelines some of the REOs felt they were virtually meaningless. Yet, the REOs were optimistic that with decentralization there was the potential of differential district development, genuinely responding to local community needs.

The issues of devolution seemed more remote to the REOs than was expected. This may be due in part to the pace of change in devolving services to community and *iwi* groups which had slowed considerably despite initial activity in the devolution of funds to COGS and a few *iwi* authorities. The REOs of Alternative Care were anticipating renewed activity with the decentralization of Community Services funding to the districts.

It was in the area of participation with the community that the highest level of debate was evident. There were considerable arguments that policy followed practice with poignant examples of community oriented efforts in community development teams, volunteer programs, specialized community work initiatives funded by the Department, and joint projects with voluntary agencies and community groups. Still, all the REOs recognized the predominance of casework and offered quite comprehensive explanations, many with strong parallels to the findings of Black, et al.[34]

The impact of biculturalism on social work practice was seen by all the REOs as pervasive and intrinsically intertwined with all four principles of the restructuring. Social work within the Department had embraced biculturalism. Intervention was focused on *whanau* decision-making, support of existing family networks, preventing children coming into care, moving children out of residential institutions to community placements, and releasing funds to local programs rather than host agencies. But it was clear that the REOs were attempting to reframe these changes in terms of good social work practice, and some fitted very well. Yet, the REOs expressed concern that because they perceived cost-cutting was a major motivator, further reductions in allocations would occurto pressure Departmental social workers to retreat into casework just to cope with the demands for mandated statutory services in child protection and youth justice.

Only one REO saw no future for social work within the Department. The remainder felt the Assistant Director's Conference in Hamilton in August 1988 clearly indicated that social work within the Department would focus on child protection and youth justice. Despite this generalized view, many of the REOs still considered the community work and development role of statutory social workers under discussion. It was unclear whether the Department's monitoring, funding and servicing role to community agencies would be defined as a social work role. Only one REO addressed this debate.

Thus, the REOs saw the Departmental policy with regard to the social work task as in flux but with clear signals that the role of social work within the Department was heading toward primarily child protection and youth justice roles. The REOs were quite knowledgeable about the debates, the conflicting views, and the implications of the conflicting directives. It was clear that they were well aware of difficulties in practice and were willing to assist Head Office and Districts to find 'new ways of working' that better served clients.

NOTES

1. Department of Social Welfare, *Management Plan, 1986* (Wellington: Department of Social Welfare, 1986a).

2. See Figure One for the DSW Head Office organizational chart prior to 1986.

3. New Zealand Planning Council (NZPC), *The Welfare State* (Wellington: Government Printer, 1979); NZPC, *Directions* (Wellington: Government Printer, 1981); New Zealand Council of Social Services (NZCSW), *Establishing District Councils of Social Services* (Wellington: Department of Social Welfare, 1978); Judith Davey and Maire Dwyer, *Meeting Needs in the Community: A Discussion Paper on Social Services* (Wellington: New Zealand Planning Council, 1984).

4. DSW.

5. Ibid, 1.

6. See Appendix V.

7. DSW, 1.

8. Administrative Review Committee, *Performance and Efficiency in the Department of Social Welfare* (Wellington: Government Printer, December, 1987).

9. DSW, 1986a.

10. See Appendix VI.

11. These perceptions were reconfirmed in reviews of the regional office structure subsequent to this research. See Barretta-Herman, Jeff Dougal and Alastair Spearling, *The Relationship Between Regional Office and District Offices in the Central District* (Palmerston North: Department of Social Welfare, 1989); *Review of Regional Offices* Report of Assistant Director-General: Programmes and Services (Wellington: Department of Social Welfare, April, 1990a).

12. DSW, 2.

13. Ibid.

14. Administrative Review Committee, 18.

15. See Appendix IX.

16. DSW.

17. Administrative Review Committee.

18. A perception confirmed in the review of Barretta-Herman, Dougal and Spierling.

19. DSW, *Review of the Regional Offices.*

20. DSW, *Report of the Department of Social Welfare for the Year ended 31 March, Presented to the House of Representatives* (Wellington: Government Printer, 1987b).

21. See Chapter Four for a discussion of this point.

22. See Appendix for a copy of the Demographics Information Sheet.

23. Ministerial Advisory Committee on a Maori Perspective for the Department of Social Welfare, *Puao-Te-Ata-Tu:The Day Break Report* (Wellington: Department of Social Welfare, 1986).

24. See Appendix 1 for a copy of the Interview Schedule.

25. Refer to Chapter Three for a full description of the methodology.

26. These reports and events were described in Chapter Four.

27. A. H. Johnston, *Report to the Minister of Social Welfare on the Current Practices and Procedures Followed in Institutions of the Department of Social Welfare in Auckland* (Wellington: Department of Social Welfare, October, 1982).

28. See Barretta-Herman, et al.; DSW, *Review of the Regional Offices.*

28. DSW, *Contracting for Social Services: Principles and Guidelines* (Wellington: Department of Social Welfare, July, 1988c).

30. Ibid.

31. Ministerial Advisory Committee.

32. See Appendix VII for a summary of the recommendations.

33. DSW, *Institutional Racism in the Department of Social Welfare: Tamaki-Makau-Rau, Auckland (Revised)* (Wellington: Department of Social Welfare, May, 1985b).

34. J. Black, R, Bowl, D. Burns, C. Critcher, G. Grant, and D. Stockford, *Social Work in Context* (London: Tavistock, 1983).

VI

PERSPECTIVES OF PRACTICE: THE NAPIER DISTRICT OFFICE COMMUNITY DEVELOPMENT TEAM

This chapter which presents the Napier District Office Community Development Team's perspectives of practice begins with a sketch of the Napier District before describing the members of the team and reviewing the data collection techniques employed.

The Napier District Office serves the Pacific Ocean seaside city of Napier and the eastern half of the Hawkes Bay Region. The *tangata whenua* of this area are Ngati Kahungunu. Economically the region, which has been traditionally a wealthy area, has suffered under five years of drought, the national rural downturn, and seasonal unusually high unemployment levels. This District Office had a national reputation of receptivity to innovation and a community orientation which was traced to the early 1970s.[1] The Napier Office was characterized by its Director as having a highly trained and experienced staff with relatively low turnover.

The office had the typical district office structure. The District Director had responsibility for the District's overall operation and its three Assistant Directors: Social Services (previous to the restructuring, Social Work), Corporate Services (previous to the restructuring, Administration) and Benefits and Pensions and their staffs. The Assistant Director: Social Services, as the only Assistant Director interviewed in this research will be refered to in this chapter as the 'Assistant Director.'

The Napier District Office's Social Services Division at the time of the research study had 30 positions: four clerical staff, seventeen basic grade social workers occupying sixteen full-time positions, seven senior social workers, two supervising social workers and one assistant director. The Division was broadly divided into two teams. The Personal and Family Services Team provided supportive, child protection, adoptions and court services to youth. The Community Development Team was responsible for community work, development activities including support to community organizations, Maatua

Whangai, the volunteer program and the budget service. At the Staff Development Day in April 1987, the staff had agreed to adopt in principle the Head Office recommended social service division structure with two exceptions. The staff group suggested a further division of the Personal and Family Services Team into a Casework and Court Work team. Secondly, they rejected the 'Community Welfare Services' team label and suggested retention of the 'Community Development Team' as ore accurately reflecting the philosophy of the Napier District Office. The structure of Social Service Division appears in the figure below.

Figure Three

Napier District Office
Social Services Divisional Structure

Assistant Director: Social Services(AD)

Personal and Family Services			Community and Preventative Services	
Children in Care	Court	Intake	Community Development	Alternative Care
SSW:SW:2	SSW	SSW	**SSW:CD**	**SSW:AC**
4.5 SWs	3 SWs	4 SWs	**4 SWs**	1 SW

Key: SSW=Senior Social Worker
SW=Social Worker
Respondents in Bold

The field study objectives were to elicit from the respondents their perceptions of changes in social work practice subsequent to the implementation of the principles of the restructuring. As was explained in the chapter on methodology, this team was purposefully chosen because it reputedly had a community focus exemplified by their support of existing voluntary agencies and support of community initiatives. Briefly, data was drawn on the Community Development Team utilizing several methods.[2] Each member of the team was interviewed using the structured questionnaire. The tapes were transcribed, the content analyzed and presented below.

In addition to the interview, each team member was asked to present a piece of their work that they felt demonstrated their way of working and were asked how this piece of work reflected the new practice principles defined as 'the new way of working'.[3] The Senior Social Worker: Community Development (SSW:1) presented his process of negotiating with a community agency's request for support. The researcher accompanied the Budget Liaison Worker as he set up a community awareness project on credit with the help of volunteers. The community social worker planned a visit to the Women's Health Centre she was instrumental in establishing and arranged a planning meeting with the volunteer collective that managed the center. The Maatua Whangai worker arranged for the researcher to meet with the twelve *kuia* (Maori women elders) who were the core of a developing *whanau* support group in a large state housing district. The Employment Related Social Worker obtained permission for the researcher to accompany him to an all day *hui* (meeting following formal protocal) on the Petane Marae where Regional Employment Action Committee Training Programmes for Maori unemployed were the focus of discussion.

In addition, the researcher participated in the life of the agency during the week-long research period. This included a District Management Team meeting, a staff meeting and a special social work meeting to discuss the reports of the National Assistant-Directors' Meeting on the future of social work. District documents, including circular memos, practice reports, statistical reports and organizational documents were examined for relevant material. Corollary interviews, using the structured questionnaire, were held with the Assistant-Director: (AD:1), and the Senior Social Workers of Alternative Care and Casework (SSW:2; SSW:3). Following the initial approach to the Napier Office, the researcher presented the proposal to the entire staff and invited any staff who wanted to comment on the restructuring to meet with the researcher during the research period. Several staff and the Executive Director of the District Executive Committee utilized the opportunity providing valuable verifying data.[4]

HISTORY OF THE COMMUNITY DEVELOPMENT TEAM

The Senior Social Worker of the Community Development Team (SSW:1) gave the following brief history of the team which was augmented by comments from the Assistant Director and the District documents made available to the researcher. The Senior Social Worker traced the beginnings of the team to a 1969 church sponsored city-wide initiative called 'Helping Your Neighbour'. This initiative included government agencies and voluntary agencies working together to provide community based preventative and support services on a formal and informal basis. The District responded by deciding in 1970 to extend the voluntary social work scheme and allocated resources for recruitment, training and support services. The volunteer scheme was only one of several preventative community based programmes put in place in the early 1970s.

In 1976, the Napier District Office Assistant Director wrote a paper describing the preventative social work activities in his division in response to a 1973 Social Advisory Council's *Working Party Report on Social Welfare*.[5] Wilson outlined the argument presented by the Report for shifting the emphasis of social work from casework to family-oriented counseling and welfare services supported by close consultation and coordination with community agencies, particularly the schools. Wilson then demonstrated that such a practice model was functioning in the Napier Office. The active volunteer program with over ninety volunteers had been in place for over five years:

> The utilizing of volunteer personnel as suggested by the Working Party has proven to be a most worthwhile addition to the existing Departmental staff, as much of the grassroots family-oriented work could be taken over by these skilled workers . . . training and support through group supervision and the sharing of experiences for such volunteers, is seen as being essential in the Napier Office and this is an ongoing regular activity.[6]

The second preventative welfare program Wilson described was the joint effort of the schools, the justice system and the Department. The 'Discussion in Schools' program was aimed at early identification of 'at risk' children, at coordinating early prevention efforts through information, at providing counselling and supportive services in the community and at increasing cooperation and consultation among the various government departments to improve service delivery.

In 1978, the Napier Office set up the 'Contact Centre' as a multi-purpose community drop-in center with a primary focus on unemployed youth. The program included information referral, job-readiness and training programs. By 1988, the center was a community run and sponsored enterprise funded through the Community Organisation Grant

Scheme (COGS). Five years after the Contact Centre was first established, the Napier Office set up KNEECAP (Kids Needing Educational, Environmental, Cultural Activities Programme). This community based trust provided activities for pre-adolescent 'at risk' youth. These programs were four of the initiatives sponsored in part or wholly by the Napier District Office that contributed to its national reputation as a community oriented district.

In 1984, a report prepared by a Napier District Office Community Worker noted that:

> It is apparent that Napier is one of only a few offices that has set up Community Development Teams with social workers released from casework. . . . There are a group of people at Head Office who are committed to the concept of community development and who will endeavour to see this area of work further develop.[7]

In 1988 the community development programs included the development of the Social Work Community Resource Manual, the Home Liaison Programme at a local school, Parent Effectiveness Training, a social skills program, and supportive services to community groups. Individual social workers with a community orientation, recruited and supported by the management were the two factors that insured continuation of this community orientation despite contrary national trends and the adoption of the unsupportive workload formula discussed earlier. The two directors during the period were committed to the community work/community development function as an integral part of statutory social work services.

These two directors hired and a number of social workers with a community orientation. The Senior Social Worker, with responsibility for the Community Development Team at the time of the research, had been granted a bursary to earn his qualification in social work and upon completion assumed supervision of the Community Development Team in 1983.

THE COMMUNITY DEVELOPMENT TEAM

The Community Development Team of five members included a senior social worker (SSW:1) and four social work positions filled by a Budget Liason Officer (SW:1), a Community Worker (SW:2), an Employment Related Social Worker (SW:3) and a Maatua Whangai worker (SW:4).[8] The Senior Social Worker of this team had been continuously with the Department since 1975 except for his two years at Victoria University to obtain his qualification. He had been the senior of this team for five years. The Budget Liaison Worker joined the Department in February, 1984. The community worker had a qualification in social work and a work history in psychiatric social work. She was appointed to the team in March, 1987. The Employment Related Social Worker, appointed in November 1987 after twelve years as a union representative in the meat industry and came with the support of his *whanau*. The Maatua Whangai worker had been appointed with the support of her *whanau* in February 1987 after five years as a volunteer with her *iwi*. The team had recently lost two part-time positions, a Volunteer Coordinator's position, a wage worker and a Budget Advisory Service Coordinator's position. The wage worker positions were lost in the budget cuts of late 1987 and early 1988.

There are several notable characteristics of this particular Community Development Team. Except for the team senior, the team members were relatively new to the Department and to social work. The team was a team with clearly designated specializations. Three of the four positions on the team had been established with targeted funding from Head Office initiated programs. Two of the team members had strong links with with their *whanau* who had supported their appointment to the Department.

During the six years the Senior Social Worker had responsibility for the Community Development Team, he felt that the the team had had to deal with recurring internal cohesion issues and constant threats to its continued existence. Despite the support of the Assistant Director over its seventeen year history, the Community Development Team had never been a particularly large or strong team. The size of the team fluctuated between four and six positions. The function of the team and its composition had been less a result of planning than of expediency. For example, when Head Office established the employment related social work positions in the early 1980s, this position was attached to the Community Development Team. The same process occurred with the the Budget Liaison Officer in 1984 and subsequently with the establishment of a Maatua Whangai position. Although a strong argument could be been made for the appropriateness of these assignments to the Community Development Team, they were management 'top down' decisions that brought together individuals from diverse backgrounds with quite distinct tasks and very different orientations to their work. The establishment of a team approach had became increasingly problematic. Each individual had been employed for a specific task, with little, if any, interchangeability of skills, common professional orientation, or Departmental work history.

> We are a 'team' in name only, each job has a specific focus. . . . We hardly see each other except for scheduled supervision and team meetings. . . . Our work is not interdependent and is mainly 'out there' in the community (SSW:1).

The one common task was support, advice and development services to community groups and agencies. The Senior Social Worker had developed a four category schema to describe the services the team members offered to community agencies and groups:

TRUSTEE RELATIONSHIPS: the team member had a legal and/or management responsibility for the group or agency

ADVISORY RELATIONSHIP: the team member had coaching, supervisory, education, specialist input role responsibilities

LIAISON RELATIONSHIP: the team member had a facilitating role as the main contact person with the Department for the group, often for a specific reason

COMMITTEE MEMBER: the team member had a developmental/ supportive role.

Each of the four categories of service had a visiting standard that specified the frequency and the level of skill the intervention required. The senior social worker used this scheme in workload allocation and as an evaluative tool. The expectation was for the team member to gradually play a less integral role with the community group or agency as the group assumed increasingly more responsibility for itself. In addition, the team provided one-off funding information and general information/referral services to emerging groups and community organizations with whom it did not have a more formal role.

The Senior Social Worker viewed the continued existence of the community development team as tenuous. Another Senior Social Worker in the District (SSW:3) reinforced this view by explaining that there was less of an assumption that the positions on the Community Development Team would be automatically filled when vacated by transfer or resignation than was the situation with casework positions.

> While staff feel community development is important, when it comes down to positions, the

> attitude of most management and practitioners is that if there's going to be cuts, community development is where the cuts should be. . . . The statutory work, the cases are priority (SSW:3).

Filling each vacancy in the Community Development Team required strong justification and was subject to multiple delays. In the budget cuts of 1987-1988, Department policy was to avoid competition between teams. The alternative chosen, to discontinue the wage worker positions, only affected the Community Development Team since it was the only team with wage workers. One of those wage workers was the volunteer coordinator. This occurred despite Department policy expressing support of a community social work model and encouraging volunteer programs. Allocation to preventative social work activities had to compete with allocations to casework services fulfilling statutory requirements. The team had difficulties recruiting team members because its social work activities were considered by many as 'fringe' and because career prospects were not seen to be enhanced by community work/development experience. It was this non-support, and, at times the thinly veiled hostility expressed by the rest of the staff towards the Community Development Team, that presented a periodic threat to its continued existence.

> It has been a constant struggle to explain our role to the rest of the staff. . . . We have not been able to clearly show how we can make their job [the casework job] easier. . . . They want our staff allocation. . . . They think we have [it easy] and just go to meetings (SSW:1).

> People can understand casework and they can also see the figures. . . . This team can't really play the numbers game and that seems the way a lot of people judge things (SW-1).

The Senior Social Worker reflected on his work in the Tamatea suburb of Napier prior to his training. There he applied a 'community casework' model which included many features of the 'patch approach'[9] to the social work he would become familiar with in his training. He made himself available to the agencies and volunteers in his area, was part of the "Discussion in Schools" programs operating in his area, and demonstrated his commitment to this particular geographical community.

> I would regularly go to the local drop-in centre a half day a week and stay there, visiting the solo mums or getting the solo mother's group together, just the little basic things. . . . I'd liaison with the local medical centre and follow-up on any concerns. . . . I set up the liaison system between the school, the school principals, the district health nurses, and the Plunket Society to identify possible problems early (SSW:1).

These activities contributed to the development of his philosophy of community work while in University. Basic to this philosophy was a belief in self-determination and the ability of individuals and communities to help themselves:

> While I believe in the importance of the welfare state, in the government taking responsibility, I also think there has been an aspect of people being relieved of their responsibilities. . . . So it is a sort of awakening people to the possibilities they have in their own fingertips. . . . It is empowerment (SSW:1).

He addressed himself to the difference between community work and community development, a difference, he argued, was both in emphasis and in degree.

> They differ in terms of the percentage of time the worker is emeshed in the project or community. The worker is much less directly involved in community development and much more involved in community work. My team could do more community development if the caseworkers adopted a more 'community case-work' perspective (SSW:1).

He contended that Departmental policy had not been explicit: "the term *community development* is used frequently but the intent is for *community work* that is directly serving our existing clients" (SSW:1). The Senior Social Worker felt that community activities must increasingly be capable of demonstrating their direct relevance to reducing referrals to the Department, to mitigating the seriousness of the referrals made or to establishing resources for existing clients clearly "within the boundaries of our statutory obligations." Such guidelines he saw as a double bind since reduction in referrals might be used to justify further budget cuts. The guidelines represented a narrowing of the operationalization of the Departmental mission as it had been interpreted before the restructuring. The Napier District Office Assistant Director (AD:1) was quite clear on this point:

> We really do need to look at our areas of responsibility, our goals, our result areas and try and get our services and our community development to fit in with the results we are expected to achieve as a Department. And those results need to be tied in very closely with the clientele. We're achieving results for our clients (AD:1).

The implication was that community development activities for the general well-being of the community was not justifiable. Activities were to be clearly linked to clients. That was assumed to mean current clients, not potential or 'at risk' of becoming clients.

> I think we were almost at the stage where if something was happening in the community, we had some how to be involved. . . . I don't think we will become the 'trash can' agency, where everything that the other agencies didn't want to do gets dumped onto Social Welfare, because we have such a wide mandate. I do think we are going to be far more selective (AD:1).

The Assistant Director predicted that the size of the Community Development Team would continue to shrink as community work and development activities were 'contracted out' or devolved to the community.

> I think we'll have at least one, possibly two positions in the office. One responsible for funding decisions and one position for the inspection of facilities and the monitoring for effectiveness of service (AD:1).

She pointed to the policy directive indicating the intention to eventually shift ultimate responsibility for Maatua Whangai to the *iwi* and the readiness of the local *iwi* in Napier to have the Department Maatua Whangai worker sited in their Roopu-a-Iwi premises.

STATUTORY - VOLUNTARY BALANCE

The Senior Social Worker expressed an ambivalence about the shift of provision of services to the voluntary sector.

> While the Department is fully responsible for these services, there is some semblance of commitment to their continuation. Once they are devolved to the 'community,' whoever and whatever the 'community' is, that commitment is weakened if not eliminated. . . . This team is being threatened by devolution and I am in conflict. While being philosophically supportive of the move to do things differently, I fear transfer of service provision to the community makes those services vulnerable to fluctuations in community support and funding (SSW:1).

For example, he and the Budget Liaison Worker were supportive of the budgeting service being devolved to the community. They recognized that the involvement of the Department and paid staff may have a negative effect on voluntary involvement:

> Hastings [a neighbouring District Office] has an autonomous budgeting service, they have the same sort of team, but they have a committee that runs it. So I think the fact that I have have been here and am available, has made me more involved with the day-to-day operations and the volunteers less involved (SW-1).

Discussion was underway for the transfer of the Budget Advisory Service to the community although the Senior Social Worker was attempting to slow down the process until adequate funding for a coordinator and administrative costs could be guaranteed through local or Departmental funding.

SERVICE DELIVERY

Regionalization and Decentralization

The Community Development Team members had little comment in response to the questions on regionalization and decentralization. In fact, the team members expressed little interest in these processes apparently since they did not perceive any immediate effect on their work. Three of the respondents holding management positions (AD:1; SSW:1; SSW:3), however, felt themselves directly effected by both regionalization and decentralization. It was the Assistant Director's opinion that the restructuring of the Department was initiated by the Fourth Labour Government to:

> Bring services closer to the people who need the services. . . . They went in with the ideas of getting decision making closer, doing more briefing and consulting, and implementing management by consensus...They had the view that there are resources people didn't use effectively and would continue to use ineffectively if they were controlled from a remote point (AD:1).

She felt the Auckland Region had provided a opportunity to examine the implications of a regionalization process. The Assistant Director reported an assistant director's meeting in the early-1980's expressed strong objections to a regionalization plan that created another layer of hierarchy.

> However, in 1985, it seemed very clear that we were going to go to regionalisation and that was, I think, when the decision was made but there certainly was discussion before then. . . . I think *Puao-Te-Ata-Tu* was the final push that was required to make it happen. . . . People did see the Department as being a bureaucracy that was remote (AD:1).

The Assistant Director lamented the loss of specialized services, such as legal and international adoption services, that occurred under regionalization. These highly specialized services were infrequently utilized by the districts. To maintain professionals on a regional basis to provide these services would be financially prohibitive to the regions in her opinion. These services would have been better retained as centralized services.

> A national perspective on issues like foster care and adoptions is gone. It really has not been well replaced in the Regions. . . . There's nobody that has replaced the programme side, there's just this broad

> overview, but nobody who is a specialist in the region (AD:1).

Her view was echoed by the Senior Social Worker Casework:

> I'm not at all impressed by regionalisation. . . . For adoptions it has meant chaos. . . . I don't know who is responsible. . . . Two and a half months ago we were told to do a job which included temporary workers and to use them to do it properly and now without an explanation, the money is not there for those workers. Head Office apparently issued a press release that despite the cuts, we would be offering the same service. Now how can we possibly do that? How can you have any respect for people who have said that? (SSW:2).

The Assistant Director expressed concern that the Regional Office staff, who characterized themselves at one point as a 'courier between the Districts and Head Office', were in fact operating in that manner:

> They [the REO's] have no line authority. If we want to find out something or clarify a policy, we have to write to them and *they* [sic] will write to Head Office. We are worse off in this regard than we were under the old system when we could contact Head Office directly (AD: 1).

The Assistant Director acknowledged that under the decentralization policies, the District Offices had been granted delegations that meant managers had more direct control over their operation.

> In relation to staff, I can decide how many social workers I'm going to have. I can decide the grading of the social workers--with approval of my director. I have to satisfy the director I can do it within the budget and the reason for those particular gradings. . . . *I am managing the division but I am only managing the division so long as my management fits the district management plan* [italics added] (AD:1).

She noted the limits of management in centrally determined budget expenditures and the realities that, not only, was the district budget function added on to an already full-time job it was assumed by individuals without skills in financial management:

> It has become quite stressful because we [middle managers] don't have terribly much training in financial management . . . and the money allocated is less than adequate to provide the standard level of service we have had up to now. *So a lot of the anger, the reaction against the curtailment of service comes against the local person* [sic] (AD:1).

The increase in workload for the Assistant Director was noted by all three Senior Social Workers who felt that the new management tasks delegated through decentralization to the AD's position meant that either those tasks had to be done along with the already full-time job, or some tasks of the AD's job would not be done or, as was already happening, some tasks would be delegated further down the hierarchy, i.e., to the Seniors, increasing the workload for everyone:

> At a time when all of us are being asked to work differently, learn different skills and save expenditure, at the same time our jobs are expanded. . . . Innovation is balanced against the constraints of time, money and the rising demand for services (SSW:1).

The delegations to the District Office were initially in the area of casework decisions so the Seniors over the Casework Team and Alternative Care were more directly affected by increased workload. The Community Development Team had few delegations passed to them as district officers but the plan to decentralize community services funding in the next year was expected to alter the Team's responsibilities dramatically.

Devolution and Participation

The proposed decentralization of community funding to the Districts[10] was expected to bring problematic issues to the District Office. Despite the stated Head Office support of community services, the Assistant Director did not foresee additional funds being made available for community initiatives nor an increase in the transfer of funds for devolution that many community groups expected (NZASW, 1986). She expected that the amount of funds available to community groups would be reduced at least by the costs of the administrative structures created for monitoring and evaluation of the expenditure. As well, the District Office would be expected to play a more prominent role in the funding process:

> We are going to be responsible for recommending certain services not be funded in the future and others are. . . . So although we are expecting the community to take initiatives, we are also going to monitor their performance (AD:1).

The Executive Secretary for the District Executive Committee[11] was of the opinion that decentralization actually *decreased* the ability of the community to influence decision making.

> While the Department was centralised you could go down to Wellington and make a 'big stink.' Now you have to make one here and you don't really know what the avenues are to get to those in power . . . it isn't the District Director. You really are not much further ahead (Executive Secretary)

The June 1988 statement of the Napier District Management Team Standards defined the aim of the Management Team as operating in a way that "provides for participation by all members" and "where possible, the method of decision making will be by consensus." It was important to note that the management team had wide membership. It was composed of the District Director, the Assistant Directors of Social Services, Corporate Services and Benefits and Pensions, two Whanau Group representatives (basically a Maori employee group), a Public Service Association representative and the Director's Secretary. The District Executive Committee Secretary was also present at the Management Team meetings in an apparent attempt to open the process to the community but did not have permanent membership.

Management Style

The management philosophy of the Assistant Director was consistent with the District Management Team philosophy.

> I have always really liked the idea of participatory management. . . . It is important to listen, to brief and to consult staff . . . but [as management], we reserve the right to make the final decision. . . . The

> process depends as well, on the level of staff experience (AD: 1).

The principle mechanisms for staff participation the Assistant Director outlined were the monthly staff meeting and the individual weekly team meetings. The senior social workers were charged with the liaison responsibility between basic grade staff and management. As well, written memos, comments, reports, etc., were periodically utilized as information exchange methods. The Assistant Director maintained what she described as an 'open door policy' but insisted that issues be dealt with within the chain of command first. She felt that the recommendations of the Administrative Review[12] and the Departmental Plans urging a participatory style of management only confirmed the style of management already operating in her division. This view was confirmed by the respondents holding management positions (SSW:1, 2, 3).

Within the Community Development Team, the Senior Social Worker characterized his role as a *coordinator* rather than as a *supervisor* with control and monitoring functions. Each of his team members had a specialized function and had been recruited to perform that specialized task. The only exception was the Community Worker who because of her qualification in social work and her commitment to community development, functioned in a more traditional supervisor-supervisee relationship with the Senior Social Worker. The other workers, particularly the Maatua Whangai worker and the Employee Related Social Worker, felt a dual accountability to their *whanau* and *iwi*. This dual accountability redefined their relationship with their Senior and increased their autonomy in task planning and performance. The modified participatory management model utilized in this team reflected these team realities.

SOCIAL WORK

All those interviewed acknowledged that social work practice in the Department had undergone radical changes and more change was still to come.

> I think there were some staff with no involvement at all in the community development initiative. They now are beginning to work to deflect children away from the services traditionally provided . . . 'The new way of working' does require new skills and brings with it new stresses (AD:1).

The Assistant Director acknowledged that despite the acceptance of change as inevitable, some social workers remained resistant to the shift to a community oriented service model because of the need to respond to the daily demands for care, protection, supportive services. She acknowledged her own resistance to the name change from Social Work Division to Social Services Division that occurred with the restructuring:

> I think with 'Social Services' the Department services were being given a wider perspective and involved more of a community sort of view and a community role. . . . [It implied] the expectation of a generic sort of approach to families. . . . But I was not involved in the decision, my opinion wasn't even asked. . . . There was a feeling almost of betrayal. . . . For awhile I even refused to sign [my new title]. . . . The acronym AD:SS was distasteful. . . . Social Work had had its own line structure and several strong managers [in Head Office who] were made redundant and with them clear identification of social work in Head Office disappeared (AD:1).

Social work practice was seen to have changed not only in the demand for a bicultural model of practice but in requiring a true power-sharing in decision making with the family in a *whanau* decision making process. The Maatua Whangai worker was explicit in setting her priorities: "I don't look at the rights of the mother, I look at the rights of the baby and its bloodline" (SW-4). The implementation of this model was just beginning and faced complex overt and subtle dilemmas:

> We're trying to work in a bicultural way, to involve the *whanau*, yet people refuse to respond. We thought it was perfectly acceptable to invite the Departmental *kaumatua* to comment on a particular case but it was not with the particular family. . . . There is a lot of confusion about the proper protocol and how you are to go about unraveling it (AD:1).

The *kaumatua* (Maori elders) group that the Maatua Whangai worker arranged for the researcher to meet felt that the Department was changing and that there were concrete examples of the Department's commitment to Maori people. They pointed out the work of the Maatua Whangai worker with the families in the housing suburb and particularly expressed their appreciation of her in bringing them together to share their cultural heritage. The Maatua Whangai worker explained that she had been encouraged by Departmental policy to engage in community development of her *iwi*. Her work with the kaumatua group was an example.

The Maatua Whangai worker was both optimistic about Departmental policy regarding *iwi* development and pessimistic about implementation of true partnership. She felt that trained social workers were more hesitant to implement power sharing in *whanau* decision making, yet the newly trained social workers were less hesitant to embrace biculturalism. The *Pakeha* community worker expressed a reluctance to practice bicultural social work because she felt that it was inappropriate for her as a *Pakeha* to offer support to the Maori community. In her work with a community agency, it was her responsibility to link with the *Pakeha* community and her Maori colleague's responsibility to link with the Maori community:

> That's how we work at the Centre. . . . The Maori women come to her [the Maori worker], not to the Women's Health Centre. . . . I recognized that pretty early on. . . . I was white in the Department like everybody else and it was inappropriate for me to approach the Maori community (SW:2).

The Senior Social Worker felt strongly that social work philosophy has always supported getting:

> People together to try to decide their own destiny rather than making decisions for them. . . . The knowledge has been there and the desire to work that way has always been there. . . . Now it is supported by policy *if not by resources, the workload formula, or training* [italics added] (SSW:1).

Three of the team members including their senior social worker felt that the initial Departmental policies issued as part of the restructuring indicated the Department was taking a broad view of the social work task in which community development and community work were seen as integral to the Department's social work services. They felt those initial policy statements supported and legitimized the work of the team. The senior had assumed that the policies were a reflection that the work of the Community Development Unit, established in Head Office in 1984, had influenced policy.

> It was only when the second wave of directives began to flow, that we realized that the intention was to devolve community development activities to agencies, groups and *iwi* authorities outside the department (SSW:1).

The Community Worker spoke of her work with the Women's Health Collective as being initially supported by the new policy statements and now clearly she was being told she must pull back from active involvement in community development activities and from community and work activities not clearly linked to the department's clients. Not only was her work with the collective seen as community development and better done 'in the community by the community' but it was clearly seen by the Assistant Director: Social Services as a health related service not a social welfare service. The community worker felt that the task of social work was being expanded in the general sense but, for social work in the Department, restricted to a very narrow range of statutory tasks.

BICULTURALISM

The Report on *Institutional Racism*[13] "was quite a shock, really, to people in top management" (AD:1). The result has been "an all out effort to try and recruit people who have got a very definite knowledge of Maoritanga" (AD:1). The recruitment of Maori people for social work positions brought new dilemmas:

> I'm not sure if they are really quite clear in their own minds as to their Departmental responsibilities, and what is essentially a personal responsibility to their *iwi* and *whanau*. . . . Some think they should be able to do almost anything, even though they are employed here to do a specific job (AD: 1).

The Assistant Director asserted that the Department had a higher profile with Maori clients and the Maori community as a result of the implementation of a bicultural perspective and the establishment of positions in the Department aimed at improving relationships with the Maori community such as a Departmental Kaumatua and a Maatua Whangai worker. Such efforts have produced a *Pakeha* backlash:

> Some of the *Pakeha* clients haven't got that sort of intermediate link that the Maori people are now having through the Maatua Whangai volunteers and staff. . . . European clients do not feel they've got a bridge between them and the Department (AD:1).

As far as casework services are concerned it is clear that "before you go anywhere about a Maori child, you must consult Maatua Whangai" (SSW:1). The increase in Maori staff as a result of afirmative action policies was seen to be having significant impact on the implementation of a bicultural perspective:

> I've found it started before *Puao-Te-Ata-Tu*, with the Permanency Planning Programme. It's been a gradual process that has speeded up in the last eighteen months. I mean policy has initiated the increase in Maori staff and just having these people amongst us has made a difference to the service (SSW:2).

A Maatua Whangai position was allocated to the Napier District in 1983. The worker at time of the research, had only been with the Department officially less than a year but had been a volunteer with her *iwi* for many years, was a respected member of her tribe, and was mature enough to command an acceptable level of respect from her people to perform her tasks. She was strongly supportive of the Maatua Whangai *kaupapa* (purpose) and expressed acceptance of the policy changes that emphasized *iwi* development over the placement of Maori children. She did however, acknowledge that because of the present capabilities of her *iwi*, the simultaneous implementation of both policy objectives was not problematic. Other *iwi* who were not as well established were in need of *iwi* development resources and activities before attention could be given to the placement of Maori children.

> We hold families responsible for their own and let them know we are here with support. . . . We are collating a register of all Maori, of all the marae and the *whanau*, *hapu* and *iwi* that are attached [to Departmental clients]. . . . Our aim is to make sure that the social workers are able to make the contacts themselves. This is part of biculturalism (SW:4).

The Maatua Whangai worker described significant changes within the Department:

> Twelve months ago social workers were not prepared, it was not in the manual, they were suspicious, it was quite new to them . . . but now we can sit and discuss Maori/*Pakeha* issues quite comfortably. It's also good for those in the *iwi* to remember that the Department has an obligation. If a child has been abused the Department has a role to play and they are responsible. . . . But there is no reason why as a *whanau* you can't make the decision as to where the child is going to be . . . with the Department having a monitoring role (SW:4).

Although she believed that the Department has taken a "a big step forward in biculturalism" (SW:4), she expressed concern that some Maori traditions were inappropriately usurped in the desire to embrace a bicultural perspective. She gave as an example the use of the title, *Rangitira* (chief) by district administrators who assumed the title by right of their position rather than recognizing it was a title only to be conferred by the *iwi*.

The Employment Related Social Worker pointed to his work with the training programs and the Contact Centre as examples of the Department's commitment to both the community and to Maori people, in this case the Maori unemployed. He acknowledged that the District Office had a long-standing commitment to the Centre but current policies reconfirmed the importance of that work. He was disheartened about the more recent policy directives that seemed to indicate that positions like his would be devolved to the community for he did not believe that there would be community resources to support the work he and the other employment related social workers were doing.

SUMMARY

Despite the long history of a Community Development Team in the Napier District and the continued support of the Assistant Directors for its continued existence, the Team members perceived the team as precariously linked to the District Office and under constant threat. The support the Team felt when the Department established a Community Development Team in Head Office in 1984 did not materialize as anticipated following the restructuring of the Department in 1986. Initially, Community Development activities were supported but further refinement of the restructuring policies clearly recommended such activities be more properly sited outside the Department. This was clearly indicated in the policy directives to site the Maatua Whangai worker in the *iwi* as the first step in devolving the Maatua Whangai program.

The reported inability of the Community Development Team to establish itself as an integral part of the District's infrastructure of services, equal in importance and in claims for District resources, supports the findings of Black, et. al.[14] The Team perceived itself as 'marginal' in the views of the staff in the Social Services Division and perceived casework with children and families as the core of Departmental service provision. The stated support of preventative activities in the initial restructuring directives did not materialize in resources or staffing support. The restructuring policy of 'partnership with the community' meant that what support there was for community development and community work in the Department and in the District was defined as support for moving preventative services out of the Department to voluntary agencies, groups and the *iwi* and restricting the team to funding and monitoring roles. At the time of the research, the funding role at the Districts was minimal and consisted of allocations on a pre-determined schedule. This would change in 1989, when community services funding was to be delegated to the districts for allocation according to local needs rather than by the previous system of pre-set priorities.

The management plans advocating a participatory management style[15] was perceived as emphasizing the briefing and consultation mechanisms already in place. However, it must be noted that the smallness of the Social Services Division, the relative staff stability, the new building with its common tea room and the management philosophy of the Assistant Director and the District Director were all factors that minimized the impact of this policy directive. That is not meant to imply that staff perceived themselves as possessing real power in decision making. Rather the respondents perceived management as approachable. It also must be said that some team members did not want to participate in management decisions feeling that was the manager's job. Some expressed resentment with the constant requests for consultation meetings when no resources were offered to deal with the work that was delayed. For example, when the Assistant Director suggested further discussion on the social work plan, some staff offered their apologies saying they had too much work to do and could not afford to be away from their desk yet another hour.

There was no doubt that the policy of biculturalism had had a profound effect on all social services and social work provided in the

Napier District. Two of the Community Development's five member team were strong in Maoritanga and committed to Maori development. The Maatua Whangai worker, in particular, was in constant consultation with the social work teams to assist in the development of a bicultural model of practice. The District's *whanau* group brought a Maori perspective to the District's operations with support of a *whanau* consultant, the District Kaumatua and the District Executive Committee which was charged to monitor implementation of *Puao-Te-Ata-Tu.*[16] The 'new way of working'[17] included a heightened awareness of Maoridom and institutional racism:

> We are now aware that everyone is not the same; there are different cultures and by treating everyone the same, you're treating them as *Pakehas* . . . that sort of awareness affects everything you do (SW:1).

The adoption of bicultural social work in the Napier District Office, although perceived by the respondents as consistent with social work values, was seen as requiring immense effort in the development of new skills and expertise at a time of diminishing resources. Some of the respondents expressed concern with the recruitment policies recommended by both *Institutional Racism*[18] and *Puao-Te-Ata-Tu.*[19] The recommendations were aimed at encouraging the hiring of personnel into social work positions without a social work orientation, without knowledge or understanding of the tasks to be performed and without a viable orientation and on-going training program within the District. The result was that the statutory work (referrals of child abuse, family disruption, youth court proceedings) which was on the rise, had to be handled by fewer and fewer staff as the casework positions were filled with Maori people knowledgeable in *Maoritanga* (knowlege of Maori culture and protocal) but not necessarily in social work skills. Paradoxically, these policies had a negative effect on race relations since the decreasing number of experienced, social work staff who were predominantly *Pakeha*, had to assume more and more service responsibility. This was to be a much more serious source of tension in the Porirua District Office then it was in the Napier District Office as will be shown in the next chapter.

NOTES

1. I. G. Wilson, *Napier Department of Social Work and Voluntary Work* (Napier: Department of Social Welfare, 1976).

2. See Chapter Three for more detail on respondent team selection and data analysis techniques utilized.

3. Department of Social Welfare, *Future Direction for Social Work* (Wellington: Department of Social Welfare, July, 1988d).

4. See Appendix IX.

5. Wilson.

6. Ibid, 6.

7. Napier District Office, *Report of the Community Development Team* (Napier: Department of Social Welfare, 1984).

8. See Figure Eight.

9. Roger Hadley and Stephen Hatch, *Social Welfare and the Failure of the State: Centralized Social Services and Participatory Alternatives* (London: George Allen and Unwin, 1981).

10. DSW, *Future Direections.*

11. This structure was obstensively set up under restructuring to increase the role of the community in decision making.

12. Administrative Review Committee, *Performance and Efficiency in the Department of Social Welfare* (Wellington: Government Printer, 1987).

13. DSW, *Institutional Racism in the Department of Social Welfare: Tamaki-Makau-Rau, Auckland (Revised)* (Wellington: Department of Social Welfare, May, 1985b).

14. J. Black, R. Bowl, D. Burns, C. Critcher, G. Grant, and D. Stockford, *Social Work in Context* (London: Tavistock, 1983).

15. DSW, *Management Plan* (Wellington: Department of Social Welfare, 1986a); DSW, *Management Plan* (Wellington: Department of Social Welfare, 1987c); DSW, *Report of the Department of Social Welfare for the Year Ending 31 March 1988* (Wellington: Government Printer, 1988b).

16. Ministerial Advisory Committee on a Maori Perspective for the Department of Social Welfare, *Puao-Te-Ata-Tu:The Day Break Report* (Wellington: Department of Social Welfare, 1986).

17. DSW, *Future Directions.*

18. DSW, *Institutional Racism.*

19. Ministerial Advisory Committee.

VII

PORIRUA DISTRICT OFFICE THE GENERIC TEAM

The same procedures for collecting data were utilized with this second team. Each member of the team, the Senior Social Worker (SSW:4) and the four social workers (SW:5-8) plus the Supervising Senior Social Worker (SSSW, a middle management position with administrative responsibility for the team) and Assistant Director: Social Services (AD:2) were interviewed using the interview schedule. Each of the team members was asked to present a piece of their work which demonstrated 'the new way of working'. The researcher took part in a multi-disciplinary conference at a short-term stay group home regarding permanency planning for an adolescent. A second worker had the researcher accompany her in the provision of preventative services to a mother under stress. The worker had helped the mother plan for day-care services in a community based childcare center. We transported the child on his first day while the social worker assisted in settling him in to the center. The researcher participated in the planning of an intervention in a reported child abuse case where the child was 'at risk'. The decision-making aimed at answering the safety of the child was complicated by contrary wishes of two factions within the *whanau* who disagreed on the placement of the child.[1]

One corollary interview was conducted with the Assistant Director: Social Services, hereafter referred to as the Assistant Director (AD:2). Informal discussions were held with the Seniors in the Court and The Coast Teams, with The District Director and the Senior Social Worker in charge of the Pacific Island Team. Members of the Maori Team and the Youth Aid Officer approached the researcher to present their views on the restructuring.

During the week long research period the researcher took part in the life of the agency including a team meeting, a seniors' intake allocation meeting and the management meeting. As well, the researcher was provided with District Office documents, memos, statistical reports, circular memos (Head Office or Regional Office generated), the 1987 planning day notes and the staff meeting minutes available from 1987 and 1988.

In the negotiation process prior to the team agreeing to participate in the research, the researcher made a presentation to the entire staff and requested their support. There was less spontaneous comment from staff not directly involved in the research than in the Napier District Office. Several explanations can be offered. The office was visibly under more pressure with the demands of the workload in this urban environment. Tensions around the new team structure and its implications for workload and staff cooperation were high, making people reluctant to discuss matters with an outsider. The office, because of its proximity to Head Office felt it was often the subject of study and the research was conducted with Head Office endorsement. Lastly, there were a few staff who expressed thinly veiled hostility to a *Pakeha* professional social work educator with a non-New Zealand accent.

THE PORIRUA DISTRICT OFFICE

The District Office serves Porirua, a suburban community of 83,000 people, contiguous with Wellington, New Zealand's capital city. It was the site of one of the first state housing projects following World War II and continues to support substantial state housing tracts within its boundaries. The District itself stretches for fourty-four kilometres along the west coast of the North Island from Waikanae to Tawa, encompassing quite distinct communities in terms of class and race. It has a significant multi-cultural mix of Maori, Samoan, Cook Island, Tongan, Tokelauan and European peoples. The District crosses the tribal boundaries of Ngati Toa, Te Atiawa and Ngati Raukawa, each with their unique history and protocol.

In 1988, the District was struggling with fast growing unemployment. The estimated unemployment rate of 15% was reflected in the increasing rate of applications for unemployment benefits, growing awareness of domestic violence, increasing referrals for child protection and the multiple needs of its relatively young population. For example, applications for domestic purposes benefits (needs based assistance to families with dependent children) had reportedly increased 7.1% over the previous year.

The Porirua District had a typical district office organizational structure set out in Figure Four. The District had one satellite office, the Paraparaumu Area Welfare Office which provided a limited range of social work services by a small team of a senior and three social workers.

THE SOCIAL SERVICE DIVISION

The Social Services Division had twenty-six full-time social work positions including the Assistant Director. In contrast to the Napier office, clerical staff were 'pooled' and, hence were not considered part of the Social Services establishment. There were six teams, five based in the Porirua Office and the sixth working up the coast at the Paraparaumu Area Welfare Office. In 1985, the division had one Maori and two Pacific Island social workers. By 1988, six Maori and three Pacific Islanders were on staff as a result of affirmative action efforts. In late 1987, the Social Work Division made the decision to change the structure of the division's teams based in Porirua from teams based on the patch system to ethnicity based teams. The redeployment of staff was nearly complete at the time of the research. Staff had been reorganized into a Maori Team with Maori staff, a Pacific Island Team with Pacific Island Staff, and two Generic Teams with all *Pakeha* Staff except one. The generic team under study included one Maori staff who objected to the concept of ethnic based teams. She was however, supportive of biculturalism and argued for racially and culturally mixed team composition. The fifth team, the Court Team was also ethnically mixed.

Figure Four

PORIRUA DISTRICT OFFICE

SOCIAL SERVICE DIVISIONAL STRUCTURE

Assistant Director Social Services(AD)

Supervising Senior Social Worker-105 (SSSW)		Supervising Senior Social Worker-105	
Youth Justice SSW-104 4SW	Generic **SSW-104** **4SW**	Nga Kaitiaki SSW-104 3SW	PacificIsland 2SW
Community Services Team SSW-104 2SW		The Coast Team SSW-104 3SW	

Key: SSW=Supervising Senior Social Worker
SSW=Senior Social Worker
SW=Social Worker
Respondents in bold

HISTORY OF THE TEAM STRUCTURE

The Porirua District Office, prior to 1983 was organized along specialist lines with teams for adoption, court work, long term foster care and generic social work with children and families. The Assistant Director (AD:2) described himself as dissatisfied with the ability of the specialist teams to provide a comprehensive service. This concern raised in Britain's Barclay Report on Social Work Services[2], was debated in the Assistant Directors Conference that year. The debate was one factor that led to the invitation to Roger Hadley to come as a consultant to the Department and address the Assistant Directors' Conference in September, 1982. It was after these discussions and presentations that the Porirua Assistant Director embarked on a plan to introduce a modified patch system[3] into the Porirua office structure.

> The implementation was difficult. . . . The notion of a 'patch system' is not exactly comparable to our [geographically] large, comparatively sparsely populated district. . . . We decided to abandon specialization, which had a number of advantages, in terms of training and extent of expertise required [and move] to a community based social work model based on a geographical community in which the social worker would know the neighbourhood, the life of the people there and be able to use community resources . . . and we were successful (AD:2).

In the Assistant Director's view the patch system brought a renewed awareness to social workers and to the clients, themselves, that they could be effective in dealing with their own problems, that common problems were affecting people in their geographical patches, and that "some forms of lower order social action responses could be more effective than dealing with them individually" (AD:2). The principles of the patch system as implemented in the Porirua District Office and delineated by the Supervising Senior Social Worker were:

1. Identification of the helping capacities in lay people, kith and kin to provide care or self-care.
2. A proactive, not a reactive, response to need and hence preventative rather the curative role.
3. A focus on teamwork utilizing professional and communitypeople rather than individual casework.
4. Workers gaining detailed knowledge of their patch, its history, characteristics, its formal and informal helping networks, agencies, groups and individuals.
5. Localized services both highly visible and accessible.
6. Participative services, rather than alienating services.

All social workers were assigned to teams designated to provide social work services to a geographical patch. Characteristics of the different patches resulted in quite different service provision. The patch in a lower socio-economic area with extensive state housing was overloaded by child protection referrals and, consequently, did less community based networking than the team in an area with a more mixed socio-economic composition which also had more helping agencies and groups.

> For us, the patch system, was a bit of a dream. . . . We did get to know the local helpers, like the Plunket Nurse and the schools, teachers, youth aid officers. . . . We were able to get some good relationships going and pitched in for some training . . . but the press of child protection work slowly eroded our efforts till we were basically doing casework (SW:5).

The patch system would have continued to be the team structure of the office if "we had not been forced by the the requirements of o consider other options" (AD:2).

In 1987, the Maori social workers in the District Office put forth a proposal for a Maori team and a client allocation system based on ethnicity. The proposal recommended joint responsibility with *Pakeha* social workers for existing Maori clients. All new clients were to be allocated on the basis of ethnicity. The proposal was discussed at the District's planning day in October of 1987 and implemented incrementally. The Maori team, Nga Kaitiaki, was set up in late October and the Pacific Island Team, in early 1988. There were three interrelated factors which made the implementation problematic. The first was the tension over "the performance levels of the Maori team" (SSW:4). Many Maori staff were hired to conform with the recommendations of the *Institutional Racism* [4] and *Puao-Te-Ata-Tu*.[5] That is, their employment was based on their cultural knowledge as a major criteria. Because of the fragmentation of the training function in the Department and its disestablishment of the training institutions as part of the restructuring, it was the perception of many staff that these workers were not adequately inducted into the Department nor trained to assume the statutory responsibilities of a Departmental social worker.

> [There has been] a frustration with the slowness with which some of the culturally appropriate client groups have been able to be shifted to culturally appropriate workers and the lack of preparation of those culturally appropriate workers in terms of training to take up their new work load (AD:2)

As well, Maori staff were often in double-binds with the Department and their *whanau* or *iwi*. The Department was often unclear in their expectations for the newly hired Maori staff, telling them on one hand their role was to 'bring a Maori perspective to the Department' and at the same time expecting them to carry traditional caseload responsibilities. The Maori team, for example, refused to be rostered for front desk duty. This decision further deepened the resentment of some *Pakeha* social workers who felt they were carrying the District's workload with an ever decreasing social work establishment. Maori staff expressed their conflict with the expectations of their *whanau* to be involved in *iwi* development activities, some of which were not sanctioned by the Department. There was some resentment about Maori staff attendance at *hui*, particularly if they were frequent or lasted several days. Their absence further highlighted the perceived disparity between Maori and *Pakeha* staff because the responsibility to deal with day-to-day client requests fell to the decreasing number of *Pakeha* social workers left in the office. Lastly, when Maori staff assumed a community/*iwi* development role, they refused to carry caseload responsibilities. Such moves were seen as effectively overloading the *Pakeha* social workers who remained responsible for meeting statutory requirements of timely service particularly in response to reported child abuse and youth justice cases.

> They [Maori social work staff] occupy a social work positions in a fixed establishment but do not perform social work tasks---that means more work for the rest of us (SW:6).

At the October 1987 staff Planning Day, staff created a Bicultural Development *Komiti* (Committee) within the District Office in an effort to respond positively to some of these difficulties. The Komiti had the following terms of reference:

1. To promote and monitor bicultural development within the office

2. To provide a forum for the discussion of issues, for the exchange of ideas and increase of understanding to facilitate the implementation of biculturalism

3. To insure a gap does not develop between Nga Kaitiaki and the rest of the social work staff

The meetings of the *Komiti* were to be open to all staff and to have decision making powers based on power sharing and consensus principles. This group was torn by strife and conflict and was all but dysfunctional by the time of the research took place in November 1988.

THE GENERIC TEAM

This team had been the responsibility of the Supervising Senior Social Worker (SSSW) until her promotion in July 1988. She had been with the Department since 1966 but was in University earning her Diploma in Social Work during the critical 1985-1986 period. The Senior Social Worker (SSW:4) was appointed to her position in October just two weeks before the research commenced. This senior social worker, who qualified with an advanced degree in social work in 1982, had been with the Department for about four years with two breaks in her work with the Department. One of her team members had been with the Department since 1979. Two joined the Department in 1983 and 1985 respectively. The fourth team member had been with the Department since 1981 but absent from the Department during 1986 and 1987 while on bursary earning her degree. The team was so new that it did not have a shared identity and each team member called the team by a different name, i.e., child protection team, the generic team or Sara's team (the newly appointed SSW:4). However, they did perceive their team as distinct from the ethnically based Maori and Pacific Island teams and as possessing its own philosophy of practice based on generic social work principles of working across the full range of activities and modes of practice. The entire team expressed concern that their generic team was under increasing pressure to become a specialist child protective services team.

The team evolved by bringing together three *Pakeha* social workers and one Maori worker who had expressed a commitment to utilizing their experience with the patch system and/or were committed to implementing the 'new way of working' with clients.[6] The Senior Social Worker had been recruited to head up this team with these particular individuals:

> I feel quite confident about these people [the team members] . . . but if I was switched to another team and asked to supervise different people . . . I would find it very difficult (SSW:4).

She expressed concern that the intention for her team was that it would move away from a generic focus to a specialism in child protection issues only, and only if the child were clearly, presently at risk:

> I'm worried if we have to categorize [a referral] every time as being child protection. . . . Now either we are involved in a statutory way or we can't be involved . . . that is pretty dangerous (SSW:4).

There was a general feeling of uncertainty regarding the stability of the team, its philosophy and its membership. The structure of the teams in the Porirua District Office had been unsettled since the staff development day in late 1987 and seemed to the team to be still vulnerable to more change.

> I do not agree with the decision for ethnically based teams. It has intensified the tension between the teams and made some working relationships impossible. . . . I don't expect these teams to last. . . . What about our clients, some of them do not want to be forced to see a Maori social worker just because they're Maori (SSW:4).

The newly appointed senior social worker was just beginning to formulate her goals for the team but first she had to familiarize herself with the dramatic changes that had occurred with during the year of her absence from the Department. She expressed concern that the focus of her team was quickly being confined to child protection investigation. She noted that the referral rate of one crisis case a day observed during the research week was not unusual. These cases required immediate attention and decisions about protection and usually intensive intervention over a minimum of two to three weeks for each case. She lamented that preventative services and community development was either being devolved to the community or limited to designated occupants of social work positions, such as the Maori community worker. "The 'cop type' jobs are the only ones left to Departmental social workers" (SSW:4).

The team membership was under constant threat from staff reorganizing efforts further complicating team-building efforts. The most experienced team member was considering tendering her resignation due in part to changing role of social workers in the Department.

> When we were structured into patches I felt as if I was able to use formal and informal helpers in response to my clients needs. I knew the other helping

> professionals in my area, I knew the families that I worked with, and I knew several of the church leaders, that is so important when you work with Samoan people, particularly. . . . I am not saying it was the perfect system. . . . The patch system was not adequately resourced or staffed, but at least I knew more about my clients and their lives, now, I am working in a vacuum . . . hate it. I know I am not doing the best job for my clients (SW:5).

Two of the other five team members expressed concern that District management wanted the team to specialize in child protection. Neither of them wanted to do child abuse work exclusively and would consider leaving the Department if that became the sole focus of the team. "I don't actually see a future for me with the Department" (SW:6). Another team member felt constantly under pressure to join the ethnically based team, a pressure she felt as much from *Pakehas* as from her own people. She, however, contended that her contribution was best made to a generic based team that acknowledged cultural differences. Hence, she resisted any attempts to transfer her to an ethnically based team.

SERVICE DELIVERY

Regionalization

The Assistant Director offered several explanations for the 1986 regionalization. He felt that the Department had grown so large in both number of employees and functions that:

> Regionalisation was a realisation of Head Offices' need to retain, and in some some cases reclaim, control of the Department and the Districts that had grown so large (AD:2).

Regionalization would not have occurred unless the State Services Commission had determined it would approve the establishment of the management structures to support regionalization.

> The technical thing that happened, as I understand it, was that the Department, because of its overall size, was regraded to a class that allowed the department to have two additional deputy directors. . . . State

> Services did the regrading in the early 1980's but it had to wait until the wage freeze was lifted (AD:2).

The third factor in his explanation was a new management philosophy that utilized a tripartite framework for management with the Head Office controlling policy, regional offices controlling resources, and district office responsible for operations. Implementing this management structure was problematic:

> There has been a general struggle with those three role. . . . Mainly the struggle has been going on between the Head Office and Regional. . . . Head Office has retained operational control over community services funding for instance, but that is going to change (AD:2).

He did acknowledge struggles between the districts for resources and programs, commenting that in the South Central Region where three districts service metropolitan Wellington, duplication of specialist services would be neither cost effective nor efficient. Yet coordination of effort or service was seen by some as contrary to the stated goals of the restructuring effort in general and the regionalization principle in particular. The Supervising Senior Social Worker was more cynical about the Assistant Director's struggles in the two-monthly regional meetings:

> [The Assistant Director] has to go and scrap with the other AD's about who gets what in an ever diminishing resource allocation. . . . It's competitive not cooperative. . . . *It is conspiracy theory, making the workers fight each other to use up their their discontent.* [sic]. . . . It is part of the new management philosophy (SSSW).

The Supervising Senior Social Worker returned to the Department in late 1986 after her study leave to learn of the restructuring and the establishment of the Regional Offices as a result of regionalization.

> I had heard of the Pink Palace over there [the description given to the South Central Regional Office because of its comparatively lavish pink and grey furnishings] but did not know just what effect it would have on my job. . . . I soon became aware that

> the decisions that had previously gone to Head Office, were to go there. So on the face of it it looked as though decision making was moving closer. . . . Really, [it] just became another link in the chain. . . . Decisions made in Head Office used to come directly . . . now it seemed like something stuck in the middle there and it happened to be in Lower Hutt [the Regional Office] (SSSW).

It was the Supervising Senior Social Worker who voiced the discontent about the resource expenditures in the creation of the Regional Office and its highly graded staff with no noticeable decrease in the size of Head Office:

> The most galling thing for me was the fact the Head Office and Regional Office was forever making requests for us to do work they couldn't do and they wanted. . . . They were easily establishing positions [in the regional offices] and they were paid heaps. . . . Meanwhile we have to struggle to increase the social work establishment (SSSW).

Her complaints were echoed by both her team and her supervisees who noted that the office's proximity to Wellington meant that they were frequently asked to second a worker to the Head Office for preparation of discussion or policy documents without any payback in staff allocation hence, effectively increasing the workload of the social workers left behind.

Decentralization

There was clear acknowledgement, from the three district social work managers interviewed, that delegations of authority to make decisions about administrative and practice matters had taken place. "Things happen more quickly definitely. . . . You don't have have to rush off to Head Office" (SSW:4). There was equally, however, acknowledgement that the delegations had resulted in an increased workload for the managers at every district office level because although the delegations brought decision making power down the hierarchy, support systems and additional staff allocations had not accompanied the delegations.

> This whole money thing is what is the biggest change, I think. Having an office budget. . . . It was like money was a vulgar thing and you never really talked about it before, it was like this endless resource that you had. . . . Now we've got to work out where our priorities are and *we are on our own* [sic] (SSW:4).

The expectation that the district's assistant-directors assume a management role over their divisions placed heavy demands on the Assistant Directors of Social Services:

> The significant changes for me are being called upon to manage the resources that we had, where as previously that had been something that had been done by Head Office. . . . I drew my satisfaction from giving direct support to operational staff activities and almost a direct involvement with them (AD:2).

The new role for the Assistant Director meant a move from a practice or clinical director's role to a manager role with an emphasis on financial management and accountability:

> The expectations of being a manager, a financial manager, isn't something I particularly relish...I'm being expected to manage a budget and be accountable for it when my ability to control that budget, is in my view, limited. [It is] manifestly unfair (AD:2).

The Assistant Director was referring to his ability to predict the demand for requests for special needs grants, foster-care placements, clothing allowances, *koha* (gratuity) payments. The demand for these benefits are linked to the rate of unemployment and *whanau* conference expenditures. These expenditures are difficult to predict.

> The Department is saying to give as much power to basic grade social workers to get their job done as well as they can and encourage delegation of authorities down to them. A lot of those authorities relate to expenditure. Yet, as Assistant Director, I am responsible to management for those expenditures. The only way I can actually get a firm grip is to undo that, to draw the expenditures back up to me (AD:2).

The Assistant Director, then clearly outlined the paradox in the delegations of authority when coupled with the demands for financial accountability. He saw his ability to manage effectively as further hampered by an archaic reporting and computer system which "if we're lucky can tell you what happened a month ago. . . . It's like remote steering with a motor car" (AD:2).

DEVOLUTION

The structure and responsibilities of this team did not directly expose them to issues of devolution. They were aware of the implications of the closure of the pre-adolescent care facilities in their region and the alternative care report. The MacDonald and Moffatt report conveyed the concern of community groups that care of these children would be left to "the community with 'armies of non-existent volunteers'".[7] The report listed ten Maori groups in Porirua offering services to adolescents and called for the transfer of resources from the closure of the Departmental pre-adolescent institutional facilities to these groups for payment of staff and expenditures in providing care.

PARTICIPATION

The team was aware the myriad implications of the policy demand for partnership with the community. They acknowledged their skepticism, "when anyone talks about community involvement, they mean cutting resources'" (SSW:4). They raised questions about the ethics and the standards of involving community people in aspects of the Department's work. One team member described an application of the principles of 'community involvement' and 'keeping a child out of care' in which those questions were raised for her. She had been called in to investigate an alleged child abuse case. The plan had to be made for monitoring and protection over the weekend for the child. Prior to 1986, in this situation, the child would have been taken into care to insure their safety. In 1988, alternatives for care in the community had to be thoroughly investigated before a child was to be brought into care. In this particular case, the Senior Social Worker arranged monitoring through the Department's industrial chaplain. The chaplain knew a young couple with children who would be willing to support this family over the weekend by visiting and being available by phone, hence providing a safeguard that was acceptable to the parents in question. This type of community monitoring would not have been acceptable practice prior to the new directives for partnership with the community.

> I wouldn't have thought that it was appropriate to go out and ask complete strangers to do this very sensitive task. . . . I would have thought that it challenged confidentiality and privacy principles but it is a new practice being tried in other offices. . . . It challenges the reluctance a lot of social workers have to using community workers and volunteers (SSW:4).

The Senior Social Worker had a second example of community involvement that contrasted with the success of her first example. This involved the support of a 16 year-old Maori boy brought before the court for offending. A newly formed Maori group made a forceful plea in front of the judge to be granted supervision responsibility and was successful. Two months later, the group had disbanded and the boy was reoffending. Such an example, she argued, highlighted the need for evaluation and monitoring to ensure quality and continuity of care.

One of the social workers saw partnership with the community as a requirement to utilize community resources first. Community resources being defined as informal caregivers and individuals, as well as, professional caregivers and formal helping agencies. She pointed out the process in the multi-disciplinary meeting regarding permanency care for the adolescent that she and the researcher attended. She explained that in the 'new way of working', she was compelled to explore, and at times develop community based alternatives.

> Before I may have assumed responsibility within Departmental resources; now use of Departmental alternatives is last of the options (SW:6).

A second social worker argued that true partnership is "a long way from community development or community work" (SW:7). She questioned the community development efforts of the designated community workers in her office saying they defined their efforts long term but did not even know the resources in the community now:

> I had a young couple that needed housing and I called [the community worker]. His reply went like this: 'I am working in the community at the moment to develop a number of initiatives, a number of

> resources for people in the situation you describe,' and he went on to say it wasn't here yet and if I would like to put their name on a waiting list. . . . Well, it was all in the never, never, that was totally unhelpful to me and my clients (SW:7).

Her anger was based both on her perceived impression that the worker didn't have any idea of the community resources available and that his well-formulated statement was a cover-up for inactivity. Meanwhile, she was left without resources for her clients. This lack of mutual appreciation of the time constraints of both the caseworker and the community development worker was noted in the responses of the Napier Office respondents as well.

There was recognition by the team and the managers that the restructuring of 1986 did open many avenues for community based participation in Departmental activities through the District Executive Committee, the Regions' Institutional Management Committees, the appointment of non-professionals and community agency personnel to the child protection team.

The Porirua Office had abandoned their fledgling social work volunteer service in the early 1980's under pressure that the use of volunteers within the Department was exploitative. By the mid-1980's, with the demands of *Puao-Te-Ata-Tu*,[8] the practice of requesting cultural advice and consultation was well established. There were clear indications that all the members of the team were actively initiating contacts with community groups and individuals in the provision of services to their clients, but much of this effort was clearly individual case related. The team felt they had become increasingly unsupported because since the Maatua Whangai position had been vacant for over a year. Their relationship with the community workers in Nga Kaitiaki was often strained and they felt isolated and uninformed of that team's community development activities. The team felt that the increase in child abuse referrals, and their severity, greatly limited their ability to work in any effective way with the community despite policy directives and the efforts being made by others in the office.

Management Style

In 1987, the Assistant Director introduced a participatory management style in the Social Services Division of the Porirua District Office. The principles of equal power and consensus making were the cornerstones of the model based on empowerment. Comments on the year long experiment from the respondents were mixed. Some saw it as a complete waste of time and an abdication of responsibility by management. Others saw it as an opportunity to participate actively in the management of the office but felt that the process was not well managed. They expressed concern that the meetings were time-consuming and emotionally draining with few tangible results. Yet, all expressed some support for the principles of participatory management.

> We try to operate a participatory management system, and I think it works quite well, at our level [the Senior Social Work level]. But there is still a lot that comes down to us that we are just told to do. I wonder if it's possible to be truly participative in a bureaucracy. It probably isn't (SSSW).

She contended that the office and the management team are relatively non-hierarchical and share a commitment to joint decision making while recognizing that "sometimes there are decisions when its simply not feasible" (SSSW).

The Senior Social Worker had just joined the team, characterized herself as having a "colleagial, participatory management style" (SSW). The social workers agreed that the division's stated goals of participatory management were, by and large, put into practice down to the first line supervisory level. They also felt the policy of briefing and consulting followed practice as far as their office was concerned.[9]

SOCIAL WORK

The Assistant Director's view was that social workers at the management level regard community development and community work "as a natural part of social work, just another social work role"(AD:2). He viewed the name change to Social Services as unnecessary if the intent was to reflect that perspective. He acknowledged that social work in the Department, while embracing individual casework, group work and community work as equal methods in social work, did not transfer equally to practice for two reasons. First, the demands of statutory responsibilities took precedence in the allocation of time and staffing levels. Second, these levels are often inadequate to permit preventative work and the development of the competencies required to fulfil statutory responsibilities. He offered the following example:

> The Senior Social Worker prior to me led a team focused on benefit related social work. She saw it as a valuable preventative social work task. I agreed

> with her theoretically, but I knew and I think she did, that pressure to supply staff resources to meet the need for children would go on--to the point now, I would say that we contribute less than one staff member's time to benefit related social work, and most of that is client initiated, people coming with hardship problems to the social worker at the duty desk (AD:2).

A contrary view was expressed by the Supervising Senior Social Worker who did not see community development or community work as part of the task of social work in the Department.

> I don't see much evidence of community work or community development in the day-to-day work of the social workers. . . . They [community work and community development] are not office sanctioned or promoted types of activities (SSSW).

The community development positions in the office were seen by the Supervising Senior Social Worker as having a specialized function with the Maori community for the development of resources for Maori clients that did not generalize to the entire client community.

The tensions in social work came from two other sources in the view of the Assistant Director. The first was the retention of Community Services Funding in Head Office, particularly in their mandated allocations to national organizations, such as to the New Zealand Society for the Intellectually Handicapped and Women's Refuge Centres. The Assistant Directors wanted the funding decentralized and argued that the delegation to the Districts would decrease the demand for community service funding positions in Head Office. The second tension stemmed from the disestablishment or alleged forced retirement of the social work hierarchy in Head Office in 1986-1987 period. The social workers in Head Office had lent an identity and professional leadership to the department's social workers. His view was echoed by the Supervising Senior Social Worker who expressed a degree of despair with the future of social work in a Department who with apparent ease "disposed of the social work hierarchy and in its place created the administratively isolated position of the Principal Social Worker" (SSSW). The name change to social services was to the Supervising Senior Social Worker indicative of the place of social work in the Department. She saw the Department as moving from direct practice to indirect practice with selected specializations. The second aspect of this change was the reclassification of all management positions in Head Office to the Clerical-Executive Class which effectively aborted the career ladder of social workers at the middle management level.

To the team members the most significant change to their practice besides biculturalism and participation with the community was the shift in emphasis and resources from working with a child after being given a formal 'status' such as being made a ward of the court to working with a child and the *whanau* or family prior to the declaration of a formal departmental 'status.'

> Before the only way we could claim resources, such as payment for temporary care, was after bringing the child 'into care.' Now we can access the resources of the department to keep children out of care (SW:5).

Yet, they expressed some concerns as to the long term effect of this change in policy because allocation of resources was based on a quantitative management information system.

> If we work really hard, keep children in the community, with their *whanau* and out of care, will our resources be cut? Contacting *whanau*, arranging planning meetings is very time consuming . . . but is not counted anywhere (SW:5).

BICULTURALISM

All the respondents acknowledged the significance of the Ministerial Advisory Committee Report on a Maori Perspective in the Department of Social Welfare: *Puao-Te-Ata-Tu* as critical to the Department's commitment to biculturalism. They noted that awareness of ethnicity issues had been developing in the Department since the early 1980's. The Porirua District Office had been granted a Maatua Whangai worker in the original establishment. That worker had been instrumental in effectively linking Maatua Whangai groups with the Departmental social workers. The Senior Social Worker who had had a period of time away from the Department and then returned to the Department in late 1986 was struck with the change:

> Maatua Whangai groups had really grown. . . . When I came back I learned that there were all these people out there that we were answerable to. . . . Before I left it felt like there was just Maatua Whangai and we

> were just trying to get involved with groups and when I came back it felt like everybody was expected to be doing it (SSW).

The work of the Maatua Whangai came to a halt when the incumbent went on parental leave. At the time of the research, the position had been vacant for over a year due in part to a proposed transfer that did not eventuate and partly to a new Maatua Whangai policy that recommended the resource be devolved to the local *iwi*.

Application of the principles of *Puao-Te-Ata-Tu* placed a heavy burden on district resources:

> No funds came with the directive to implement *Puao-Te-Ata-Tu* No clear policy guidelines came either. . . . For example, we were told to familiarize our staff with Maori protocol, to seek invitations to marae but koha payments are culturally appropriate. Nobody knew where you were to get the money and yet we were told to get on with it (SSSW).

Although money was now clearly allocated for *koha* payments to marae for hosting *hui*, to volunteers and to cultural consultants, the Supervising Senior Social Worker thought that the "payment is a pittance and inhibits the social workers from getting into full swing" (SSSW). This is a clear example of the inconsistencies in the community partnership philosophy as perceived by these social workers. The social workers voiced a commitment to the principle of partnership but in their conceptualization it involved non-exploitation of volunteers and community groups. They expressed frustration with the lack of support and lack of discussion oni implications prior to directives to implementate partnership. Governmental policy emphasized community responsibility and the ability of people to take care of their own, but did not consider including provisions for payment for service.

The Senior Social Worker described the apprehension with the shift in relationship from one of professional/bureaucratic power with a relatively powerless client and community to sharing power with clients and the community in a partnership.

> At first I found it daunting. . . . Fancy me having to justify what I am doing to these people and after a little while I felt like it was a relief to say to the

> *whanau* and *iwi*, 'Can you help? . . . and then I could say 'that hasn't worked, we need to get together again' (SSW:4).

The change to a bicultural model of practice was exemplified in the use of Maori language in the informal every day life of the agency and in formal documentation.

> I just remember some of the forms that we used to have for kids coming into care. They had race and tribal affiliation on it but no one filled it in. . . . that started to be done and now there are family trees on the file and where so and so's mother's people come from (SSW:4).

The more fundamental change was the demand for *whanau* based decision-making which was expected to be given further impetus in the proposed Children and Young Person's Act under Parliamentary discussion at the time of the research. The Supervising Senior Social Worker saw the adoption of *whanau* decision making as a top-down process that has received qualified support by direct-line practitioners. Here again, she contended, that the lack of resource allocation hindered its full implementation:

> There should have been a fund to support *whanau* decision making: money for travel, koha, accommodation. The whole question of extra time required by social workers [to find, contact, and arrange for *whanau* to attend the decision making meeting] should have been looked at . . . two or three positions [should have been created] to accommodate the extra and time-consuming tasks that result (SSSW).

She also noted that no funds were allocated for training in the new skills that are required to arrange and plan a *whanau* decision meeting which would be bicultural and in many cases multi-cultural.

> [Departmental Social Workers] don't have a tradition of group work. . . We are required to do it without knowing about the dynamics . . . skill is required in knowing what and how to lay out the facts, the responsibilities, possible alternatives, how to be

> firm, [and] knowledgeable without either abdicating our responsibilities or retaining control that is contrary to the purpose of the process in the first place (SSSW).

The Senior Social Worker noted that in her university social work training, community work wasn't seen as an integral part of social work in a statutory agency. Community work was seen rather as a skill that would be practiced by a worker in local government or by a detached youth worker in an program sponsored by the Department of Internal Affairs. Hence, she felt a whole new set of skills had to be acquired by the social worker in the statutory setting:

> What has changed is the requirement to be knowledgeable about how to get families involved, to make links with children's families . . . how to trace families, convene meetings for decision making. . . . Whereas before you planned a desired outcome, now you take one step at a time and you take a back-seat quite often but you have a very important job in laying the ground work for the decision making (SSW:4)

The Senior Social Worker felt the *whanau* decision-making meetings require a high degree of skill and knowledge.

> The social worker feels great responsibility to these meetings . . . but then you actually have to sit back and let it go. . . . Let the process go. It is not easy (SSW:4).

Such an perspective is contrary to social work practice principles which although they provide a feedback loop for altering an intervention plan, demand that an intervention be planned, even if within broad parameters and, hence, conflicts with the traditional expectations in the role of the professional as expert. Secondly, the social worker has statutory responsibilities to uphold as clearly outlined in the 1987 report of the Independent Inquiry Team on the Ailini case.[10] The impact of that report on Departmental policy and resourcing was unclear. The Report was under embargo in late 1988 because of an injunction laid by the mother's lawyers. As well, the Children and Young Persons' Act was still under consideration in Parliament and no clear indication was given of the social workers' responsibilities and consequent liability in the proposed legislation.

SUMMARY

The issues and dilemmas of implementing the principles of the restructuring of the Department of Social Welfare were well reflected in this urban district office. The diversity of views and the intensity with which they were expressed, reflect the multiple tensions and strains that the Social Work Division, as an organizational entity and the social workers as professionals, were experiencing. The strains in implementing a bicultural approach to practice during this crucial transition period were clearly evident. The team members expressed restrained optimism about the 'new way of working' not because of philosophical differences, in fact, they welcomed an opportunity to explore a potentially more effective model. Their hesitation stemmed from their questions of the motives of the government and their fears that the demands of their statutory requirements would relegate them to a specialized and limited social work practice with child abuse cases. Their Supervising Senior Social Worker viewed the changes in the Department as:

> Reflecting a serious erosion of the concept of universality . . . which has created enormous disparities in what is done, by whom, and with whom and who has access, reflecting a shift away from ideas of the welfare state by which people have access to services by virtue of citizenship to one based on the ability to pay (SSSW).

She expressed a degree of despair with the Department's ability to provide a quality service with increasing number of untrained workers with poor or non-existing training program. Her fear was that incidents similar to the Ailini case[11] would increase as the ability to provide competent service in the Department was eroded.

NOTES

1. See Appendix X for a summary of research activities in the Porirua District Office.

2. Barclay Report, *Social Workers: Their Role and Tasks* (London: Bedford Square Press, 1982).

3. Roger Hadley and Stephen Hatch, *Social Welfare and the Failure of the State: Centralized Social Services and Participatory Alternatives* (London: George Allen and Unwin, 1981).

4. DSW, *Institutional Racism in the Department of Social Welfare: Tamaki-Makau-Rau, Auckland (Revised)* (Wellington: Department of Social Welfare, May, 1985b).

5. Ministerial Advisory Committee on a Maori Perspective for the Department of Social Welfare, *Puao-Te-Ata-Tu: The Day Break Report* (Wellington: Department of Social Welfare, 1986).

6. DSW, *Contracting for Social Services: Principles and Guidelines* (Wellington: Department of Social Welfare, July, 1988c).

7. Ian MacDonald and Makareta Moffat, *Report on the Needs Analysis and Consultation in the Porirua District Office* (Porirua: Department of Social Welfare, June, 1988).

8. Ministerial Advisory Committee.

9. See Appendix VIII.

10. J. Pilalis, S. Opal and T. Mamea, *Dangerous Situations* (Wellington: Department of Social Welfare, 1987).

11. Ibid.

VIII

PATTERNS AND PROSPECTS

In 1986, the Department of Social Welfare underwent a pervasive restructuring process that marked the most dramatic shift in social service policy since the advent of the welfare state during the first half of this century. This book reports the findings of a research study on the changes in social work within the Department of Social Welfare which occurred as a consequence of the restructuring processes outlined in the *Management Plan, 1986*.[1] This plan proposed sweeping reforms in the Department's service delivery through the regionalization of its activities, decentralization of delegated authorities to the Districts, changes in management style and the provision of "culturally appropriate social services".[2] This final chapter analyses the findings of the document review and the interviews with departmental social work administrators and practitioners using the theoretical framework contrasting welfare state and welfare society principles. The underlying patterns are identified and the prospects for social work practice within the Department of Social Welfare are discussed. The final section addresses the implications of the New Zealand experience for welfare states internationally.

This research proposed that the challenges to welfare state policies made in the 1970s and early 1980s succeeded in shifting social service policy from a welfare state model as articulated by Richard Titmuss[3] toward a welfare society model of social service delivery as promulgated by Roger Hadley and colleagues.[4] The Hadley model was reflected in the principles of the 1986 restructuring: regionalization, decentralization, devolution and partnership with the community. In this study, the change in social policy strategy from a welfare state toward a welfare society was linked to subsequent changes in the organizational design of the Department as exemplified in the implementation of the principles of the restructuring and, consequently, to the performance of social work as exemplified in the definition of the social work task and issues of professionalization. Theoretical explanation for these interrelationships was found within the model proposed by Pearce and Robinson.[5]

In the process of exploring these interrelationships, the five research questions of the study led to the development of the four organizing themes of the research. The first theme, 'statutory-voluntary balance' addressed the broad direction of social policy, that is, 'strategy' as it is used in the Pearce and Robinson model. To reiterate the central point made in the theorectical conceptualization: in the welfare state model, the key to the statutory voluntary balance is government funding and provision of social services, whereas in the welfare society model the predominant feature is the provision of services by the voluntary and commercial sector and informal care givers. The second organizing theme, service delivery, incorporates the principles of the restructuring and management style as components of organizational design. The third element of the model, performance, was explored under the thematic heading social work. Consideration was given to the definition of the social work task, that is, the role of social work in the provision of casework or community work services, and to debates on the professionalization of social work. The fourth theme, that of biculturalism, was to have a decisive influence on the entire process. The Department had responded to the report of the Ministerial Advisory Committee on a Maori Perspective, *Puao-Te-Ata-Tu* [6] by pledging a commitment to culturally appropriate services.[7] This commitment was explicitly stated in the *Management Plan, 1987* as a commitment to biculturalism within the Department.[8]

THE METHODOLOGY

The formulation of a research methodology to explore these themes within the conceptualized interrelationships was problematic. Three methods of data collection were selected with the objective of gathering data at the policy, organizational and practice levels. Documents relating to the debates on social service policy and delivery systems from 1969 to 1988 were analysed. These documents included publications by policy advisory groups, by the voluntary sector, by government appointed review committees, task forcesand commissions, by the New Zealand Social Work Association and by the Department itself. The review set out in Chapter Four analysed the data from over 120 documents under the four themes.

An interview schedule consisting of twenty open-ended questions was used to examine the perceptions of the Regional Executive Officers as middle-management social workers in the newly designed organizational structure. Two District teams of social workers, one in a rural area, the other in an urban area were interviewed using the same questionnaire. Participant observation techniques supplemented the interviews in the District Offices as each team member demonstrated an example of their work that reflected the 'new way of working'.[9] The discussion of the findings in relation to these themes and research questions is reported below.

PATTERNS

Discussion of the patterns discerned in the findings is ordered according to the four thematic headings which formed the basis of the analysis.

The Statutory - Voluntary Balance

It was the combined effects of four developments (the fiscal crisis, debates on the statutory-voluntary balance, social work and service delivery, and biculturalism) that provided the impetus to alter the welfare state provisions that had characterized New Zealand's social policy for over forty years. Each development supported the challenge that a welfare state model of social service delivery was no longer sustainable nor desirable in the 1980s. These four developments challenged welfare state policies, albeit for quite different reasons. However, it was the converging force of these developments in the economic, political, social and cultural spheres that combined to provide the impetus for the shift toward a welfare society model of social service delivery.

During the 1970s New Zealand faced a series of fiscal crises, including two major oil crises, an increasing overseas trade imbalance, and growing unemployment.[10] By the early 1980s there was growing support among economic advisors in Treasury,[11] for monetarist economic policies that emphasized the 'market place' and the responsibilities of the individual. The influence of monetarism became evident in the policies of the Fourth Labour Government, referred to as 'Rogernomics,' which reflected a major shift away from Keynesian economics.[12]

Under the National Party and Robert Muldoon, as Prime Minister and Finance Minister from 1978 to 1984, New Zealand had experienced growth in government centralization and executive power.[13] Critics of the National Development Act, 1979 contended it had been designed to "speed up the planning process and restrict public participation".[14] The highly centralized bureaucratic character of government departments contributed to a sense of powerlessness that fueled increasingly vocal demands for participation in, if not control over, social welfare service provision by the voluntary sector and community groups in the years preceding the decision to restructure.[15]

The document review traced the debates on the role of the state in social welfare services and confirmed growing support during the pre-1986 period for a welfare society model of social service delivery characterized by the decentralization of service provision, a broader role for the voluntary sector and participation of the wider community in service planning. It was the welfare society model as articulated by Hadley and Hatch that was implemented in the 1986 restructuring of the Department of Social Welfare. This restructuring represented the change in strategy from welfare state policies to the adoption of welfare society policies. In the welfare state model of social service delivery the state is viewed as the key funder and provider of social services with the voluntary sector and other non-statutory providers offering services complementary to, but not a substitute for, state provision.

Support for a welfare society model of service delivery, with its emphasis on service provision by voluntary agencies and community groups, was based on a long history of dissatisfaction with the Department of Social Welfare and its continued emphasis on individualized casework as the primary social work intervention. Throughout the fifteen years of the Department's history to 1986, queries were consistently raised about the ability of the Department to be responsive to local needs, the bias of the Department's services toward casework services of an ameliorative nature and the dominance of the state sector in service delivery. The document analysis confirmed that the New Zealand Planning Council, as a major social policy advisory body, became increasingly committed to a policy that established a more significant role for the voluntary agencies in service provision throughout the period under study.

Finally, considerable pressure was exerted by the Maori community for the Department to respond more effectively to the needs of Maori through less reliance on state provided services. Their demands dovetailed with the sentiments expressed by voluntary agencies, community groups and the New Zealand Planning Council for a change from the state as the primary provider of service toward embracing the welfare society notions of community care, self-help, community based initiatives, *whanau* support and 'community oriented social services'.

The findings of this study lend support to the contention that the decision to restructure marked a significant redirection of governmental social service policy strategy from the pursuit of a welfare state to that of a welfare society. In order to implement this strategy, the Department launched the multi-pronged processes of regionalization, decentralization, devolution and partnership with the community. All four processes were designed to realign the role of the state vis-a-vis the voluntary sector. The strategy was couched in carefully chosen terms intended to imply governmental responsiveness to the criticisms of social services delivery that had plagued the Department and hence, veiled government's intention to move toward containment of social service expenditure through adoption of a welfare society model of social service delivery. Implementation of the welfare society model was to be accomplished, in part, through a partnership in service provision with voluntary agencies and the community, particularly the Maori community who were disproportionately clients of social services. The Maatua Whangai program, Departmental support of *iwi* development, and the encouragement of community initiatives were examples of these partnership initiatives. Not only was support of these programs consistent with the welfare society strategy, but they had the potential of operating completely outside the statutory sector in the future and, thus, afforded the potential of budgetary reduction and reduced state responsibility.

The restructuring of the Department was, then, part of a broader thrust toward monetarist policies, cost containment and promotion of notions of individual responsibility. This analysis lends strong support to the propositions of Scott, Lincoln, and Weick[16] that organizational analysis must consider the organization in its widest social, political and economic contexts.

Service Delivery

Pearce and Robinson[17] argue that for a change to be effective the three components of strategy, design and performance must be congruent. This proposition suggests, then, that changes in one component of the model will entail corresponding changes in the other two elements if congruence is to be optimized. Hence, changes in strategy must be reflected in changes in organizational design to support the strategy and ensure the desired performance. From an application of the model, therefore, it was possible to predict that the changes in the strategy discussed above as the change from a welfare state to a welfare society should be reflected in changes in organizational design to support the new strategy. This appears to have occurred with the restructuring of the Department of Social Welfare in 1986. The principles of the restructuring exemplified the desired characteristics of a welfare society strategy. In the analysis of service delivery, the implementation of the principles of the restructuring are analysed in terms of the changes to the components of organizational design critical in the Pearce and Robinson model. The principles of regionalization and decentralization are analysed together because they were inextricably linked in the restructuring process.

Regionalization and Decentralization

Initiation of the restructuring efforts was assisted by a long-standing proposal within the Department to regionalize. The Regional Executive Officers (REOs) noted that the Department had experimented with regionalization with the creation of a Regional Office in Auckland in 1980 and had made an application to the State Services Commission for a reclassification that would permit the establishment of Deputy Director-General positions. Although the reclassification was approved in principle, allocation of funding for regionalization was not approved due to the wage and price freezes imposed by the National Government during the period 1981 - 1984.

Although regionalization did take place in the restructuring through the establishment of the six regions, its effect was confounded by the decentralization process that was initiated concurrently. The establishment of Regional Offices as an administrative structure was seen by the District Office respondents as a costly exercise that drained resources from service provision at the District level and placed another layer of management between the Districts and Head Office. The role ambiguity of the Regional Officers was depicted in the organizational chart included in the first *Management Plan, 1986*.[18] It was the stated intent that the REOs would further the objectives of the decentralization by assisting the Districts to develop as much autonomy as possible in the operations of Departmental functions.

However, all of the REOs questioned the underlying motivation for the regionalization and decentralization processes. Ten of the eleven REOs saw the processes as an attempt by top management to *regain* control of the organization rather than to decentralize authority despite the formal statements in the Management Plans and Departmental directives to the contrary. There were several justifications for their perception.

The REOs cited examples of Head Office pressuring them if their districts were not 'coming on board' with new policy despite the fact that their administrative positions were established as advisory staff positions without line authority. The REOs, themselves, perceived their role as untenable and ambiguous. They pointed to the conflicting messages they received from Head Office about their roles and responsibilities. The role ambiguity led to misunderstandings, conflict and inappropriate task expectations by Head Office, the Districts and the REOs themselves.

The reluctance of Head Office to relinquish power to the Districts was revealed in the organizational structures depicted in the organizational charts and in the designation of positions to reflect changes in Departmental strategy. Change in structure, Pearce and Robinson[19] argue, is necessary to ensure the optimum fit between strategy and organizational design. However, the structural changes as depicted in the organizational charts reflect Head Office's ambivalence in the regionalization and decentralization processes by indicating hierarchical direct line authority relationships between Head Office and the regions. Hence, there was a lack of 'fit' between the strategy of decentralization and the organizational structure established.

As well, the reorganization of Head Office staff into five directorates (Older People and People with Disabilities; Youth and Employment; Maori, Community and Pacific Island Programmes; Families in Special Circumstances; and Family Development and Support) was intended to:

> Emphasize the complementary nature of income support and social work services [and provide] the structure for an integrated approach to social welfare policy development and monitoring.[20]

The present analysis argues that the reorganization of Head Office appeared to follow the characteristics of a functional organizational structure as defined by Pearce and Robinson and Robbins.[21] Head Office was no longer organized by a combination of professional (social work) and task (benefits and administration) groupings but along functional lines as exemplified in the directorates.

However, the reorganization of Head Office realigned working relationships and effectively weakened well established leadership patterns. For example, the label 'social work' or 'social services' did not appear on the organizational charts of 1987 or 1988 beyond the District level[21] and was seen by several of the respondents as indicative of the trend away from direct social work services in the Department.[22] It also meant the individuals assuming responsibility for those programs were not identified by their professional affiliation. De-emphasis on professionals in service delivery is consistent with the welfare society model of service delivery and represents a deprofessionalization of social work within the Department of Social Welfare. This point will be elaborated further below.

The respondents contended that the creation of the regional structure was promulgated on the premise that Head Office staff establishment would be substantially reduced. None of the Regional Executive

Officers nor the management staff in the Districts perceived that the staff establishment had reduced substantially despite the initial disestablishment of positions in Head Office during the 1986 - 1987 period. In fact, several of the respondents contended that staff establishment in Head Office had grown both in number of staff positions and total personnel expenditure as a result of staff promotions, the creation of new positions, and payment to consultants. This was to be confirmed in reviews of the regional structure subsequent to this research.[23] The regionalization, then, not only created another layer of management during a time when the stated objective was to delegate more authority to the districts, but apparently created that layer of management at the expense of the Districts Office allocation since the District Offices *did* experience both allocation cuts and hiring freezes during the 1986 - 1988 period.

Furthermore, as part of the restructuring, the major responsibility of each layer of management was delineated. Head Office and the Executive Management Group were responsible for policy development and overall leadership. The Districts were responsible for the 'operations' of Departmental functions. It was the designated role of the Regional Office staff to provide the vital link between the two. The split of policy and practice threatened to further alienate Head Office from the Districts who questioned how the policy makers could make good policy without clear integrative links to the service providers. Pearce and Robinson[24] warn that in a divisional structure the development of sub-unit autonomy and the consequent distancing of top policy makers from performance can be a major disadvantage. This was seen to be particularly true in the fast-changing and politically sensitive area of social services.

The comments of the respondents indicated supportfor decentralization of selected 'delegated authorities' such as eligibility for specific benefits and changes in status categories. They expressed concern with the effectiveness of decentralization of specialized services, such as international adoptions and legal services, and with the realities of exercising the delegated authorities without attendant support services and budget allocations.

Considered together, these findings point to an apparent 'paradox of decentralization'. Decentralization processes, such as the delegation of authority to the Districts, masked a more pervasive concentration of decisive control at the center through the simultaneous implementation of accountability and control mechanisms which effectively limited the exercise of the decentralized authority. For example, the decentralization of the Department occurred simultaneously with major policy changes accompanied by policy directives and a shrinking budget allocation causing the one of the District Assistant Directors to comment that her plan must fit within the parameter of the District plan which in turn must fit within the Region's plan, and so on up through the hierarchy. Her point was that the scope and range of her decision making was so closely circumscribed that her flexibility in creative and innovative response to local needs was *more* limited than under the previous centralized system.

Secondly, the stated objective of decentralization was to increase District autonomy. However, because the decentralization process was initiated at a time of budgetary constraint, the scope for decision making was limited by shrinking resources. As the Assistant Director explained, the diminishing budget only served to further restrict the District's service responsiveness. Furthermore, because she was responsible for expenditure as the local manager, she was responsible for cutting or restricting service to ensure a balanced budget. Hence, it was the District staff that had to face client dissatisfaction with service cuts rather than top management. The strategy of decentralizing during economic constraints so as to displace negative reaction to service cuts on to local government officials is described in the work by Lowi and Ginsberg.[25]

This paradox of decentralization was also revealed in the comments of the Regional Executive Officers who argued that much of their time was spent in servicing Head Office needs rather than supporting district operation. The Assistant Directors in the Districts perceived their own jobs as expanding in part because the District Directors were drawn on to participate in the management of the Region. Hence, each layer of the hierarchy was being drawn up to the next layer of the hierarchy to assist in the higher level management task. This brought into serious question the substance of the decentralization. Although the 'delegations' might indicate the transfer of decision making power to lower levels in the hierarchy, the development of the Regional Executive Management Teams to manage the Regions and the Executive Management Group to manage the Department nationally, had the perceived effect of further *centralizing* decision making rather than *decentralizing* decision making within the Department despite formalized statements to the contrary.

The present analysis also highlighted two disadvantages of decentralization noted by theorists: an increase in specialized competencies and an increase in competition between sub-units.[26] The increase in competition between regions and among Districts has already been noted[27] and was expected to continue and intensify as loyalty to the Department shifted to loyalty to the region or district, as the career prospects of staff become more confined to their region and linked to their knowledge of the local community and its needs, and as, at both the regional and the district level, resource allocation became more dependent on the skill of the individual manager to 'present and argue' the case for resources.

An increase in specialized competencies in response to local needs was encouraged at the District level. However, because the allocation for District social welfare services was cut twice in 1988, an increase in resource allocation was perceived by the respondents as highly unlikely. Both Districts in this study were experiencing exponential growth in statutory child abuse case referrals, the sheer volume of which precluded the development of additional specialisms in response to local demands. Similarly, the Black, et al.[28] study of statutory social work in Britain found the demands of meeting statutory child protection requirements and the limitations of resources, precluded the development of a range of specializatopms in statutory social work.

The results of the document review also provided support for Wineman's argument that "centralization, with its tendency to homogenize and to produce mass culture, is equally opposed to indigenous culture and community life".[29] Critiques of the Department had emphasized its inability to respond to minority needs.[30] Theorists, policy analysts, the Maori activists and the respondents alike, were optimistic that decentralization had the potential of promoting a high degree of responsiveness to community needs.[31] Nevertheless, some of the respondents were pessimistic about the Department's capacity to respond at the local level. These respondents viewed decentralization as part of a 'conspiracy theory' to promote competition among the lower level managers for diminishing funds. Five of the District Office management respondents explained that the decentralization effectively further limited the ability of the District to respond to community needs because these changes diverted financial resources to service another level of management.

Findings of this study supported the contention that the strengthening of Head Office staffing to assume a policy, development and monitoring role was consistent with the welfare society strategy. Policy makers in Head Office would need to be sensitive to practice realitites in the Districts. The financial constraints imposed on the Districts would limit their service responsiveness capability and encourage the development of service providers outside the state sector.

Devolution

The analysis of the documents and the interviews with the respondents revealed little commentary on the implementation of the third principle of the restructuring. At the time of data gathering, the only example of devolution, in the sense of a "movement of mutually agreed power . . . for programme design/delivery/evaluation from a government to a group outside government",[32] was the Community Organisation Grants Scheme established in 1985 to replace a number of subsidized employment programs.[33] Thus, it was established *prior* to the 1986 restructuring.

The Regional Executive Officers had little information about the meaning or implications of devolution and expressed the opinion that devolution had stopped. Certainly, the Task Group on Devolution which consisted of Permanent Heads of the nine government departments providing social services, was not supportive of full-scale devolution in their report:

> A client centred approach does not, however, automatically favour devolution through power-sharing as being the best means of meeting client's needs.[34]

The District Office respondents were unclear about the distinctions between devolution and the proposals for the contracting out of services. The effect of the Department's intention to expand the contracting for service provisions announced in July, 1988[35] were as yet unclear. The expansion of the contracting out capability clearly reflected the adoption of the Hadley and Hatch[36] model which emphasized high levels of contractural arrangements with voluntary organizations and individuals for service provision.[37] The REOs who commented on the contracting out policies noted the difficulty in distinguishing between devolution and contracts, questioned whether they were two distinct processes in practice and expressed concern that the contracting out policies were designed to further deplete statutory service provision.

Partnership with the Community

The initiatives implementing the fourth principle of the restructuring, partnership with the community, further reflected the adoption of welfare society principles as espoused in the Hadley and Hatch model. The creation of the District Executive Committees and the Institutional Management Committees provided mechanisms for the community to participate in service planning and for the Department to exercise the accountability to the community explicitly demanded for in the Hadley and Hatch model. When the Regional Executive Officers were asked if the Department had become more 'community oriented,' none mentioned the District Executive or Institutional Management Committees as examples of a community orientation or partnership. This may have been because these administrative officers were once removed from direct involvement in the Districts and Institutions, a similiar community based advisory structure was not in place for the Regional Offices, or because many of these committees had been in operation for less than a year and as newly created committees had not yet made their influence felt beyond the District level. However, the District staff referred positively to the work of the District Executive Committees in bringing community representatives into the District Office. They were seen as a resource for culturally appropriate program development, as an aid in recruitment and selection, particularly of Maori staff, and as providing a forum for discussions between the community and the Department on matters of policy and practice.

As well, a majority of the respondents remarked on an increased openness of the Department to scrutiny by community representatives on the monitoring committees; to increased willingness and support by the Department management and practitioners for participation in community forums and *hui*; to informing the community of developments in the Department and to responding to the advice and counsel of Maori *kaumatua* and Samoan elders. These developments were a result of the commitment to implement the recommendations of *Puao-Te-Ata-Tu* by involving cultural advisors in Departmental activities.[38]

The moves toward partnership in service provision were also clear in the restructuring principle of devolution and the moves toward contracting out services just discussed. The respondents noted directives from Head Office to utilize community supports, including voluntary agencies and informal caregivers (particularly the *whanau* and the *iwi*) in service provision.

The picture regarding participation in the provision of service was complex. All of the respondents providing casework services acknowledged significant changes in the planning process and in social work decision making. This was encouraged through the involvement of the *whanau* initiated in anticipation of the mandate expected to be part of the Children's and Young Person's Act awaiting Parliamentary confirmation. Both teams indicated that the restructuring policies legitimated coordinating service provision with community groups and agencies in a more explicit manner than had been true in the past. For the Napier Community Team, these policies meant a confirmation of their efforts that pre-dated the restructuring. For the Porirua team, it meant further legitimation for their pre-1986 efforts to implement the Hadley and Hatch 'patch system' and their current efforts to utilize both formal community agencies and informal caregivers in service provision.

Thus, these initiatives established mechanisms for involving the community in a partnership for service planning in the Districts. They represented a clear application of the Hadley and Hatch participatory model that demands mechanisms for involvement of the community in service planning and provision.

Partnership with the community in service provision was expected to be given further impetus in the Department's intention to complete the decentralization of community services funding to the Regions and the Districts by March 1989.[39] Although the decentralization of community service funding was not yet officially in place at the time of this research, the respondents voiced concern about the implications of this process for the local districts. While there was considerable philosophical support for the decentralization of the community grants voiced, one senior social work respondent, for example, expressed concern that the process of decision making at the local level might not be equitable and the competition for resources might negatively effect coordination of services and threaten lack of continuity in services and the maintenance of service standards.

The uncritically positive view of the role of the voluntary sector in service provision and of the benefits of competition for funding has been heavily criticized by Pinker, Greycar, Kramer and Flora.[40] As Pinker[41] argued, localized decision making does not guarantee equity or responsiveness and may in fact, further disadvantage the disadvantaged by removing centrally mandated universal services. The realities of decentralized funding was appreciated by the District management respondents who expressed skepticism about their ability to equitably allocate what they expected would be diminishing funds at the district level.

Furthermore, a majority of the Regional Executive Officers were concerned by the splitting of the funder and provider roles germane to the decentralization of community services funding. They feared that the role split was a further step in reducing government responsibility for service provision and for containment of social service expenditure. They expressed concern that diminishing the role of the state in provision through contracting out and funding of community based services might result in a diminishing sense of state responsibility to social service funding. Events subsequent to this study are instructive.

For example, the revised regulations regarding Special Needs Benefits, the staff hiring freeze of 1990 and the restrictions imposed on community services funding not only appear to justify this concern in the New Zealand context, but corroborate Johnson's[42] claim that in Britain, where the changes associated with the separation of the funding and provider roles are more advanced, the government's sense of responsibility for social services has been undermined.

Management Style

The Department's management plans had given high priority to 'participatory management' as exemplified in the establishment of a formal system of two-way communication. In the Department's first formal *Management Plan,1986*, the Director General announced his intention to "create a sense of corporate identity" through managerial accountability for "achieving tasks, building teams and developing individuals".[43] He acknowledged that staff had been inadequately briefed and consulted in the past and pledged the development of formal systems "backed by the kind of informal system that is generated by a willingness to co-operate in the work-place".[44] The management plan pledged management to:

> Brief (and check understanding) and to consult (and report back on outcomes) both within a formal system and informally as a normal feature of working relationships.[45]

These commitments reflected the expectation of staff participation inherent in the Hadley and Hatch model which views the involvement of staff as "indispensable if available resources are to be maximized and variations in need/demand are to be recognized".[46] The *Management Plan, 1986* stated the themes to be emphasized in the 1987-1988 year:

> Policy review and development based on effective use of community and departmental collaboration in Districts, Regions and nationally.[47]

Although, the respondents gave mixed evaluations of that commitment, they were particularly negative about the 'briefing and consulting' policies.[48] The policies were seen as time consuming and unproductive; moreover, they created further pressures on the effective provision of service to clients. The net effect appeared to be ever increasing levels of stress on both practitioners and clients.

The majority of the respondents reported participatory management styles emphasizing joint decision-making between management and staff on policy interpretation, practice procedures and workload management were more prevalent in their work setting. They argued that social workers have a commitment to participation in decision making with clients which should also apply to decision making in their work setting. One Regional Executive Officer expressed the opinion that the social workers within the Department were professionally supportive of joint decision making.

The District social worker's assessment of participatory management developed briefing and consultation process, they perceived themselves as less a part of it. Three of the district office social workers reported that they felt either that decisions were had made prior to the consultations or they were drawn into making managerial decisions that the manager was being paid to make, for example, on staff allocation expenditure. The Assistant Directors and the Regional Executive Officers expressed concern that the meeting time demands of the Regional Executive Team Meetings on District Directors and the of the Executive Management Group on the Regional Assistant Director-Generals were removing them for several days a month from their responsibilities in the Districts and Regions and placed a further burden on the remaining staff. All the respondents acknowledged the time commitment required for a participatory management style to be implemented while expressing concern with its effectiveness and efficiency. Thorough investigation of the effectiveness of the participatory management policies requires further research analysis.

SOCIAL WORK

The restructuring which occurred in 1986 had a profound effect on the definition of the social work task within the Department and on the course of social work professionalization. It was clear from the analysis of the documents and the interviews that despite the Department's references to community development and community oriented practice, the social work task in the Department became restricted to direct service provision in the two areas of child protective service and youth justice. As a step toward the narrowing of the definition of the social work task within the Department, social workers were being encouraged to utilize community, *whanau* and immediate family resources as a means of involving the community in service provision and limiting the provision of service by the Department. Five of the respondents expressed the opinion that the Department was rapidly becoming an 'agency of last resort,' that is, referrals would come to the

Department only if no community resource was available or only after all community resources were expended.

Utilization of *whanau* and community resources as the first course of action was established as a practice principle.[49] For example, rather than bringing children into care, social workers were authorized to expend financial resources and social work services in support of children in their *whanau* or family setting utilizing the support of community agencies and informal care givers. Social workers were to utilize Departmental based services only after all efforts to retain children in their community had been expended.

The community development role which had been supported in the initial restructuring directives was rapidly being relegated by the Department to the voluntary sector and community groups or *iwi* authorities. These moves clearly reflected the adoption of a welfare society model of social service delivery which places more emphasis on non-statutory providers and limits the role of the state. These developments further confirm the findings reported in the section on the statutory-voluntary balance discussed early in this chapter.

It was during the period of centralization, beginning with creation of the Department through to the decision to restructure in 1986 that the Department of Social Welfare became increasingly more bureaucratized and social work in the Department become professionally oriented. The professionalization of social work within the Department was reflected in personnel practices that rewarded social work educational qualifications, in policies that supported social work training within the Department and in tertiary educational institutions and in the opportunities provided for in-service social work training programs to those employed in voluntary agencies through the Department's three training centers. The professionalization of social work was further evidenced by the creation of the Social Work Training Council in 1973 under the Department's auspices. These findings support the hypothesis of Hollingsworth and Hanneman[50] which proposed a positive relationship between bureaucratization and professionalization.

Decentralization, combined with demands to meet the recommendations of *Puao-te-Ata-Tu* , marked a trend away from social work professionalization. New policies were introduced that lessened emphasis on tertiary qualifications and emphasized cultural sensitivity and knowledge as a, and in some cases *the* primary qualification for hiring and promotion. In addition, policies were implemented that aimed to change the role of the social worker from one of 'expert' and direct service provider to one of coordinator of *whanau* based decision making and broker, that is, offering skilled assessment and referral services.[51]

These policies effectively undermined the professional authority of the social worker. According to Hadley and Hatch in bureaucratic social service organizations there are two sources of authority: the organization and the training and expertise of individual staff. In the present research, the Department's support for professionalization was evidenced in the various training programs and bursary schemes of the Department already noted. The restructuring had crucial consequences for these historical commitments. The loss of support for social work professionalization was perceived by the respondents as a loss of support for social work in the Department. This loss of support would eventually further reduce the scope for professional judgement as the demand for compliance with the organizational requirements increased and the professional expertise of social work within the Department decreased.

The District staff members, particularly those on the Porirua team providing direct services, felt their legitimised authority had also altered character with the implementation of a partnership relationship with clients and the community. The teams did feel a degree of legitimated authority in their negotiated relationships with the community. The Porirua team reported individually negotiated relationships with community groups and individuals for specific cases but not the established networks envisioned by the Hadley and Hatch model. It was evident that there were several positive relationships in existence, many predating the policy directives but there was little evidence of district wide negotiations presented and few formalized, consistent relationships with community groups or agencies.

Conversely in the Napier office, the Community Development Team had formal negotiated relationships with over one-hundred community groups and agencies. However, further research would be required to determine to what extent these agencies provided services immediately supportive to the other social workers in the District Office and between service providers in the community. The Napier Community Development Team complained of the lack of understanding of their task by the rest of the social workers whom they felt they could better serve if there was a stronger working relationship between those social workers providing casework services and the Community Development Team members.

It is important to note that despite the long history of a community development team in the Napier District Office and the well developed negotiated relationships with community groups, the team never felt integrated into the service delivery infrastructure of the

District Office. They reported feeling periodically under threat and dispensable. This raises serious questions as to whether a statutory social work service can have a broad based approach to its practice and to the requirements that must be in place to insure a broad based approach becomes adequately integrated into the infrastructure of a statutory organization.

In the Hadley and Hatch model, expert knowledge is acknowledged; however, for this to be truly effective the practitioner must also have the capacity to recognize, and work with the non-expert. The Napier Team's close involvement with non-experts in community groups and agencies pre-dated the restructuring as does the Porirua Office's efforts with implementing the patch system. However the extent, depth and consistent involvement with non-experts, except in the case of Maatua Whangai worker and cultural advisers, was not clearly discernible. All the members of the Porirua Team claimed involvement with community non-experts that pre-dated policy directives but pointed out that under the 'new way of working' work with non-experts outside the Department was at last clearly legitimated by top management policy.

The moves toward negotiated relationships between the social workers as providers of service and the community as consumers is consistent with the patronage type of profession conceptualized by Johnson.[52] It seems reasonable to argue that the state mediated professional relationship which characterized social work under the centralized system could be expected to assume features of the patronage type of profession as a result of the implementation of the policies advocating accountability and responsiveness to the community. Such moves are in direct opposition to the characteristics of the traditional professions as conceptualized by Johnson and toward which social work in the Department had been heading prior to the 1986 restructuring.

The professionalization of social work had been intricately intertwined with Departmental policy and had become increasingly dependent on the Department during the 1969 - 1988 period. In the Department of Social Welfare Act , 1971 the Department was charged with the responsibility of supporting and providing social work training to both the public and voluntary sector. As a result of its direct and indirect support of social work training, the Department was the primary influence in setting the direction for social work professional development. When the Minister of Social Welfare placed the Social Work Training Council in remission and then set in its place the Council of Education and Training in the Social Services, not only was social work professionalization dealt a strong setback but the term social work was superseded in the Department by the more amorphous, generalized, non-occupationally linked designation 'social services.' The debates on social work effectiveness of the 1970s and the criticisms by radical social workers[53] intensified a 'crisis of confidence' among social workers.

This 'crisis of confidence' was further deepened by the critique of professionalism offered by the keynote address of the 1978 NZASW Biennial Conference.[54] Findings from the present research suggest that the critique of social work from divergent sources was particularly devastating because social work's hold on professionalism in New Zealand was so tenuous. This vulnerability was deepened by the ACORD and Johnston Report[55] which heavily criticized social work as racist in its practice. Social work training institutions and the New Zealand Association of Social Workers, as well as individual social workers in practice, were challenged to re-examine the basic assumptions of their practice. Many social workers engaged in the personally demanding exploration of personal racism along with an examination of social and institutional racism. For example, eight social workers authored the Report on *Institutional Racism*[56] that recommended sweeping reforms within the Department of Social Welfare. Their recommendations were later echoed by the Ministerial Advisory Committee[57] and subsequently accepted by the Department.

The pressure from social work to respond to Maori and minority interests may be an important contributing factor to its loss of power within the Department as evidenced by the deprofessionalization processes initiated by the loss of social work professional leadership and social work identity in Head Office and by the disestablishment of the training centres. In Chapter One, Wilding[58] is quoted as proposing that the privileges of professional status are the result of an alliance between the state and the profession. It could be argued that social work within the Department violated the alliance by advocating for minority interests through social work support for biculturalism and hence, social work lost its hold on professional status within the Department.

As discussed earlier, the moves which the Department made to regionalize training were perceived as deleterious by the respondents because they effectively suspended training opportunities during the 1986-1988 period. These moves within the Department were significant because of the leadership, funding and influence the Department had traditionally exercised in social work professional development. This loss of what might have been perceived as a dependent relationship was to lead to a resurgence of social work professionalism that was independent of Departmental sanction and support. This resurgence was evident in the increasing membership in the New Zealand Association of Social Work which began in late 1988.

The Association's moves toward the development of certificates of competency generated a new sense of commitment to the professional association.[59] It is ironic that the loss of support for social work professionalization within the Department led to support for social work professionalization in the Association. To what extent this was a paradoxical effect on the loss of Departmental support which resulted in a determination to achieve independence from the state or another example of a reactive response to the Departmental policies on accountability and contracting out demands further study.

BICULTURALISM

Partnership with the community as it was defined within the Department included a commitment to biculturalism and to the development of models of bicultural social work practice. In the wide sweeping reforms recommended by the Ministerial Advisory Committee on a Maori Perspective, *Puao-Te-Ata-Tu*,[60] social workers were advised to give due regard to maintaining Maori children within their *whanau* and hapu, to make inquiries as to the child's heritage and family links, to undergo training with regard to customary cultural preferences, Maori circumstances and Maori aspirations and to consult with *whanau* and *hapu* regarding the care and protection of Maori children. All of the respondents acknowledged major changes in social work practice in the Department as a result of these commitments. They reported a heightened awareness of Maori culture and some had further developed or acquired specific cultural knowledge and language skills. Social workers in both District Offices acknowledged that their approach to every social work task was now evaluated in terms of cultural appropriateness. It was expected that every social worker would develop and maintain contacts with the Maori community, consider the implications of *whanau* and *whanau* decision making with each client, and invest the bulk of resources in maintaining a child with the *whanau* prior to the child coming into care. The changes were seen as implementing the commitment to biculturalism and hence, to the recommendations of *Puao-Te-Ata-Tu* .

However, it must be noted that the Director-General announced key changes to the Department's organizational design *prior* to the release of the recommendations of *Puoa-Te-Ata-Tu.* It can be argued that because the Director-General was a member of the Advisory Committee and aware of the recommendations, he was able to pre-empt the recommendations of the Committee by announcing the changes from his position as Director-General in an effort to retain organizational integrity. Alternatively, the dynamic may have been the reverse.

Perhaps, it was the intention of the Department to regionalize, to decentralize, to devolve and to enter into a partnership with the community as part of the strategy for the adoption of a welfare society model of social service delivery and hence, the changes were merely confirmed by the Ministerial Advisory Committee's recommendations as one of the respondents contended.

Both Districts studied reported on-going relationships with local *kaumatua* who were consulted on Maori protocol issues. The Districts had paid positions for Maatua Whangai workers and for Maori Advisory Officers who offered a range of consultative services from translations to cultural training for staff. Both offices had a cultural group who were given release time in return for their commitment to participation in Departmental *powhiri*. There were reportedly similiar developments in District offices nationwide.

For the social workers the commitment to biculturalism meant they had to examine the basic assumptions of their practice not only in relation to Maori clients, but to all clients.[61] All of the direct-line practitioners were daily confronting issues of race and culture as they attempted to reconcile their practice with professional and cultural demands. The major changes they identified in their practice were a move toward recognizing cultural identification as an factor in planning; legitimation of resource expenditure before a child came into care rather than having to bring a child into care before expenditures, such as board payments, could be authorized, sharing decision making with *whanau/* regarding planning for the care and protection for a child in a child abuse case, taking a coordinator's role in family conferencing and the legitimation of involving informal care givers, volunteers, and voluntary agencies and groups in service planning and provision.

IMPLICATIONS FOR FURTHER RESEARCH

This study is a contribution to research on the origins and effects of the changes enacted under New Zealand's Fourth Labour Government. Findings from this study suggest several potentially fruitful areas for further research.

First, replication and extension of the analysis undertaken in this study is imperative in order to corroborate the patterns in service delivery and social work practice delineated. The collection of data for this research was completed in December 1988. Since then, the pace of change within the Department has continued, unabated. Perhaps, the most significant development was the decision in July of 1990 to disestablish the six regions and their two hundred and forty staff and to replace them with four operational units with the major responsibility of providing information for policy and development to the Head Office of the Department.[62] Subsequent to this decision in 1990 have been several identifiable 'restructurings.' Pearce and Robinson[63] suggests that a change in organizational design may signal a change in strategy. A study of the extent to which these restructurings signal changes in the strategy regarding the delivery of social services promises an important contribution to understanding the relationship between strategy and practice.

Another related avenue of research could address a key assumption of the welfare society model. The model is predicated on the assumption that the voluntary sector and other non-statutory providers can and will provide services previously provided by the state. Johnson[64] noted growth in the commercial sector as a result of welfare pluralism in Britain, but no significant growth in the voluntary sector. Careful analysis of the impact of the implementation of welfare society principles on the growth of voluntary social service agencies is required to ascertain to what degree this assumption by the welfare society proponents is valid in the New Zealand context particularly because the voluntary sector is not extensive, well-developed, nor independent of state funding.

The third area for potential research is related to management. The designation of the function of Head Office as policy and development and of the Districts as 'operations' has some similarities to an hypothesis of Meyer and Scott.[65] In their study of educational institutions, they describe a 'decoupling' process whereby top management in educational institutions distanced itself from the controversial realities of service delivery in the classroom. Study of developments in the Department of Social Welfare, given subsequent restructurings since 1988, might reveal a similar process as Head Office re-establishes its position as policy development and the Districts are expected to deal in a semi-autonomous fashion with the demands of service delivery.

A crucial area already highlighted in the previous discussion, is the promotion of research designed to shed further light on the development of social policy by studying key power holders in government and management. An associated line of research could focus on the interlocking committee memberships on the various reviews, committees and task forces of this period. It has already been noted that such interlocking memberships may have contributed to the apparent consensus of approach so evident in the many reports of the period 1984-1988. Also, an analysis of expenditure associated with financial costs of the 1986 and subsequent restructurings, including associated personnel costs such as retraining and redundancy options offered to staff deemed 'surplus to requirement', would generate the data that would be required to validate the claim that the restructuring occurred at the cost of service provision in the Districts.[66]

The principles and procedures applied in the restructuring of the Department of Social Welfare were also applied to education and health. In education, schools were decentralized into semi-autonomous Boards of Trustees responsible for the overall management of the school. In the health sector, Area Health Boards replaced the old Hospital Board system. The restructuring which occurred in these two crucial sectors warrants careful research in its own right; moreover, such research would provide an excellent opportunity to explore similarities and differences on the effects of the restructuring.

Finally, the restructuring of New Zealand's Department of Social Welfare and its redefinition of the statutory social work task into child protection services and youth justice parallels trends elsewhere, particularly in Britain. Comparative research, with reference to the impact of decentralization on service provision would provide a fruitful source of data for both an understanding of how social policy is developed and implemented but also about the interface between practitioner and client.

PROSPECTS

The late 1930s witnessed the enactment by the First Labour Government of the progressive legislation that was the foundation of what came to be termed the Welfare State. Some forty years later, the Fourth Labour Government initiated sweeping policies of economic deregulation and social restructuring that dismembered both the frameworks and provisions that had evolved over the previous decades. By focusing on a segment of social reality that was circumscribed both temporally and organizationally, the Social Welfare Department in the period 1986-1988, this research has attempted to theorize and analyse some of the consequences of these changes. Although, the explanatory nature of this research and the immediacy of the changes which were its focus require that any generalizations arising from it should be drawn with care, the implications of the research are poignant for more than social services and social work in New Zealand.

When the Fourth Labour Government was elected to office in 1984, New Zealanders had acknowledged to varying degrees, that change was inevitable. They were aware of the country's deteriorating economy. But once the changes began, they seemed to come so quickly and from so many directions that many felt the country was out of control. Easton,[67] for example, perhaps somewhat extravagantly argued, that changes in economic policy gained their own momentum without anyone, even the Minister of Finance, Roger Douglas, quite knowing what the objectives were, let alone how to get there!

This sense of pervasive change without time to reflect on its possible implications was evident in many sectors, including the social services. It was obvious that the Treasury espoused cuts in government spending as a way of stimulating the weak economy. But, the initial directives from the Department of Social Welfare, targeting as they did, long standing criticisms of the Department's bureaucratic structures and highly centralized style of management did seem to be progressive harbingers of better things to come. Indeed, the initiatives were hailed as such by diverse groups. Voluntary agencies and community groups welcomed the apparent willingness of the Department to acknowledge and more fully utilize their contribution to service provision. Social workers within the Department welcomed the establishment of a Community Development Unit in Head Office because it was perceived as recognition of the community development role as a facet of the social work task. The Maori community also responded favourably because the introduction of anti-racism training in the Department, the creation of the Maatua Whangai program, the acceptance of the Report on *Institutional Racism*[68] and the establishment of a Maori Advisory Unit in the Auckland Region were seen as major steps toward dealing with their critique of the Department's monocultural service delivery. These initial responses were strengthened when the Department accepted the recommendations of *Puao-Te-Ata-Tu* and made a commitment to biculturalism in the *Management Plan., 1987.*[69]

Even if one assumes that the Director General was able to engage in a significant face saving operation by announcing the changes recommended in *Puao-Te-Ata-Tu* as part of the Department's management plan prior to the release of *Puao-Te-Ata-Tu*, there appeared to be meagre grounds for accepting these sweeping recommendations. There are several possible explanations. First, the acceptance of the recommendations permitted the regionalization the Director General had been trying to implement since 1980. Second, the acceptance of the recommendations could be seen as instrumental in curtailing social service spending without engendering a political backlash by appearing to respond to requests by Maori to take care of their own. This possibility was particularly significant since research findings and official information confirmed the dire circumstances of Maori in New Zealand with respect to health, welfare and justice. Any scaling down of care in welfare institutions would, consequently, remove a resource which had over time become disproportionately utilized by Maori. This does not address the appropriateness of institutional or residential care for Maori children and youth but does serve to alert the reader to the convenient match between efforts to curtail governmental spending and the requests of Maori people to care for their own.

Within the management of these restructured services, the policies of the Department of Social Welfare were intended to foster 'participatory management' and create structures that would encourage community participation in social service planning and provision. As has already been suggested, Johnson's[70] assessment of welfare pluralism in Britain pointed to more growth in the commercial rather than in the voluntary sector as a result of the adoption of welfare society principles. These trends could be precursors of similiar developments in New Zealand as evidenced by the expansion of the Department's contracting out policies,[71] the development of a certificate of competency for social workers,[72] and the growth in the number of private practitioners. These developments appeared to provide not only their own legitimation, that is, they were at once responsive and progressive, but they seem to open up attractive alternatives to those most affected by them. However, there were darker underpinnings that are now becoming apparent. Most of these center on the availability of already scarce human and economic resources. Just what are the limits to the capability of voluntary agencies and community groups to plan and provide services that were once almost the sole responsibility of the Department?

In a similar view, it seems important to try and establish just how much participation is possible, let alone desirable at the interface between the community and Department. Will increased levels of participation result in, for example, services that are based on strong interest groups or local prejudices? Certainly, it seems reasonable to argue that the demands for community participation in the whole range of social services in New Zealand from education to health and welfare were already showing signs of disadvantaging minority interests by the end of the 1980s.

The effects of the restructuring that were the focus of this research, exposed yet again the incompatibility between the major functions of the Department: financial benefits and personal social services. This incompatibility was inherent in the amalagamation which was the birth of the Department of Social Welfare and has haunted the Department throughout its history. The implementation of the principles of the restructuring only served to exacerbate the differences between the two functions. This tension is exposed in the following comment from one of the respondents:

> The hidden hope of most of the managers . . . is that we will one day get through this experience of being a department of social welfare. This is not a properly set up organisation, that is it is neither one nor another. It doesn't provide an integrated social welfare service because so many functions lie outside our orbit and it has forced the child and family services in with the income maintenance services in an unnaturally overmanaged kind of way (Regional Executive Officer).

The incompatibility of the two major functions of the Department was emphasized by so many of the respondents that it raised the question of the appropriateness of the placement of social work services within this government department. The history of tensions and dilemmas faced by social work services within the Department strongly supports the separation of the provision of financial services from the provision of social work services. Such a proposal would, however, need to address the fundamental conflict between targeted, limited access, means tested services and universal services as a right of citizenship.

The trends evident in the period immediately after 1986-1988, suggest that the accountability and control systems now in place continued to inhibit the development of social work by pushing its practice into ever narrower specializations, specifically in child protection and youth work. If social work is to effectively enact its dual commitment to individual and social change, the potential for integration of that commitment must exist in the work setting. Clearly that potential was denied by the policies following the 1986 restructuring since the changes did not create an organizational environment supportive of the dual focus of social work. The policies explicitly stated that community development and community work--the social change interventions--were to be tasks of voluntary agencies, community groups and the *iwi* authorities. Social work without community work/development is not social work. It might be counseling or therapy, but it is not social work. The prospect for the practice of social work within the Department of Social Welfare is, at best, dim.

What of the efforts made to deflect or ameliorate these changes? One can only speculate about the possible effect of criticism from social workers in the Department. Social work staff in their various reports and reviews during the years immediately preceding the restructuring[73] had recommended changes in social work services.

Perhaps the most controversial of their efforts was *Institutional Racism Within the Department of Social Welfare*[74] which was authored by eight social work staff. The respondents characterized top management's response to the report as an 'embarrassment' that generated in some a feeling of betrayal of organizational loyalty. There is sufficient evidence in the findings to suggest that several of the initiatives in the restructuring process effectively curtailed the power base of social work within the Department. To what extent this might have been a reaction to social workers' efforts for change is impossible to assess. However, it is reasonable to assume that the actions of social workers to advocate for minority interests worked against their own professional self-interest in the Department. Social workers lost further ground in the processes of decentralization which progressively separated social workers into smaller and smaller groups, thus eliminating the 'critical mass' that is deemed necessary for professional development and growth. Most importantly, social workers lost their professional reference group within the Department. This was evident in the removal of the line social work management position in Head Office and the redesignation of the Social Work Division to Social Services Division, a step which effectively eliminated an identifiable social work presence at the top management level in the Department.

Regardless of the motivation for the restructuring, changes in social work practice were clearly indicated in the findings: the emphasis on using community support networks, expenditure of resources prior to a child coming into care rather than after the fact, *whanau* or family oriented decision-making, the emphasis on biculturalism, the reorganization of teams along cultural lines, and the redefinition of the social work task in the Department to the specializations in child protection and youth justice.

It was through these changes in strategy and design that the changes in social work practice within the Department occurred. The analysis of the findings suggest that the Department was dominant in the social service ystem because it exercised control over training and evaluative bodies, and hence, was in a powerful position to dictate practice directives as Howe observed.[75] The present analysis of the Department of Social Welfare has provided a further demonstration of the interrelationship between organizational setting and professional social work. Without a strong independent professional identity, social work was particularly vulnerable to the demands of the organization.

If social work is to retain its commitment to the goals of social justice for disadvantaged groups in society, it can not afford to be unduly dependent on one governmental structure. The uncoupling of their dependent relationship could lead to the development of professional social work in New Zealand--a professional social work that can more completely pursue its commitment to individual and social change. Furthermore, the findings provide support for the claim that a strong independent social work lobby, such as the New Zealand Association of Social Work, is imperative if social work in New Zealand is to achieve the degree of autonomy necessary for it to pursue the dual commitment of social work.

The First Labour Government introduced progressive social legislation motivated by a genuine concern for the well-being of all New Zealanders. Such a concern was much less apparent in the policies of the Fourth Labour Government. Given these circumstances the practice of social work was inevitably more diminished. The musing of a social work practitioner who was part of the restructuring process captures that sentiment:

> On my cynical days, I really think that the welfare system as we know it has been dismantled under our very eyes, the community are going to be overwhelmed with a sort of do more on less ideology. . . . There will be no role for social work in the Department.

NOTES

1. Department of Social Welfare, *Management Plan, 1986* (Wellington: DSW, 1986).

2. Ibid, 1.

3. Richard Titmuss, *Social Policy: An Introduction* , ed. Brian Abel-Smith and Kay Titmuss (London: George Allen and Unwin, 1974); Richard Titmuss, *Essays on 'The Welfare State"* 3rd ed. (London: George Allen and Unwin, 1976); David Reisman, *Richard Titmuss: Welfare and Society* (London: Heinemann, 1977).

4. Roger Hadley, Mike Cooper, Peter Dale and Graham Stacy, *A Community Worker's Handbook* (Bungay, Suffolk: Richard Clay, Ltd., 1987); Roger Hadley, Peter Dale and Patrick Sills, *Decentralising Social Services* National Council of Voluntary Organisations (London: Bedford Square Press, 1984); Roger Hadley and Stephen Hatch, *Social Welfare and the Failure of the State: Centralized Social Services and Participatory Alternatives* (London: George Allen and Unwin, 1981); Roger Hadley and Morag McGrath, ed., *Going Local: Neighbourhood Social Services* National Council for Voluntary Organisations, Occasional Paper 1 (London: Bedford Square Press, 1981); Roger Hadley and Morag McGrath, *When Social Services are Local: The Normanton Experience*. (London: George Allen and Unwin, 1983).

5. John A. Pearce II and Richard B. Robinson, Jr., *Management* (Singapore: McGraw-Hill International Editions, 1989).

6. Ministerial Advisory Committee on a Maori Perspective for the Department of Social Welfare , *Puao-Te-Ata-Tu:The Day Break Report* (Wellington: DSW, 1986).

7. DSW, *Management Plan, 1986.*

8. DSW, *Management Plan, 1987* (Wellington: DSW, 1987c).

9. DSW, *Future Directiors for Social Work* (Wellington: DSW, 1988d).

10. Brian Easton and N. J. Thomson, *An Introduction to the New Zealand Economy* (St. Lucia: University of Queensland Press, 1982); Stuart Birks and Srikanta Chatterjee, eds., *Introduction to New Zealand Economy* (Palmerston North: Dunmore Press, Ltd., 1988).

11. Paul Dalziel, "The Economic Summit," in *The Making of Rogernomics,* ed. Brian Easton (Auckland: University Press, 1989), 53-67.

12. Brian Easton, "The Unmaking of Roger Douglas" in *The Making of Rogernomics,* ed. Brian Easton (Auckland: University Press, 1989), 171-187; Hugh Oliver, "The Labour Caucus and

Economic Policy Formation, 1981-1984" in Brian Easton (ed) *The Making of Rogernomics* (Auckland: University Press, 1989),11-52.

13. Jonathan Boston, "Democratic Theory, Devolution and Accountability" in *Devolution and Accountability,* eds. J. Martin and M. Harper (Wellington: G. P. Books, July, 1988), 46-71.

14. Chris Wilkes, "Development as Practice: The Instrument of Reason" in *Development Tracks,* ed. Ian Shirley (Palmerston North: Dunmore Press, 1982), 117-134.

15. New Zealand Planning Council, *Directions* (Wellington: Government Printer, 1981); Judith Davey and Maire Dwyer, *Meeting Needs in the Community: A Discussion Paper on Social Services* (Wellington: New Zealand Planning Council, 1984); Ministerial Task Force on Social Welfare Services, *Social Welfare Services* (Wellington: Department of Social Welfare, July, 1986); Ministerial Task Force on Social Welfare Services, *Social Welfare Services: The Way Ahead* (Wellington: Department of Social Welfare, July, 1987); Sue Driver and David Robinson, *Voluntary Social Services: A Review of Funding* (Wellington: New Zealand Planning Council, 1986); Royal Commission on Social Policy, "Social Provision: Access and Delivery" in *The April Report*, Royal Commission on Social Policy, Vol. II (1988), 773-811; Task Group on Devolution, *Sharing Control: A Policy Study of Responsiveness and Devolution in the Statutory Social Services* State Service Commission (Wellington: Government Printer, February, 1988).

16. W. Richard Scott, "The Organization of Environments: Network, Cultural and Historical Elements" in *Organizational Environments: Ritual and Rationality,* eds. John Meyer and W. Richard Scott (Beverly Hills: Sage Publications, 1983a), 155-178; Yvonna Lincoln, ed., *Organizational Theory and Inquiry: The Paradigm Revolution* (Beverly Hills: Sage Publications, 1985); Karl Weick, "Sources of Order in Underorganized Systems: Themes in Recent Organizational Theory" in *Organization Theory and Inquiry: The Paradigm Revolution,* ed. Yvonna S. Lincoln (Beverly Hills: Sage Publications, 1985), 106-136.

17. Pearce and Robinson.

18. DSW, *Management Plan, 1986.*

19. Pearce and Robinson.

20. DSW, *Corporate Management Plan, 1988* (Wellington: Department of Social Welfare, 1988e), 20.

21. Pearce and Robinson; Stephen Robbins, *Organization Theory: The Structure and Design of Organizations* (Englewood Cliffs, NJ: Prentice-Hall, Inc., 1983).

22. DSW, *Management Plan, 1987*; DSW, *Corporate Management Plan, 1988.*

23. Barretta-Herman, Jeff Dougal and Alastair Spearling, *The Relationship Between Regional Office and District Offices in the Central District* (Palmerston North: Department of Social Welfare, 1989); DSW, *Review of Regional Office:Report of Assistant Director-General: Programmes and Services* (Wellington: DSW, 1990a).

24. Pearce and Robinson.

25. Theodore Lowi and Benjamin Ginsberg, *Poliscide* (New York: The Macmillan Publishing Company, 1976).

26. See Stewart Clegg and David Dunkerley, *Organization, Class and Control* (London: Routledge and Kegan Paul, 1980) for a further discussion of this point.

27. Refer to Chapter Five, Six and Seven.

28. J. Black, R. Bowl, D. Burns, C. Critcher, G. Grant, and D. Stockford, *Social Work in Context* (London: Tavistock, 1983).

29. Steven Wineman, *The Politics of Human Services* (Boston: South End Press, 1984), 3.

30. A. H. Johnston, *Report to the Minister of Social Welfare on the Current Practices and Procedures Followed in Institutions of the Department of Social Welfare in Auckland* (Wellington: Department of Social Welfare, October 29, 1982); DSW, *Institutional Racism in the Department of Social Welfare: Tamaki-Makau-Rau, Auckland (Revised)* (Wellington: Department of Social Welfare, 1985b); Ministerial Advisory Committee on a Maori Perspective for the Department of Social Welfare, *Puao-Te-Ata-Tu:The Day Break Report):* (Wellington: DSW, 1986).

31. See for examples the arguments made in Hadley and Hatch; Barclay Report, *Social Workers: Their Role and Tasks* (London: Bedford Square Press, 1982); NZPC, *The Welfare State* (Wellington: Government Printer, 1979); NZPC, *Directions.*

32. Task Group on Devolution, 11.

33. Allan Levett, Josie Keelan, and Velma McClellan, *Making Devolution Work: Report on the Community Organisations Grant Scheme* (Wellington: Department of Social Welfare, June, 1988), 3:1.

34. Task Group on Devolution, 8.

35. DSW, *Contracting for Social Services: Principles and Guidelines* (Wellington: DSW, 1988c).

36. Hadley and Hatch.

37. See Table One.

38. Ministerial Advisory Committee.

39. DSW, *The Organisation of Social Work Services at the District Level: Report of the Working Party* (Wellington: Department of Social Welfare, 1986b).

40. Robert A. Pinker, "Appendix B: An alternative view" in the Barclay Report, *Social Workers: Their Role and Tasks* (London: Bedford Square Press, 1982); Robert Pinker, "Populism and the Social Services" *Social Policy Administration*, 18(1) (1984) : 89-99; Adam Graycar, "Informal, Voluntary and Statutory Services: The Couples Relationship" *British Journal of Social Work*, 13 (1983): 379-393; Ralph M. Kramer, "The Welfare State and the Volunteer Sector: The Case of the Personal Social Services" in *The Welfare State and Its Aftermath*, eds., S. N. Eisenstadt and Ora Ahimeir (London: Croom Helm, 1985), 132-142; Peter Flora, "On the History and Current Problems of the Welfare State" in *The Welfare State and Its Aftermath*, eds. S. N. Eisenstadt and Ora Ahimeir (London: Croom Helm, 1985), 11-30.

41. Pinker, "Populism and the Social Services".

42. Norman Johnson, *The Welfare State in Transition: The Theory and Practice of Welfare Pluralism* (Brighton, Sussex: Wheatsheaf Books, 1987).

43. DSW, *Management Plan, 1986*, 2.

44. Ibid, 2.

45. Ibid, 7.

46. Hadley and Hatch, 147.

47. DSW, *Management Plan, 1987*, 3.

48. See Appendix VIII

49. DSW, *Future Directions for Social Work* (Wellington: DSW, July, 1988d).

50. J. Roger Hollingsworth and Robert Hanneman, *Centralization and Power in Social Service Delivery Systems* (Boston: Kluever, Nighoff Publishing, 1984).

51. Administrative Review Committee, *Performance and Efficiency in the Department of Social Welfare* (Wellington: Government Printer, December, 1987); DSW, *Contracting for Social Services*.

52. Terence J. Johnson, *Professions and Power* (New York: Macmillan Publishing Company, 1972).

53. Mike Brake and Roy Bailey, eds., *Radical Social Work and Practice* (London: Edward Arnold, 1975).

54. New Zealand Association of Social Workers, *Biennial Conference: Conference Papers* (Palmerston North: NZASW, 1978).

55. Johnston.

56. DSW, *Institutional Racism*.

57. Ministerial Advisory Committee.

58. Paul Wilding, *Professional Power and Social Welfare* (London: Routledge and Kegan Paul, 1982).

59. Sarah Fraser, "President's Report" *Social Work Review: NZASW*, 1(1) (July, 1988) : 30-31.

60. Ministerial Advisory Committee.

61. DSW, *Future Directions.*

62. DSW, *Review of Regional Offices.*

63. Pearce and Robinson.

64. Norman Johnson, *The Welfare State in Transition: The Theory and Practice of Welfare Pluralism* (Bighton, Sussex: Wheatsheaf Books, 1987).

65. John Meyer and W. Richard Scott, eds., *Organizational Environments: Ritual and Rationality* (Beverly Hills: Sage Publications, 1983).

66.This would be particularly illuminating because the National Government has since reversed the deprofessionalization policies of the Fourth Labour Government by allocating $5 million dollars for social work training and education.

67. Easton.

68. DSW, *Institutional Racism.*

69. DSW, *Management Plan, 1987.*

70. Johnson.

71. DSW, *Contracting for Social Services.*

72. Fraser.

73. DSW, *Review of the Social Work Division: Report of a Working Party* (Wellington: Department of Social Welfare, December, 1982); DSW, *Institutional Racism*; DSW, *The Organisation of Social Work Services*; Raoul Ketko, *Social Work Developments in England 1981/1982: The Nuffield Report* (Wellington: Department of Social Welfare, July, 1982).

74. DSW, *Institutional Racism.*

75. David Howe, *Social Workers and their Practice in Welfare Bureaucracies* (Hants, England: Gower Publishing Company, 1986), 2.

Postscript

Although the Fourth Labour Government lost the election in 1990, the restructuring of New Zealand social services from a welfare state to a welfare society continued unabated by the policies enacted by the new National Government. In fact, the restructuring swiftly accelerated under the new Ministers of Finance and Social Welfare. There are few remnants of the welfare state remaining in New Zealand. Most universal benefits have been abolished. In the first sweep of National Government changes the family benefit was discontinued, means testing was applied to all but a few social services and the waiting period for unemployment benefits was extended. National's Minister of Finance openly declared her expectation that the top third of all income earners in New Zealand would assume full responsibility for their own costs of housing, health, higher education and social welfare services. This removes them from receiving the benefits of state supported welfare services and threatens to diminish any commitment to their continuation.

Extension of means testing has resulted in narrowly defined criteria effectively limiting the number of eligible applicants. Under the guise of more effectively targeting those in need, scores of individuals have been excluded from benefits for which they were eligible just months before. The National Government has announced plans to adopt what is called the core family unit as a basis for calculating need. Details are not yet available but is is likely that women and children will be disadvantaged further. The National Party has further developed their concept of a *Kiwi Card* as a type of identity card designed to permit careful monitoring of service eligibility. The benefit levels that have been adopted approximate subsistence levels of support and preclude any possibility that those on a benefit will have the means to feel a part of and participate in New Zealand society. This expectation was reaffirmed by both Royal Commissions and aceepted by most New Zealanders.

The Department of Social Welfare has undergone several more restructurings since 1988. The six regional offices were reduced to four and reorganized. The administrative structures established in the first restructuring of 1986 were abolished as the Department assumed a more pervasive corporate identity. Managers are expected to produce outcomes based on quantifiable data. Predictably, rivalry issues and glaring examples of lack of coordination are reported with growing regularity in the press as loyalty to public service is replaced with loyalty to compartmentalized units.

A powerful and potentially effective means of participation in decision making and mechanisms to establish a true partnership with the community were lost when the National Government made the decision to dis-establish the Social Welfare Commission, the District Executive Committees and the Institutional Management Committees. The Government felt these structures demanded a too high level of expenditure and could be replaced by informal consultation based on existing networks and relationships.

The practice of social work in the Department has been further limited to investigation of child abuse and neglect with increased monitoring and coordination functions as the provisions of the *whanau* decision making process mandated by the Children, Young Persons and their Families Act of 1989 are implemented. The efforts to establish a bicultural model of practice has made considerable process despite numerous setback in funding, staffing and logistics. The dilemmas of high work load, ever increasing demands for child protection services, staff turnover and loss of experienced and qualified staff continue to plague the Department.

Perhaps the dark underpinnings of the policies of the Fourth Labour Government mobilized the social work community. The National Association of Social Workers reported a 30% rise in membership and a more active than ever association rank and file. Their efforts were given an added impetus when the Minister of Social Welfare expressed concern with the low number of qualified social workers in the Department and announced funding to support social work education and training. The package was estimated to be worth $5million and represented support for the continued professsionalization of social work but more importantly, it was viewed as governmental recognition of the contribution of social work to the social services.

The New Zealand Association of Social Workers' *Social Work Review* devoted its entire January 1993 issue to developments in social work professionalization. The Association's Board of Competency reported considerable success in gaining recognition for their work in fulfilling their commitment to competency and biculturalism in their assessment process.

The New Zealand Council on Education and Training in the Social Services essentially deregulated social work training by encouraging training pluralism and a three tier approach to social work courses. Their aim was to increase access for those already in the social services through programs outside the University system while supporting the responsiveness and initiatives of that system. The Council is beginning work on guidelines and procedures for accreditation since no accreditation process has been in place since the Social Work Training

Council was placed in remission by the Fourth labour Government's Minister of Social Welfare in 1985. The question of registration is once again being considered while at the same time educational programs are considering the merits of the *Recognition of Prior Learning* initiatives as a way of improving access for non-traditional and minority students.

Not all of the social work community is supportive of the revitalized professionalization effort. Some are concerned that the partnership with the community in decision making and service provision will be lost as social work regains and extends its professional power. Many social workers are supportive of the *whanau* decision making process mandated by the Children, Young Persons and their Families Act passed in 1989 as a valid effort toward partnership. They fear that the new emphasis on professionalism may threaten the progress that has been made toward a true partnership in decision making with the community. Considerations of the relationships between professionalization, centralization and a narrow definition of the social work task addressed in this book are acutely relevant as professionalization of social work develops under the conservative, New Right, policies of this National Government.

There is some evidence of public opposition to the extension of a tightly targeted means tested system of social welfare benefits and to the intrusiveness of eligibility requirements. New Zealanders are aghast at the exponential growth in requests for food and shelter. Voluntary agencies can not meet the increasing demands for service. Families are struggling to care for their ill, disabled and aged members without support from the state. Without benefits of right, as was the case under the welfare state, New Zealanders are struggling under an extreme interpretation of welfare society principles that demands they seek assistance from voluntary agencies and their communities. Many individuals and families are finding that assistance is not freely given nor without stigma, that giving is often arbitrary and selective and that they must be seen as 'deserving' in the eyes of the giver--often a difficult and humiliating experience.

The National Government policies have served to further accentuate income disparities to the benefit of a few at the cost of the many. Not only are low-income families burdened by the costs of essential services but moderate income families are struggling as well. The National Party came to office promising to 'redesign the welfare state'. They have effectively dismantled the remnants left by the Fourth Labour Government.

There are some glimmers of hope. Such dramatic change in less than a decade means many can easily recall what once was to compare with what is now. The energy of the memory might be harnessed, not to return to the past, but to informs a new future. The restructuring of New Zealand's social services must be reversed so that a majority of New Zealanders can participate, contribute and enjoy the benefits of society. This implementation of welfare society principles is particularly divisive, grossly unequal in its accruing benefits to a few and destroys the sense of community critical to a just society. New Zealand may have the energy and determination to reverse the current social policy direction and to embrace a more equitable one. It has shown itself capable of resourcefulness in the past. The scars of divisiveness, alienation and human suffering are not easily healed. New Zealand will have to deal with the folly of the last decade. It can only be hoped that other countries will learn by their experience. The welfare state and the principles upon which it is based have been shown to be fragile. They need to be nurtured and carefully monitored lest community responsibility give way to an individualism that threatens the social fabric. New Zealand is a prime example of what can transpire when the principles of the welfare state are abondoned and those of a welfare society are recklessly adopted.

Appendix

I	Research Materials: Demographic Information and Interview Schedule
II	Sample Letter of Negotiation
III	Correspondence with Dame Ann Hercua
IV	Excerpts from *Management Plan, 1986*
V	Excerpts from *Management Plan, 1987*
VI	Excerpts from *Corporate Management Plan, 1988*
VII	Summary of Recommendations: *Puao-Te-Ata-Tu*
VIII	Circular Memo, 1986/240: New Direction in Management
IX	Summary of Research Activities: Napier District Office
X	Summary of Research Activities: Porirua District Office
XI	Excepts from *Future Direction in Social Work*

Appendix I
Research Materials: Demographic Information and Interview Schedule

DEMOGRAPHIC INFORMATION

1988 Research Project
Angie Barretta-Herman
Massey University

Name____________________
Position____________________
Date of Appointment________
Acting____Permanent________

Employment History

1. Please list below your social services employment history prior to joining the department:

From - to (in years)	Employer	Brief description of responsibilities including number of supervisees

continue on separate page if necessary

2. Please list below your employment history with the Department by position and listing the District Office

From - to (in years)	District Office	Brief description of responsibilities including number of supervisees

continue on separate page if necessary

3. How do you describe your professional affiliation? Administrator, Social Services Administrator, Social Worker, Community Worker, Residential Social Worker, other?____________________

4. List any professional organisations to which you belong:

____

____

____

____

5. Do you hold a CQSW?yes__no___If yes, year awarded___________

6.List below any academic qualifications or training or certifications you have acquired

Qualification	Year Completed	Name of Training Institution

7. List below the meetings, conferences, seminars, or reports you see as significant in the development of decisions within the department about regionalisation, bi-culturalism, community approaches, ect.:

Year	Meeting, conference, seminar, report etc.	How were you involved?

____________________continue on separate page if necessary

Please complete and return to me prior to your scheduled interview if possible. Allow 5-7 days transit time.

Thank you for your cooperation

abh

INTERVIEW SCHEDULE

JUNE 1988

Below is the schedule of open-ended questions to be addressed to the Regional Directors of Alternative Care and Social Services. The interviews will be taped(if permission is obtained) and transcribed. Content analysis of the interviews will followed accepted methodological procedures. Confidentiality, of course, is an objective but is limited because of the small number of individuals involved and their position.

The interviews are part of the research project on the impact of regionalization on social work services. The objective is to gain an understanding of the process of organizational change as outlined in the reviews, reports and plans published by the Department over the past two-three years which outline the philosophy and operationalization of the move to regionalization as part of the implementation of Puau-te-Ata-tu recommendations, the move to "community"/community development activities and devolution or responsibility for social services.

The interviews with the REOs are preceeded by a questionnaire to elicit statistical and demographic information. This is done to facilitate the interview by removing the necessity to obtain basic factual information during the interview itself.

The interview will focus on "public" information but of necessity will elicit attitudes, comments and evaluations that might be considered by the interviewee as "private". Throughout the interview, the interviewee is as in control and able to ask not to be quoted, etc. As well the researcher is bound by professional ethics to insure that any quotes are not identifiable. As well, any interviewee can request to view the draft of the interviews for vetting.

The Questions

PHILOSOPHY

1. What do you see as the objectives of regionalization? Why was it proposed at that particular time?

2. How does regionalisation reflect the recommendations of Pua-te-Ata-tu? the move to community/community development? devolution?

3. What do you think are the essential aspects of the move from a "case-oriented" social work to a "community oriented" social work?

4. What changes have been implemented in your region as a result of these initiatives?

5. What has been the positive reactions of the social work staff to the implimented changes? the proposed changes?

6. What has been the negative reactions of the social work staff to the implemented changes? the proposed changes?

7. How has the philiosophy guiding the provision of social services and particularly social work services changed? changing?

8. What do you see as the objectives for social work services that were proposed at the A.D.'s August Conference in Hamilton on "Future Directions for Social Work"?

ORGANISATIONAL CHANGES

1. What impacts has the regionalization made on the delivery of social work services?

2. In what areas do you think regionalization has moved the departments services closer to being more responsible? accessible? community oriented?

3. What types of accountability mechansims have been put in place to reflect the community focus? What is being planned?

MANAGERIAL SUPPORTS

1. Participatory Management has been seen as an essential ingredient of this process. How is this change from an administrative management style to a participatory one being planned?

2. What reactions to this style have been encountered?

3. How available is in-service training &/or support for outside training?

SOCIAL WORK SERVICES

1. How would you characterize the approach to social work services in place in this department? and how do you see it changing?

2. There has been a substantial increase in trained social workers at the direct service level in DSW over the past six -eight years. Do you think this is influencing the acceptance of a more community based approach to social work services.

3. The "patch system" has been utilized in DSW social work for years. What are its basic principles? Is a "community based approach" different? How?

That is all the questions that I have for you. Are there some points you would like to make that would further my understanding of the issues, dilemmas or conflicts that are facing statutory social work services during this period of major reorganization?

abh

Appendix II
Sample Letter of Negotiation

22 September 1988

Dear

Enclosed you will find a copy of the research proposal and the selected bibliography. Your interest in the project and willingness to consider you and your staff participating in the research is most appreciated particularly because of your interest in Hadley's theories. From our discussion Tuesday it is clear to me that you and your staff could provide valuable insights into a community approach to social work practice.

The format of the participant observation phase would include semi-structured interviews with you as the director, the senior social worker and each of the team members, as well as with key members of staff critical to the team's operation. These interviews would be audio-taped if permission is granted by the interviewee and conventional confidentiality guidelines would be observed in the handling, transcription and summaries of the tapes.

The format of the participation with the individual team members would be by negotiation. The focus of the participation would be to provide for research purposes an opportunity to see "practice in action."

Also, a review of relevant documents, such as monthly reports, reports to special meetings, case notes, etc. would be necessary. You mentioned some reports on the implementation of a "patch system"/community approach that you felt would be relevant as well.

Because of work responsibilities at the university, it would be preferable if the week I was there with you was the first week in November (beginning with October 31st). If this is not possible, a split week would have to be arranged to coincide as much as possible with the first two weeks in November.

I appreciate the consideration you and your staff are giving to this request which I am certain can contribute to the field of social work. I look forward to your reply.

Sincerely,

Angie Barretta-Herman

Appendix III
Correspondence with Dame Ann Hercus

NEW ZEALAND MISSION
TO THE UNITED NATIONS
ONE UNITED NATIONS PLAZA
NEW YORK, N. Y. 10017

22 September 1989

Ms Angeline Barretta Herman, MSW MBA
Lecturer in Social Work
Massey University
PALMERSTON NORTH

Dear Ms Barretta Herman

Thank you for your letter of 7 August 1989. I regret that I am unable to assist you with an interview; nor (in part because I am not in New Zealand) can I give you copies of speeches, etc., or access to my archives. I made a decision not to give interviews about my previous positions as a Cabinet Minister when I retired from politics (this includes academic interviews) and this is a firm decision to which I am holding, certainly for as long as I am the UN Ambassador, and possibly longer. I hope you understand.

My kind regards to Graeme Fraser.

Yours sincerely

Ann Hercus
Permanent Representative

Appendix IV
Excerpts from *Management Plan, 1986*

This is the Department of Social Welfare's first formal Management Plan. I have decided to produce the plan to provide both management and staff with a single statement of the extensive changes which are being made in the Department's administrative structure and style of management. The issuing of the plan is one of the new developments planned for the year ahead.

It may be helpful for me to introduce this first plan by describing the challenges which confront the Department, and the rationale for the developments I have set in train.

The Department of Social Welfare was formed in 1972 to bring together the Child Welfare Division of the Department of Education and the Social Security Department. This was a complex operation — and while much progress has been made in forming a new entity, some of the early and inevitable tensions are not yet fully resolved.

Further, the Department has had to cope with the effects of a period of major social change, the rapidity of which is without precedent. It is hardly surprising then, that the Department has come under increasing fire for inadequate performance of its mission and inadequate feeling for its clients and staff.

I accept that the Department is seen as bureaucratic, impersonal and mono-cultural — and that communication is a problem. But, though such an image does not do justice to dedicated staff who have coped with heavy work demands under very difficult conditions, we must make substantial changes.

> **We need a positive, action-oriented organisation, an organisation more flexible in operation, and more sensitive to clientele and staff.**

To achieve this goal I have been grappling with two sets of problems: (1) how to create a structure for the organisation that will make major improvement to the delivery of service possible and, (2) how to develop the Department as an organisation.

Structural Change: The Six Regions

I had to accept responsibility for making an urgent decision about what the department's basic structure should be. The principle guiding my decision was one that surfaced in many criticisms of our performance. This was that decision-making had to be taken closer to clients and staff — hence the establishment of the six regions.

The structure being implemented now will allow delegation of authority to match responsibility so that District Offices can have the necessary autonomy. It will permit a much clearer definition of function and give substance to the management of people as a firm commitment. It will also allow for management reappraisals, and for consultation with staff on the organisation detail.

Our mission is to provide a service which gives best effect to the social welfare policies of Government.

Our Commitment
Our commitment is to maintain a Department which is efficient and flexible in operation, ethical and sensitive to the needs of clientele and staff, and which provides services which are culturally appropriate.

Our Approach
Our approach to this mission will be a "people approach".

We believe that our organisation will work best when it is suitably organised, well managed and adequately staffed:

— to give good service to clients.

— to enhance the chance that each member of the staff will grow in his or her job.

THE NEW DIRECTION IN MANAGEMENT

The Management approach we have adopted is:—

- To provide leadership:
  — which demonstrates a commitment to the maintenance of good morale.
  — in the development of a Department that is flexible, and sensitive and responsive to the needs of clientele and staff.
  — which helps develop a staff in which managers meet the obligation to achieve tasks, build teams, develop individuals and promote the interests of the organisation.
- To brief (and check understanding) and to consult (and report back on outcomes) both within a formal system and informally as a normal feature of working relationships.
- To monitor and evaluate the performance of tasks, and of compliance with the goals and objectives of the Department, balancing this against the need to give personal support to individuals and groups.
- To accept the responsibility to ensure that the training needs of personnel are met.

DEPARTMENT OF SOCIAL WELFARE STRUCTURE

(The regional grouping of social welfare districts and associated facilities)

NOTE:
This is a provisional grouping for Regions until the Regional Directors take up their appointments and final decisions can be made.

HEAD OFFICE

- **Northern Region**
  - Whangarei
  - Takapuna
  - Auckland
  - Special Purpose Offices (3)*
  - Community Care Assessment Centre
  - Staff Training Centre
- **South/West Auckland Region**
  - Henderson
  - New Lynn
  - Manukau
  - Otahuhu
  - Papakura
  - Special Purpose Office**
  - Child Care Institutions (5)
- **Central North Region**
  - Hamilton
  - Taumaranui
  - Paeroa
  - Tauranga
  - Whakatane
  - Rotorua
  - Gisborne
  - Child Care Institutions (2)
- **Central Region**
  - Wairoa
  - Napier
  - Hastings
  - New Plymouth
  - Wanganui
  - Palmerston North
  - Child Care Institutions (4)
  - Staff Training Centre
- **Central South Region**
  - Masterton
  - Wellington
  - Porirua
  - Lower Hutt
  - Blenheim
  - Nelson
  - Child Care Institutions (2)
  - Staff Training Centre
- **Southern Region**
  - Greymouth
  - Christchurch
  - Timaru
  - Dunedin
  - Invercargill
  - Child Care Institutions (4)

Organisation Development

In December last the Department began a programme to impress on all senior management the practical implications of our Mission Statement. All management will be made aware of the goals that all Divisions of the Department have in common; all management will develop a common vocabulary — and thus common expectations of managerial performance. And the change is from the "top" down.

As part of the new direction in management, managers will not only be accountable for achieving tasks, building teams, and developing the individual, but will also be accountable for promoting the interests of the organisation. Not the least of their concerns, then, will be to develop a spirit of co-operation and a sense of common purpose. High priority will be given to remove sources of tension and to create a sense of corporate identity.

Staff have been inadequately briefed and consulted in the past. We will develop formal systems of briefing and consulting backed by the kind of informal system that is generated by a willingness to co-operate in the work-place.

There are other improvements that must be made if there is to be better delivery of service to clients and greater job satisfaction for staff. Those that have been accorded greatest priority feature in the timetable of this Management Plan.

The achievement of all these changes will require a special commitment to training throughout the organisation. Training needs created by the new directions in management will be met. Induction and specialist training will be improved. Training throughout the Department will be co-ordinated.

Finally, the Department will be making a commitment to forward planning based on sound research.

For the staff of the Department, the changes set out in this plan will alter the familiar organisational framework and familiar ways of doing things. Inevitably this will produce some discomfort and even feelings of threat — but it will also pose a challenge. The commitment of staff, at all levels of the Department, will be necessary for that challenge to be met and the purposes of the change to be achieved.

J. W. Grant
Director-General

Appendix V
Excerpts from *Management Plan, 1987*

ORGANISATIONAL STRUCTURE

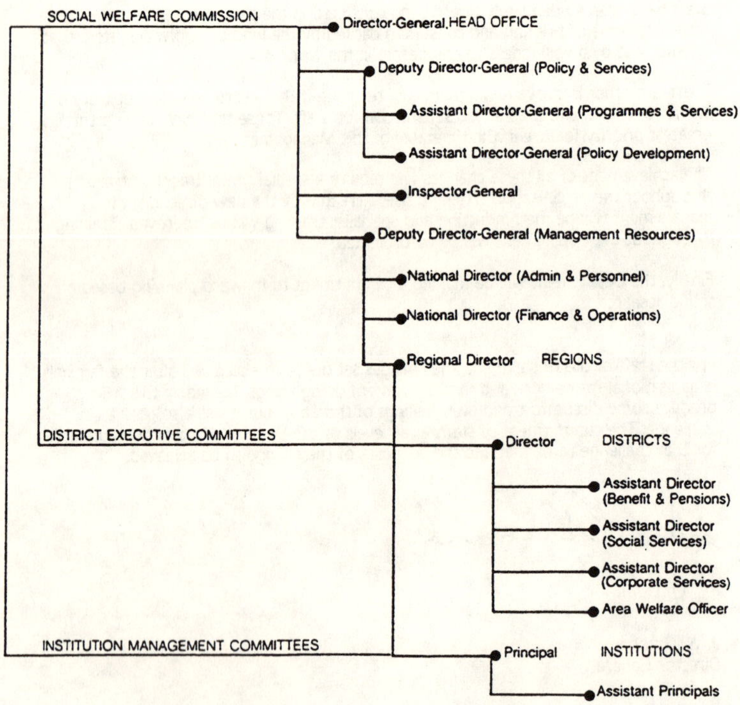

Appendix VI
Excerpts from *Corporate Management Plan, 1988*

MISSION

OUR MISSION is to provide a quality service to clients which gives best effect to the social welfare policy objectives of the government.

The Department of Social Welfare is **accountable** to its Minister for the efficient performance of its mission.

To provide a quality service the Department is required to be **responsive** to its clients by:

- ensuring that client needs are understood and met;
- involving local communities in the planning and delivery of services.

The Department is **committed** to assist staff to achieve their potential by training and development and reward them appropriately for their effort and performance.

GUIDING PRINCIPLES

THE ACHIEVEMENT of our mission is guided by two principles:

PUAO-TE-ATA-TU

- To attack all forms of cultural racism in New Zealand that result in the values and lifestyle of the dominant group being regarded as superior to those of other groups, especially Maori, by:

  (a) Providing leadership and programmes which help develop a society in which the values of all groups are of central importance to its enhancement; and

  (b) Incorporating the values, culture and beliefs of the Maori people in all policies developed for the future of New Zealand.

- To attack and eliminate deprivation and alienation by:

  (a) Allocating an equitable share of resources;

  (b) Sharing power and authority over the use of resources;

  (c) Ensuring legislation which recognises social, cultural and economic values of all cultural groups and especially Maori people; and

  (d) Developing strategies and initiatives which harness the potential of all people, and especially Maori people, to advance.

EQUAL OPPORTUNITY

- **Eliminate** all discriminatory practices, based on gender, race, ethnic origin, sexual preference, disability or age.

ORGANISATION

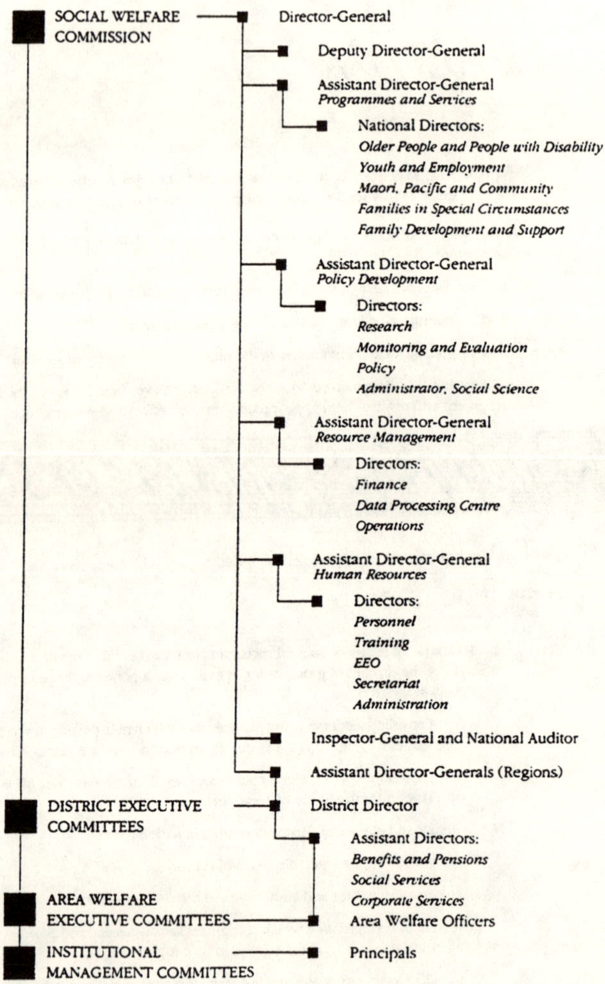

Appendix VII
Summary of Recommendations: *Puao-Te-Ata-Tu*

Recommendation 1 (Guiding Principles and Objectives)

We recommend that the following social policy objective be endorsed by the Government for the development of Social Welfare policy in New Zealand:

"Objective

To attack all forms of cultural racism in New Zealand that result in the values and lifestyle of the dominant group being regarded as superior to those of other groups, especially Maori, by:

(a) Providing leadership and programmes which help develop a society in which the values of all groups are of central importance to its enhancement; and

(b) Incorporating the values, cultures and beliefs of the Maori people in all policies developed for the future of New Zealand."

Recommendation 2

We recommend that the following operational objective be endorsed:

"To attack and eliminate deprivation and alienation by:

(a) Allocating an equitable share of resources.

(b) Sharing power and authority over the use of resources.

(c) Ensuring legislation which recognises social, cultural and economic values of all cultural groups and especially Maori people.

(d) Developing strategies and initiatives which harness the potential of all of its people, and especially Maori people, to advance."

Recommendation 3 (Accountability)

We recommend that:

(a) The Social Security Commission be abolished and be replaced by a Social Welfare Commission. The new Commission shall consist of four principal officers of the department, two persons nominated by the Minister of Maori Affairs after consultation with the tribal authorities, and two persons nominated by the Minister of Women's Affairs. The Minister of Social Welfare may wish to consult the Minister of Pacific Island Affairs on the desirability of a ninth appointee.

(b) The Social Welfare Commission, either at the request of the Minister or on its own motion shall:

(i) advise the Minister on the development and changes in policy and scope relating to social security, child and family welfare, community welfare of disabled persons and other functions of the Department of Social Welfare;

(ii) advise the Minister on the co-operation and co-ordination of social welfare activities among any organisations, including Departments of State and other agencies of the Crown or by any other organisations or tribal authority; and

(iii) consult at least once a year with representatives of tribal authorities in a national hui;

(iv) recommend to the Minister the appointment of and oversee the work of District Executive Committees for each Social Welfare District Office, and Management Committees for each Social Welfare Institution, and allocate appropriate budgets according to priorities set by these Committees.

(c) District Executive Committees should be formed in each Social Welfare department district. Each Committee shall consist of up to 9 persons appointed from the community on the nomination of the Maori tribal authorities and the nominations of other community interests. The Director of Social Welfare (in person) and the Director of Maori Affairs are to be members. The Chairperson shall be one of the non-public service members. Members are to be paid in the normal way.

(d) The District Executive Committees shall be appointed by the Minister of Social Welfare under S13 of the Department of Social Welfare Act 1971, and shall report to the Social Welfare Commission and be responsible for assessing and setting priorities in consultation with the various tribal authorities for the funding of specific family and community welfare projects and initiatives in their areas; for preparing draft budgets for these projects for final approval by the Social Welfare Commission; and for monitoring and reviewing the effectiveness of such projects and initiatives and the appropriateness and quality of the Department's range of services to the district it serves.

Recommendation 4 (Deficiencies in Law and Practice)

We recommend the following amendments to legislation:

(a) The Social Welfare Act 1971 be amended to provide for the establishment of the Social Welfare Commission.

(b) The Social Security Act 1964 be amended to provide for the following:

(i) Abolition of the Social Security Commission.

(ii) Clarify the law so that there is no impediment to verification of age and marital status being established from Marae or tribal records and that a Maori custom marriage is recognised for the purposes of the Social Security Act.

(iii) Restructuring of the unemployment benefit so that it can provide greater incentive to work, whether part time or full time, training or entrepeneurial initiative and to provide the flexibility through discretion for the Social Welfare Commission to develop variations of or alternatives to the unemployment benefit that are tailored to the needs of the individual.

(iv) Social Security benefit child supplements be made more readily available where the care of Maori children is transferred from natural parents to the grandparents or other relatives.

(v) Eligibility to orphans benefit provisions be extended to include the claims of unsupported children, so that payment can be made to whanau members who are looking after these children.

(c) The Children and Young Persons Act 1974 be reviewed having regard to the following principles:

(i) That in the consideration of the welfare of a Maori child, regard must be had to the desirability of maintaining the child within the child's hapu;

(ii) that the whanau/hapu/iwi must be consulted and may be heard in Court of appropriate jurisdiction on the placement of a Maori child;

(iii) that Court officers, social workers, or any other person dealing with a Maori child should be required to make inquiries as the the child's heritage and family links;

(iv) that the process of law must enable the kinds of skills and experience required for dealing with Maori children and young persons hapu members to be demonstrated, understood and constantly applied.
The approach in recommendation (iv) will require appropriate training mechanisms for all people involved with regard to customary cultural preferences and current Maori circumstances and aspirations;

(v) that prior to any sentence or determination of a placement the Court of appropriate jurisdiction should where practicable consult, and be seen to be consulting with, members of the child's hapu or with persons active in tribal affairs with a sound knowledge of the hapu concerned;

(vi) that the child or the child's family should be empowered to select Kai tiaki or members of the hapu with a right to speak for them;

(vii) that authority should be given for the diversion of negative forms of expenditure towards programmes for positive Maori development through tribal authorities; these programmes to be aimed at improving Maori community service to the care of children and the relief of parents under stress.

Recommendation 5

We recommend that the Social Security Act be reviewed by the Social Welfare Commission with a view to removing complexity of conditions of eligibility and achieving rationalisation of benefit rates.

Recommendation 6 (Institutions)

We recommend that:

(a) Management Committees drawn from local communities be established for each Social Welfare institution;

(b) The Committees shall be appointed by the Minister of Social Welfare under S13 Department of Social Welfare Act 1971 and shall be responsible to the Social Welfare Commission for the direction of policy governing individual institutions, allocating resources, making recommendations on the selection of staff and for ensuring that programmes are related to needs of children and young persons and are culturally appropriate;

(c) Each Committee shall consist of up to 9 persons appointed to represent the community on the nomination of the Maori tribal authorities and on the nomination of other community interests and with one member to represent the Director-General of Social Welfare and one to represent the Secretary of Maori Affairs. The

Chairperson will be a non-public servant member. Members are to be paid in the normal way;

(d) As a priority the Committees shall address the question of alternative community care utilising the extended family;

(e) The Committees shall have the right to report to the Social Welfare Commission on matters of departmental policy affecting the institutions.

(f) Funds be provided to enable children from institutions to be taken back to their tribal areas for short periods to give them knowledge of the history and nature of the areas and to teach them Maori language and culture;

(g) Provision be made to enable young people to be discharged to home or community care and to continue to attend schools attached to Social Welfare institutions.

Recommendation 7 (Maatua Whangai)

We recommend that:

(a) The Maatua Whangai programme in respect of children return to its original focus of nurturing children within the family group;

(b) Additional funding be allocated by the Department to the programme for board payments and grants to tribal trusts for tribal authorities to strengthen whanau/hapu/iwi development;

(c) The funding mechanism be through the tribal authorities and be governed by the principle that board payments should follow the child and be paid direct to the family of placement, quickly and accurately and accounted for to the Department in respect of each child. The programmes should be monitored for suitability of placement and quality of care;

(d) The level of the reimbursement grant for volunteers be increased to a realistic level.

Recommendation 8 (Funding Initiatives)

We recommend that:

(a) The Departments of Social Welfare, Education, Labour and Maori Affairs in consultation with tribal authorities promote and develop initiatives aimed at improving the skill and work experience of the young long term unemployed;

(b) The proposed Social Welfare Commission meet with Maori authorities to consider areas of needed investment in urban and rural districts to promote the social and cultural skills of young Maori people and to promote training and employment opportunities for them.

Recommendation 9 (Recruitment and Staffing)

We recommend that:

(a) Job descriptions for all staff acknowledge where appropriate the requirements necessary for the officer to relate to the community including the needs of Maori and Maori community;

(b) Interview panels should include a person or persons knowledgeable in Maoritanga;

(c) The Department provide additional training programmes to develop understanding and awareness of Maori and cultural issues among departmental staff;

(d) Additional training positions be established for training in Maoritanga;
(e) Provision be made for the employment of staff to provide temporary relief while other staff attend training;
(f) Assistance be provided to local Maori groups offering Maoritanga programmes for staff; and
(g) The Department accredit appropriate Maori people to assist in field and reception work.

Recommendation 10 (Training)

We recommend that:

(a) The Department take urgent steps to improve its training performance in all aspects of its work;
(b) The State Services Commission undertake an analysis of the training needs of all departments which deliver social services;
(c) The State Services Commission assess the extent to which tertiary social work courses are meeting cultural needs for those public servants seconded as students to the courses;
(d) The Department in consultation with the Department of Maori Affairs identify suitable people to institute training programmes to provide a Maori perspective for training courses more directly related to the needs of the Maori people;
(e) (i) additional training positions be established for training in Maoritanga at the district level;
(ii) provision be made for the employment of staff to provide temporary relief while other staff attend training;
(iii) assistance be provided to local Maori groups offering Maoritanga programmes.

Recommendation 11 (Communication)

(a) The Department ensure appropriate advice to its information staff on the specific public relations and information needs of particular ethnic groups, and to assist with interpretation and translation into Maori;
(b) Immediate steps be taken to continue to improve the design and function of public reception areas;
(c) An immediate review be undertaken by an appropriate firm of consultants of the range of all application forms to reduce their complexity;
(d) That funds be allocated to Social Welfare district offices with a high Maori population to provide some remuneration to Maori people who provide assistance to Social Welfare staff in dealing with Maori clients;
(e) A toll free calling service to Social Welfare district offices be installed to enable all Social Welfare clients living outside toll-free calling areas to ring the Department free-of-charge (rural areas);
(f) A general funding programme be established which could be drawn on by rural areas for community self-help projects. These funds could be used for example, to employ a community worker, or to provide back-up funds for voluntary work.

APPENDIX VIII
CIRCULAR MEMORANDUM 1986/240 (adapted)
NEW DIRECTION IN MANAGEMENT:
COMMUNICATION: FORMAL SYSTEMS FOR BRIEFING AND CONSULTING

INTRODUCTION

1. The DSW 1986 Management Plan states that the new management approach would be to brief (and check understanding) and to consult and report back on outcome) both within formal systems and informally as a normal feature of working relationships. The Department is committed to develop the briefing and consulting processes.

2. This circular sets out how the department's formal systems for briefing and consulting are to operate.

2.1 The purpose of briefing is to ensure that information moves "downwards" in the organisation so that staff are informed in advance of forthcoming changes and that they understand what, if anything, is expected of them.

2.2 The purpose of consulting is to ensure movement of information "upwards," thus enabling the advice and opinion of staff to be sought as a guide to decision making.

2.3 Formal briefing and consulting systems are designed to cause the least possible interference with the very effective systems which exist in some offices.

6. Consultation will occur when there are events of major significance such as proposed changes in departmental policy or administration which, if implemented, will lead to significant changes in the working environment for departmental staff.

When this is to happen, staff will whenever possible, be given the opportunity to comment on the implications of the proposals and plans *before* final decisions are made thus enabling departmental management to be better informed about staff views of likely consequences if a certain policy or administrative change is implemented. Sometimes for reasons such as timing, consultation will occur after a decision has been taken. In this instance consultation becomes the seeking of advice of information on the outcome of the original decision so that changes can be make, if appropriate.

7. The process of consultation is ongoing and takes place at various levels in the department. Sometimes everyone in the department is consulted, on other occasions only group(s) which have a direct interest will be consulted. The decision on who is to consulted and at what level has, of necessity, to be left to the judgment of Head Office management which will only use the consultative process for major discussion papers. it is expected that *all* managers will have a consulting process for issues which are confined to their own region, office or institution.

WHEN CONSULTATION WILL NOT OCCUR

8. There will be occasions (e.g. a major change in Government policy) when consultation will not occur because advice from staff will not be able to alter the outcome. In these circumstances, there is no point in asking for advice when the die is cast.

WHAT CONSULTATION DOES NOT OFFER

9. It is important for staff to appreciate that consultation provides a means for their view to be heard. Those views will be considered as an input in the decision-making process, but there can be no assurance they will be implemented. Ultimately managers are accountable and sometime it will be necessary for them to take decision which do not coincide with the views of many of the staff who have been consulted.

APPENDIX X
Summary of Research Activities: Napier District Office

Day One

8:30 Meeting with Team Members to plan theweek
9:45 Discussion with community worker
10:30 Interview with Chairperson of DEC
11:45 Discussion with Senior Social Worker regarding history of team and community development
1:00 Accompany Budget Liason Officer to community display and consumer credit
2:30 Discussion with District Director about the research and its possible implications
3:30 Interview with Assistant Director: Social Services

Day Two

8:30-12 Staff meeting followed by discussion on *Future Direction for Social Work*
12:00 Discussion with Assistant Director: Social Services regarding social work response to*Future Directions*
1:00 Discussion with Intake Supervisor regarding proposed Children and Young Persons and Families Act.
2:30 Interview with Team Social Worker
3:30 On-site visit to Women's Health Centre

Day Three

8:30 On-site visit to Contact Centre for unemployed
9:30 Visit to Petane Marae for *hui* on Join Marae Enterprises project with 65 trainees and 8 tutors
2:30 Return to Contact Centre for meeting with work coordinator, youth and volunteers
4:00 Corollary interview with child abuse social worker

Day Four

8:30 Accompany Maatua Whangai to *hui* with *kaumtua* of the Maraenui surburban development
10:30 Interview with TeamSenior Social Worker
1:00 Interview with Senior Social Worker: Alternative Care
3:00 Interview with Team Maatua Whangai worker

Day Five

8:30 Attended District Management Team
10:30 Interview with Budget Liason Worker
1:00 Review departmental documents
3:00 Closing interview with Team Senior

Appendix X
Summary of Research Activities: Porirua District Office

Day One

8:30 Plan week with Supervising Senior Social Worker
9:30 Interview with Assistant Director: Social Services
10:30 Team Meeting regarding planning child abuse intervention
11:30 Discussion of week's research activities with team
1:00 Discussion with Maori Social Work
1:30 Interview with Senior Social Worker
3:30 Interview with Pacific Island Social Worker
4:00 Travel to court with team social worker to register warrant for intervention with court
4:30 Interview with Senior Social Worker: Court Team

Day Two

8:30 interview with Senior Social Worker: Coast Team
9:00 Multi-disciplinary meeting in Family Home regarding foster children in care
11:00 Discussion with team member regarding outcome of warrant
11:30 Discussion with Youth Aid Officer
1:00 Allocation Meeting with Senior Social Workers
2:00 Management Team Meeting

Day Three

8:30 Review unreleased Ailini Report
9:00 Discussion regarding child abuse procedures
9:30 Home visit with team social worker re. child care
10:30 Interview with Team Social Worker:1
1:00 Interview with Team Social Worker:2
2:30 Team Staff Meeting
3:30 Discussion with Pacific Island Social Worker
4:00 Review district documentation

Day Four

8:30 Discussion with Pacific Island Team Social Worker
9:30 Formal interview with Senior Social Worker
11:30 Discussion with District Director
1:30 Review district documentation
2:30 Formal interview with Team Social Worker:3

Day Five

8:30 Review of district documentation
10:30 Interview with Team Social Worker:4
1:00 Discussion with Supervising Senior Social Worker
2:30 Closing meeting with team members

Appendix XI
Excerpts from Future Direction in Social Work

ALL SOCIAL WORK STAFF

FUTURE DIRECTIONS FOR SOCIAL WORK

INTRODUCTION

1. Social work in the department is in a time of change and new directions. This is an overview paper to identify policy issues to do with support for frontline staff, and to outline a process for action.

2. First it is important to affirm the dedication to the point of burn-out of social workers whose role is to intervene in situations that society would like to ignore. This work is done under the pressure of the seriousness and complexity of the new cases continually presenting at the door. The countless times when long hard hours go into preventing tragedy are seldom recognised. It is the occasions when systems and practice break down which hit the headlines.

3. Secondly is the fact that the practice of social work is undergoing a radical change. Acceptance of the principles of Puao-te-Ata-tu implies that every familiar role and activity needs to be re-examined in the light of a partnership of decision-making and resource sharing with the community and in particular with Maori whanau, hapu and iwi.

4. Thirdly, the department must acknowledge that the task of fixing perceived shortcomings in social work is a dual responsibility. Social workers strive for excellence in their practice but they depend on managers to provide adequate supervision, training and resource allocation.

THE CYCLE OF POLICY, MANAGEMENT AND PRACTICE

5. Social work practice can be effective only when it is supported by good management and informed by clear policy. Good policy arises from a sensitive practice response to client needs.

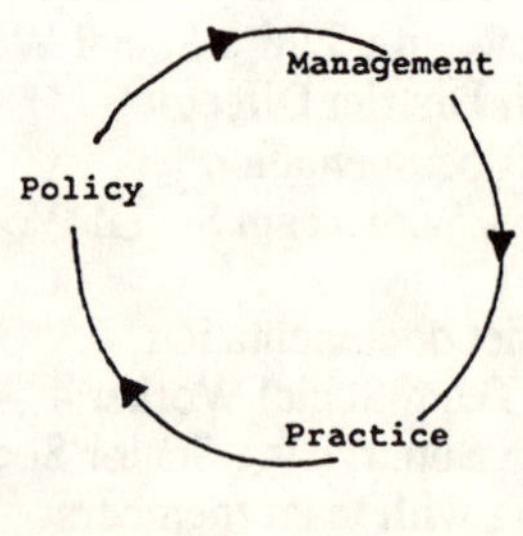

0021d/0411d

6. Restructuring and the challenge of new directions has meant that there has been a lack of policy statements for social work on:

   (a) The implications of Puao-te-Ata-tu;
   (b) goals and values for bicultural social work services;
   (c) priorities for service delivery;
   (d) knowledge and skills requirements;
   (e) training;
   (f) roles and tasks; and
   (g) workload management and resource allocation.

7. A lack of policy direction has had consequences for all levels of social work. For social work practitioners these deficiencies have led to a high turnover of staff in both frontline and senior positions, workload stress, new and inexperienced staff having to cope with crisis situations, uncertainty about what is expected of them and feelings of being unsupported and unsure about the future.

8. Social work managers have had little guidance on how to meet new expectations placed on them. These expectations include developing partnership models with the community; new approaches to staff recruitment; balancing the needs for professional and cultural skills; deciding priorities for resource allocation; and clarifying the respective roles of social work managers and supervisors.

9. District directors faced with bulk allocations and the prospect of zero-based budgeting recognise that the trend to devolution may have an impact on planning social work resources. They also recognise their responsibility to provide skilled bicultural social work services and to support their managers with adequate resources for social work supervision and training. These tasks are compounded because at this point in the department's development it is impossible to foresee what the future shape of social work will be.

10. We need to establish a set of goals and values for bicultural social work services and then use the experience of frontline social work staff as the basis for practice-based policies.

11. The outcome will be a set of policy guidelines to clarify the mutual expectations which social workers and the department have of each other. These will also provide tools for management planning and will assist decisions about service priorities and equitable resource allocation for district and regional planning.

THE CONTEXT OF CHANGE

12. Positive things are happening. Many districts have already accepted the challenge of developing bicultural social work services. This includes new practice models, the establishment of Maori and Pacific Island social work teams, the involvement of local iwi in the recruitment and selection of social work staff, and the development of strong links with the Maori community through the Maatua Whangai programme.

0021d/0411d

13. The Maori, Pacific Island and Community Services Directorate in Head Office is preparing a position paper on bicultural services and for developing partnership with iwi.

14. The Residential Services Management Plan has provided the opportunity to develop planning to move resources and responsibility to a community base.

15. Head Office restructuring targetted to client groups will provide goals for specific programme outcomes and encourage further initiatives to develop preventive community-based services.

16. Once the new C & Y P Bill is finalised and enacted there will be clear models and procedures for work in areas of child protection and youth offending.

17. Numbers of children in care are reducing. This reflects increased and intense work to achieve goals of supporting children in their families in spite of the fact that child abuse referrals are increasing.

18. Decentralisation and the process of placing accountability for services at district level invite social workers to take a more proactive role in client advocacy. These include supporting work with iwi structures and re-examining direct services to determine when preventive community based services would better meet client needs.

CONSULTATION FOR FUTURE DIRECTIONS

19. As part of this change there are generic issues for social work as a service. The fundamental issue is that the department must develop truly bicultural social work services. Our services must be examined to give answers to the question:

    What are the practical implications of Puao-te-Ata-tu for providing appropriate social work services?

20. Developing policy for the future will mean finding answers to some other hard questions:

    What is the best mix of indirect and direct social services?

    What tasks require a social worker to do them?

    What skills and training will social workers need for the future?

    What standards are required for culturally sensitive, effective and ethical social work practice both within the department and in contracted organisations?

0021d/0411d

21. During 1988/89 the Principal Social Worker will consult with social work staff and prepare a Social Work Policy Development Plan. The aims of this process are to provide:

    (a) policies that support frontline staff;

    (b) tools for planning for social work managers; and
    (c) a basis for social work input to next year's Corporate Management Plan.

22. The consultation will include:

    (a) Goals and values for a bicultural social work service;
    (b) general guidelines for service priorities;
    (c) standards for knowledge, skills and practice;
    (d) definitions of roles and tasks;
    (e) training directions; and
    (f) workload management and resource allocation.

23. The outcome of the consultation will be guidelines which will be specific about expectations and will help inform managers in their planning.

24. Appendices to this paper give some starting points for consultation. They are intended as discussion drafts only and you are invited to scribble constructively all over them and pass on your thoughts to your A.D. They are:

    (a) Draft statement of goals and values;
    (b) additional notes on future directions;and
    (c) a framework for the development of practice standards

25. Stages in the consultation process will include a national workshop for A.D.'s, Principals and interested parties from Head and Regional Offices in August to ensure national co-ordination, and set specific goals and time-frames. We will need practitioner working groups to develop the more detailed papers.

26. The Principal Social Worker team will take an active leadership role and will consult social work staff in every office and institution during July through October.

27. The development of policy papers will be overseen by a small steering committee chaired by the Principal Social Worker and including representative staff from local and regional levels, Head Office Units and the PSA. This process will include co-ordination with programme goals of the Programmes and Services Directorates and integration of social work development into the department's corporate management planning.

28. The development of policy papers will be overseen by a small steering committee chaired by the Principal Social Worker and including representative staff from local and regional levels, Head Office Units and the PSA. This process will include co-ordination with programme goals of the Programmes and Services Directorates and integration of social work development into the department's corporate management planning.

0021d/0411d

CONCLUSION

29. The department's social workers have always been in the forefront of change and have a long tradition of advocacy for their clients. The department's new directions provide a renewed opportunity to shape policies that will help frontline staff achieve the best interests of clients and develop new structures and processes. Your input to this debate and planning will be crucial for determining the social work roles and tasks for the future.

Beverley Keall
Principal Social Worker

0021d/0411d

Glossary of Terms and Abbreviations

AD: Assistant Director - District Office Managerial position, in this thesis referred to as Assistant Director of Social Services.
Administrative Style of Management: Used by Administrative Review Committee to describe a style of management characterized by "administration of instruction top-down communication, emphasis on inputs" (See Chapter Five).
Alternative Care: Designation given to the development of community care programs for pre-adolescents as an alternative to institutionalization.
Biculturalism: *Puao-Te-Ata-Tu* interprets biculturalism within the Department of Social Welfare as "the sharing of responsibility and authority for decisions with appropriate Maori people" (Ministerial Advisory Committee, 1986:19:50).
CETSS: Council for Education and Training in the Social Services.
COGS: Community Organisation Grant Scheme. A joint funding scheme of the Departments of Labour and Social Welfare for community programs.
Community Services Funding: The funding allocation for community groups and programs distributed by the Department. In 1987 over 60 million dollars was distributed (Administrative Review Committee, 1987).
DSW: Department of Social Welfare.
EMG: Executive Management Group. Established in the restructuring of 1986 to include the Director-General, the two Deputy Directors-General and the four Assistant Director Generals. In 1988, the Regional Directors were redesignated Assistant Directors-Generals: Region and included in the membership.
hui :Meeting, usually on a Marae and conducted according to Maori protocol.
Institutional Principal: The senior administrative position in the Department's residential institutions.
iwi : Tribe.
Kaumatua: Respected Maori elder.
Kaupapa: Purpose, objective.
Komiti : Committee.
Korero : Talk, conversations, interviews.
Kuia : Maori women elders.
Maatua Whangai: A program established in 1983 by joint

effort of Department of Social Welfare Services and Maori Affairs to stem tide of young Maori into care.

NZASW: New Zealand Association of Social Workers.

NZCAB: New Zealand Citizens Advice Bureau.

NZCSS: New Zealand Council of Social Services.

NZFVWO: New Zealand Federation of Voluntary Welfare Organisations

NZPC: New Zealand Planning Council.

Pakeha: White New Zealanders of European ancestry.

powhiri : Formal ceremonial welcome conducted in accordance with Maori protocol.

PSA: Public Service Association.

REOs: Regional Executive Officers. The middle management positions in the newly established regional structure. In this book, REOs refer to those positions designated for Social Services and Alternative Care.

RMT: The Regional Management Team. It was comprised of the District Directors, the Institutional Principals, the Regional Director and selected REOs.

SSDs: Social Service Departments. The centralized local authority structure in Britain changed with the provision of social services following the recommendations of the 1968 Seebohm Report.

SAC: Social Advisory Council.

Social Welfare Commission: The major advisory body to the Department established in 1986 comprised of four officers of the Department, two people nominated by Minister of Maori Affairs and two persons nominated by the Minister of Women's Affairs. Replaced the Social Security Commission created in Department of Social Welfare Act 1971.

SSSW: Supervising Senior Social Worker.

SSW: Senior Social Worker, the first line field social work supervisor usually with staff of 3-5 direct line practitioners.

SW: Social worker, used here to designate the direct line or front-line practitioner whose responsibilities are direct practice with clients.

SWTC: Social Work Training Council.

Tangata whenua : Literally 'people of the land', refers to the indigenous population of New Zealand.

VOTP: Voluntary Organisation Grant Scheme - a Labour Department training program that provided paid positions for voluntary organizations.

Whanau : Extended family group.

SPELLING CONVENTIONS

Americanized spellings are used for selected words such as organization and professionalization throughout the text with the following exceptions: when the term appears in a title or direct quote that uses the British spelling and when the term appears in a quote from the respondents who used the preferred British spelling.

BIBLIOGRAPHY

Abbott, Max. "Death of the Voluntary Sector ." *Mental Health News* (February/March 1988): 3-5.

Abel-Smith, Brian. "The Major Problems of the Welfare State: Defining the Issues." In *The Welfare State and Its Aftermath*, ed. S. N. Eisenstadt and Ora Ahimeir, 31-43. London: Croom Helm, 1985.

Adams, Gerald, and Jay D. Schvaneveldt. *Understanding Research Methods*. New York: Longman Publishing, 1985.

Administrative Review Committee. *Performance and Efficiency in the Department of Social Welfare*. Wellington: Government Printer, 1987.

Allen, Graham. "Informal Networks of Care: Issues Raised by Barclay." *British Journal of Social Work* 14 (1985): 417-433.

Aotearoa Community Workers Association. "History of the Aotearoa Community Workers Association and Community Work Training National Proposal." *Kupu Kaimahi-A-Iwi: Newsletter of the Aotearoa Community Workers Association, Inc.* 1 (1989): 2-3.

Bagnall, C. *A Department of Social Welfare for New Zealand*. Wellington: Government Printer, 1968.

Bailey, Roy, and M. Brake, ed. *Radical Social Work*. New York: Pantheon Books, 1975.

Bamford, Terry. *Managing Social Work*. London: Tavistock Publications, 1982.

Barber, Benjamin. *Strong Democracy: Participatory Politics for a New Age*. Berkeley: University of California Press, 1984.

Barclay Report. *Social Workers: Their Role and Tasks*. Bedford Square Press, 1982.

Barretta-Herman. "Social Work at the Interface: The social worker in a Bureaucracy." *New Zealand Social Work Journal* 10:3 (1983): 16-18.

Barretta-Herman, Jeff Dougal, and Alastair Spearling. *The Relationship Between Regional Office and District Offices in the Central District.* Palmerston North: Department of Social Welfare, 1989.

Billis, David. *Welfare Bureaucracies: Their Design and Change in Response to Social Problems.* London: Heinemann Educational Books, 1984.

Birks, Stuart, and Srikanta Chatterjee, ed. *Introduction to New Zealand Economy.* Palmerston North: Dunmore Press, Ltd., 1988.

Black, J., R. Bowl, D. Burns, C. Critcher, G. Grant, and D. Stockford. *Social Work in Context.* London: Tavistock, 1983.

Boston, Jonathan. "Democratic Theory, Devolution and Accountability." In *Devolution and Accountability*, ed. J. Martin and J. Harper, 46-71. Wellington: G. P. Books, 1988.

______. "The Treasury and the Origins of Economic Advice." In *The Making of Rogernomics*, ed. Brian Easton, 68-91. Auckland, New Zealand: University Press, 1989.

______. "Reorganizing the Machinery of Government in New Zealand: Objectives and Outcomes." (Faculty of Commerce and Administration): Wellington: Victoria University, 1990.

______, ed. *The Decent Society? Essays in response to National's economic and social reforms.* Auckland, New Zealand: Oxford University Press, 1990.

______, and M. Holland, ed. *The Fourth Labour Government: Politics and policy in New Zealand.* Auckland, New Zealand: Oxford University Press, 1992.

Brake, Mike, and Roy Bailey, ed. *Radical Social Work and Practice.* London: Edward Arnold, 1980.

Brochadt, D. H. "Introduction." In *Social Policy and its Administration*, ed. Joanne Marie and Adrianne Wise, vii-xvi. Rushcutter's Bay, Australia: Pergamon Press, 1977.

Brodkin, Evelyn Z. *The False Promis of Administrative Reform: Implementing Quality Control in Welfare*. Philadelphia: Temple University Press, 1986.

Brook, Jane. "The Demise of the Social Work Training Council." Masters Thesis, Palmerston North, New Zealand: Massey University, 1988.

Brosnan, P., and D. Rea. "Rogernomics and the Labour Market." In *New Zealand Sociology*, 7. Sociology Department: Massey University, New Zealand, 1992.

Brown, P., R. Hadley, and K. J. White. "Appendix A: A case for Neighbourhood-based Social Work and Social Services." In *Social Workers: Their Role and Tasks*, ed. 1982 Barclay Report, 219-235. London: Bedford Square Press, 1982.

Buurman, Gary. "Issues on Social Welfare & Economic Inequality." In *The New Zealand Economy: Issues and Policies*, ed. Stuart Birks and Srikanta Chatterjee. Palmerston North: The Dunmore Press, 1988.

Carney, Thomas F. *Content Analysis*. Winnepeg: University of Manitoba, 1972.

Carson, Richard, and Richard Hennessey. *Social Programme Evaluation Unit*. Wellington: Department of Social Welfare, 1984.

Chamberlain, Edna, ed. *Change and Continuity in Australian Social Work*. Melbourne: Longman Cheshire Pty., 1988.

Chambers, Donald E. *Social Policy and Social Programs: A Method for the Practical Public Policy Analyst*. New York: Macmillan Publishing, 1986.

Clegg, Stewart, Paul Boreham, and Geoff Dow. *Class Politics and the Economy*. London: Routledge and Kegan Paul, 1986.

Clegg, Stewart, and David Dunkerley. *Organization, Class and Control*. London: Routledge and Kegan Paul, 1980.

Cnaan, Ram A., Yeheskel Hasenfeld, Avital Cnaan, and Jane Rafferty. "Cross-Cultural Comparison of Attitudes Toward Welfare-State Programs: Path Analysis With Log-Linear Models". *Social Indicators Research*, 29 (1993): 123-152.

Cody, John. "Personal Social Services." In *The April Report*, The Royal Commission on Social Policy, Vol. IV:234-250. Wellington: Government Printer, 1988.

Collins, Simon. "Rogernomics: The Economic Aftermath." In *The Making of Rogernomics*, ed. Brian Easton, 188-206. Auckland: University Press, 1989.

Compton, Beulah R., and Burt Galaway. *Social Work Processes*. 4th ed. Belmont, CA: Wadsworth Publishing Co., 1989.

Corrigan, Paul, and Peter Leonard. *Social Work Practice Under Capitalism: A Marxist Approach*. London: Macmillan Press, 1978.

Council for Education and Training in Social Services. *Education and Training in the Social Services: Interim Report*. Wellington: Council for Education and Training in the Social Services, 1988.

Dalziel, Paul. "The Economic Summit." In *The Making of Rogernomics*, ed. Brian Easton, 53-67. Auckland: University Press, 1989.

Daniels, Ken R. "Competent Health Social Work." Christchurch: University of Canterbury, Department of Social Work,1989.

Dargill, Giles and Brian Munday, ed. *Volunteers in the Personal Social Services*. London: Tavistock Publications, 1984.

Darracott, Peter, and Terry Kilmister. *Policy and Action in Voluntary Organisations*. Wellington: Community Services Institute, 1988.

Davey, Judith A. *Social Policy Options*. Wellington: New Zealand Planning Council, 1987.

Davey, Judith, and Maire Dwyer. *Meeting Needs in the Community: A Discussion Paper on Social Services*. Wellington: New Zealand Planning Council, 1984.

Department of Maori Affairs. *He Tironhanga Rangapu, Partnership Perspectives: A discussion paper on Proposals for a New Parnership*. Wellington: Government Printer, 1988.

Departments of Education and Sociology. *Final Report: Community Education Initiatives Scheme Evaluation*. Palmerston North: Massey University, 1986.

Department of Social Welfare (DSW). *A Report on the Establishment of a New Department by the Amalgamation of the Social Security Department and the Child Welfare Division of the Department of Education*. Wellington: Government Printer, 1970.

______. *Report of the Department of Social Welfare for the Year Ended 31 March*. Wellington: Government Printer, 1973-1988.

______. *Review of the Social Work Division: Report of a Working Party*. Wellington: Department of Social Welfare, 1982.

______. *Briefing Notes for the Incoming Minister of Social Welfare*. Wellington: Department of Social Welfare, 1984.

______. *Circular Memos*. Wellington: Department of Social Welfare, 1985, 1986, 1987, 1988.

______. *Report of the Department of Social Welfare for the Year Ending 31 March 1985*. Wellington: Government Printer, 1985a.

______. *Institutional Racism in the Department of Social Welfare: Tamaki-Makau-Rau, Auckland (Revised)*. Wellington: Department of Social Welfare, 1985b.

______. *Review of the Department of Social Welfare Volunteer Programme*. Community Development Unit. Wellington: Department of Social Welfare, 1985c.

______. *Maori Advisory Unit Report*. Wellington: Department of Social Welfare, 1985d.

______. *Management Plan, 1986*. Wellington: Department of Social Welfare, 1986a.

______. *The Organisation of Social Work Services at the District Level: Report of the Working Party*. Wellington: Department of Social Welfare, 1986b.

______. *Review of the Department of Social Welfare Volunteer Programme*. Community Development Unit. Wellington: Department of Social Welfare, 1986c.

______. *Briefing Papers for the Incoming Minister of Social Welfare*. Wellington: Department of Social Welfare, 1987a.

______. *Report of the Department of Social Welfare for the Year ended 31 March: Presented to the House of Representatives*. Wellington: Government Printer, 1987b.

______. *Management Plan, 1987*. Wellington: Department of Social Welfare, 1987c.

______. *Equal Employment Opportunities: Management Plan*. Wellington: Department of Social Welfare, 1988a.

______. *Report of the Department of Social Welfare for the Year Ending 31 March 1988*. Wellington: Government Printer, 1988b.

______. *Contracting for Social Services: Principles and Guidelines*. Wellington: Department of Social Welfare, 1988c.

______. *Future Directions for Social Work*. Wellington: Department of Social Welfare, 1988d.

______. *Corporate Management Plan, 1988*. Wellington: Department of Social Welfare, 1988e.

______. *Social Work Development Plan*. Wellington: Department of Social Welfare, 1989.

______. *Review of Regional Offices (Report of Assistant Director-General: Programmes and Services).* Wellington: Department of Social Welfare, 1990a.

______. *Corporate Plan, 1990.* Wellington: Department of Social Welfare, 1990b.

______. *Report of the Department of Social Welfare.* Wellington: Department of Social Welfare, 1990c.

Department of Social Welfare Act, 1971. Wellington: Government Printer, 1971.

Dingwall, Robert and Philip Lewis. *The Sociology of the Professions.* London: Macmillan Press, 1983.

Douglas, Ian G. *New Zealand in Change: Policies and Attitudes.* Wellington: Hutcheson, Bowman and Steward, Ltd., 1985.

Driver, Sue, and David Robinson. *Voluntary Social Services: A Review of Funding.* Wellington: New Zealand Planning Council, 1986.

Drucker, Peter. *Management.* London: Pan Books, Heinemann, 1981.

Easton, Brian. *Social Policy and the Welfare State in New Zealand.* Auckland: George Allen and Unwin, 1980.

______. Introduction to *The Making of Rogernomics*, ed. Brian Easton, 171-187. Auckland: University Press, 1989.

Easton, Brian, and N. J. Thomson. *An Introduction to the New Zealand Economy.* St. Lucia: University of Queensland Press, 1982.

Eisenstadt, S. N., and Ora Ahimeir, ed. *The Welfare State and Its Aftermath.* London: Croom Helm, 1985.

Ephross, Paul H., and Michael Reisch. "The Ideology of Some Social Work Texts." *Social Service Review* 56 (1982): 275-283.

Epstein, Irwin, and Kayla Conrad. "Empirical Limits of Social Work Professionalization." In *Human Service Organizations*, ed. Rosemary Sarri and Yeheskel Hasenfeld, 163-184. New York: Columbia University Press, 1978.

Finch, Wilbur A., Jr. "Social Workers versus Bureaucracy." *Social Work* 21:5 (1976): 370-375.

Fischer, Joel. "Is Casework Effective: A Review." *Social Work* 18 (1973): 5-20.

Flora, Peter. "On the History and Current Problems of the Welfare State." In *The Welfare State and Its Aftermath*, ed. S. N. Eisenstadt and Ora Ahimeir, 11-30. London: Croom Helm, 1985.

Flowers, Mark. "Social Work Issues for the 1980s." In *The 1981 Social Work Lectures*, ed. Ken R. Daniels. Christchurch: Canterbury University, 1981.

Forrest, Jan, and Sandra Williams. *New Technology and Information Exchange in Social Services*. London: Policy Studies Institute, 1987.

Fraser, Sarah. "President's Report." *Social Work Review: NZASW* 1:1 (July 1988): 30-31.

Freidman, Robert R., Neil Gilbert, and Moshe Sherer. *Modern Welfare States: A Comparative View of Trends and Prospects*. New York: New York University Press, 1987.

Friedson, Eliot. *Professional Dominance: The Social Structure of Medical Care*. Chicago: Aldine Publishing Co., 1970.

Furniss, Norman, and Timothy Tilton. *The Case for the Welfare State*. Bloomington, Indiana: University Press, 1977.

Galper, Jeffrey. *Social Work Practice: A Radical Perspective*. Englewood Cliffs, N. J.: Prentice-Hall Publishers, 1980.

George, Vic, and Paul Wilding. *Ideology and Social Welfare*. 2nd ed. London: Routledge and Kegan Paul, 1987.

Gilbert, Neil, and Harry Specht. *Dimensions of Social Welfare Policy*. 2nd ed. London: Routledge and Kegan Paul, 1986.

Goldberg, E. Matilda. *Social Work Since Seebohm: All Things to All Men? (Eileen Younghusband Lecture)*. London: National Institute for Social Work, 1977.

Graham, Jeanine. "Settler Society." In *The Oxford History of New Zealand*, ed. W. H. Oliver with B. R. Williams. Oxford: Clarendon Press, 1981.

Graycar, Adam. "Informal, Voluntary and Statutory Services: The Couples Relationship." *British Journal of Social Work* 13 (1983): 379-193.

Green, David. "The Future Role of the Social Work Profession in Welfare." *Australian Social Work* 4 (December 1979): 32-33.

Grinnell, Richard, ed. *Social Work Research and Evaluation*. Itasca, Il: F. E. Peacock Publishers, 1981.

Grove, Chris. *Discussion Paper: Development of Training Opportunities for those working in Community Work*. The Working Party on Community Work Training. Wellington: New Zealand Association of Social Work, 1983.

Gruber, Murray L., ed. *Management Systems in the Human Services*. Philadelphia: Temple University Press, 1981.

Guba, Egon G. "The Context of Emergent Paradigm Research." In *Organization Theory and Inquiry: The Paradigm Revolution*, ed. Yvonna S. Lincoln, 79-105. Beverly Hills: Sage Publications, 1985.

Hadley, Roger, Mike Cooper, Peter Dale, and Graham Stacy. *A Community Worker's Handbook*. Bungay, Suffolk: Richard Clay, Ltd., 1987.

Hadley, Roger, Peter Dale, and Patrick Sills. *Decentralising Social Services*. ed. National Council of Voluntary Organisations. London: Bedford Square Press, 1984.

Hadley, Roger and Stephen Hatch. *Social Welfare and the Failure of the State: Centralized Social Services and Participatory Alternatives.* London: George Allen and Unwin, 1981.

Hadley, Roger, and Morag McGrath. *When Social Services are Local: The Normanton Experience.* National Institute Social Services Library, No. 48, London: George Allen and Unwin, 1984.

______, ed. *Going Local: Neighbourhood Social Services* National Council for Voluntary Organisations, Occasional Paper I. London: Bedford Square Press, 1981.

Hadley, Roger, and Ken Young. *Creating a Responsive Public Service.* Hertfordshire: Harvester Wheatsheaf, 1990.

Hage, Jerald and J. Roger Hollingsworth. "The First Steps Toward the Integration of Social Theory and Social Policy." *American Journal of Sociology* 434 (1977): 1-23.

Hall, Trish, and Ian Shirley. "Development as Methodology: Locality Development, Social Planning and Social Action." In *Development Tracks*, ed. Ian Shirley, 135-164. Palmerston North: Dunmore Press, 1982.

Halsey, A. H. "Some Lessons from the Debate: A Sociologist's Viewpoint." In *Account of the Conference on Social Policies in the 1980s*, ed. Organisation for Economic Cooperation and Development. Paris: OECD, 1981.

Hancock, Mervyn, and Beverly Barron. *Some Citizens' Views on the Quality of Life and the Welfare State in Napier : Napier Pilot City Project.* Palmerston North: Social Communications, Ltd., 1983.

Hancock-Benseman, M. *Women's Refuge Centres in New Zealand: A Research Project.* Palmerston North: Massey University, 1979.

Handy, Charles B. *Understanding Organizations.* Harmondsworth: Penguin, 1978.

Hardiker, Pauline, and Mary Barker, ed. *Theories of Practice in Social Work.* London: Academic Press, 1981.

Hasenfeld, Yeheskel, and Richard English, ed. *Human Service Organizations*. Ann Arbor: University of Michigan Press, 1978.

Hellreigel, Don, and Jr. John W. Slocum. *Organizational Behavior: Contingency Views*. St. Paul, MN: West Publishing Co., 1976.

Hessey, Eve. "Why Should Social Workers be Professionally Trained?" *New Zealand Social Work Journal* 9:1 (1982): 18-21.

______. "Professional Training and the Probation Service." *New Zealand Social Work Journal* 9:1 (1984): 6-8.

Hinds, Pamela S., Sharon Scandrett-Hibden, and Leon S. McAulay. "Further Assessment of a Method to Estimate Reliability and Validity of Qualitative Research Findings." *Journal of Advanced Nursing* 15 (1990): 430-435.

Hollingsworth, J. Roger, and Robert Hanneman. *Centralization and Power in Social Service Delivery Systems*. Boston: Kluever, Nighoff Publishing, 1984.

Holsti, Ole R. "Introduction to Part II." In *The Analysis of Communication Content*, ed. George Gerbner, Ole R. Hosti, Klaus Krippendorff, William J. Paisley, and Philip J. Stone, 109-122. New York: J. Wiley and Sons, 1969.

Howe, David. *Social Workers and Their Practice in Welfare Bureaucracies*. Hants, England: Gower Publishing Company, 1986.

Howe, Elizabeth. "Public Professions and the Private Model of Professionalism." *Social Work* 25:5 (1980): 179-191.

Hunt, Leonard. "Social Work and Ideology." In *Philosophy and Social Work*, ed. Noel Timms and David Watson, 7-25. London: Routledge and Kegan Paul, 1978.

Huse, Edgar F. *Organizational Development*. St. Paul, MN: West Publishing Company, 1980.

Illich, Ivan, Irving Kenneth Zola, John McKnight, Jonathan Caplan, and Harley Shaiken. *Disabling Professions*. London: Marion Boyars Publishing Ltd., 1977.

Ings, Katrina. "NZASW and the Professionalisation of New Zealand Social Workers." *New Zealand Association of Social Workers Journal* II:1 (1986): 3-6.

Jack, P. Avery and J. H. Robb. "Social Welfare Policies: Development and Patterns since 1945." In *Social Welfare and New Zealand Society*, ed. A. D. Trlin, 29-44. Wellington: Methuen Publications, N. Z., 1977.

Jackson, Jim. "Constant Learning: Developing Community Involvement In a Social Service Department." In *Volunteers in the Personal Social Services*, ed. Giles Darvill and Brian Munday, 63-77. London: Tavistock Publications, 1984.

Jensen, J. E. "Some Recent Developments in Social Welfare Policy in New Zealand in Relation to Children, Youth and Women: A Paper Presented to the Training Seminar on Social Welfare Policies in Asian and Pacific Countries." In *Training Seminar on Social Welfare Policies in Asian and Pacific Countries in Manila Philippines*, edited by Department of Social Welfare Chief Research Officer, Wellington: Department of Social Welfare, 1976.

Johnson, John M. *Doing Field Research*. New York: The Free Press, 1975.

Johnson, Norman. *The Welfare State in Transition: The Theory and Practice of Welfare Pluralism*. Brighton, Sussex: Wheatsheaf Books, 1987.

Johnson, Terence J. *Professions and Power*. New York: Macmillan Publishing Company, 1972.

Johnston, A. H. *Report to the Minister of Social Welfare on the Current Practices and Procedures Followed in Institutions of the Department of Social Welfare in Auckland*. Wellington: Department of Social Welfare, 1982.

Jones, Kathleen, John Brown, and Johathan Bradshaw. *Issues in Social Policy*. London: Routledge and Kegan Paul, 1978.

Jordan, Bill. *Rethinking Welfare*. London: Basil Blackwell, Ltd., 1987.

Judge, Ken. "The British Welfare State in Transition." In *Modern Welfare States: A Comparative View of Trends and Prospects*, ed. Robert R. Freidman, Neil Gilbert, and Moshe Sherer, 1-43. New York: New York University Press, 1987.

Kakabadse, Andrew. *Culture of the Social Services*. Hampshire: Gower Publishing Company, Ltd., 1982.

Karger, Howard Jacob. "Private Practice: The Fast Track to the Shingle." *Social Work* 34:6 (1989): 566-567.

Katan, Yosef. "The Utilization of Indigenous Workers in Human Service Organizations." In *Human Service Organizations*, ed. Yeheskel Hasenfeld and Richard A. English, 448-467. Ann Arbor: University of Michigan Press, 1974.

Kaufman, Franz-Xavier. "Major Problems and Dimensions of the Welfare State." In *The Welfare State and Its Aftermath*, ed. S. N. Eisenstadt and Ora Ahimer, London: Croom Helm, 1985.

Kelsey, J. *Rolling Back the State*. Wellington, New Zealand: Bridget Williams Books, Ltd., 1993.

Ketko, Raoul. *Social Work Developments in England 1981/1982: The Nuffield Report*. Wellington: Department of Social Welfare, 1982.

Kilmister, Terry. *Community Volunteers: A History*. Wellington: The Roy McKenzie Foundation, 1987.

Kirk, Stuart A., and James R. Greenley. "Denying or Delivering Services?" *Social Work* 19:4 (1974): 439-447.

Klein, Rudolf, and Michael O'Higgins. "Introduction: Old Myths-New Challenges." In *The Future of Welfare*, ed. Rudolph Klein and Michael O'Higgins, 1-8. Oxford: Basil Blackwell, Ltd., 1985.

Koontz, Harold, and Cyril O'Donnell. *Essentials of Management*. 2nd ed. New York: McGraw Hill, 1978.

Kramer, Ralph M. "The Welfare State and the Voluntary Sector: The Case of the Personal Social Services." In *The Welfare State and Its Aftermath*, ed. S. N. Eisenstadt and Ora Ahimeir, 132-142. London: Croom Helm, 1985.

Laking, Rob. "Social Policy and the Future of Bureaucracy." In *Responding to the Revolution: Careers, Culture and Casualties*, ed. Jeannette Johston and Adrienne von Tunzelmann. Wellington: Government Printer, 1987.

Larson, Magali Sarfotti. *The Rise of Professionalism*. Los Angeles: University of California Press, 1977.

Latto, S., and C. Rowlings. *Evidence to Social Work Enquiry*. Britain: University of Keele, 1981.

Lerman, Paul. *Deinstitutionalization and the Welfare State*. New Brunswick: Rutgers University Press, 1982.

Levett, Allan, Josie Keelan, and Velma McClellan. *Making Devolution Work: Report on the Community Oranisations Grant Scheme*. Wellington: Department of Social Welfare, 1988.

Lincoln, Yvonna S., ed. *Organizational Theory and Inquiry: The Paradigm Revolution*. Beverly Hills: Sage Publications, 1985.

Lipsky, Michael. *Street-Level Bureaucracy: Dilemmas of the Individual in Public Services*. New York: Russell Sage Foundation, 1980.

Litwak, Eugene. "Organizational Constructs and Mega-Bureaucracy." In *Human Service Organizations*, ed. Rosemary Sarri and Yeheskel Hasenfeld, 123-163. New York: Columbia University Press, 1978.

Lowi, Theodore J. *The End of Liberalism: the Second Republic of the U. S.* 2nd ed. New York: W. E. Norton, 1979.

Lowi, Theodore J. and Benjamin Ginsberg. *Poliscide*. New York: The Macmillan Publishing Company, 1976.

MacDonald, Ian, and Makareta Moffat. *Report on the Needs Analysis and Consultation in the Porirua District Office*. Porirua: Department of Social Welfare, 1988.

Malcolm, Margy Jean. "Restructuring the State: Restructuring Society." In *The April Report*, The Royal Commission on Social Policy, Vol. III: Part II, 407-421. Wellington: Government Printer, 1988.

Malcom, L. A. *Decentralisation of Health Services Management: A Review of the New Zealand Experience*. Wellington: Department of Community Health, Wellington Clinical School of Medicine, 1986.

Maori Economic Development Summit Conference. *A Briefing on Maori Economic Affairs*. Palmerston North: The Dunmore Press, 1984.

Marmor, Theodore, Jerry L. Mashow, and Philip L. Harvey. *Americas Misunderstood Welfare State: Persistent Myths, Enduring Realities*. (No City Given): Basic Books, 1990.

McLennan, Roy, Kerr Inkson, Stephen Dakin, Philip Dewe, and Graham Elkin. *People and Enterprises: Human Behavior in New Zealand Organisations*. Sydney: Holt, Rinehart and Winston, 1987.

Meyer, John, and W. Richard Scott, ed. *Organizational Environments: Ritual and Rationality*. Beverly Hills: Sage Publications, 1983.

Middleman, Ruth, and Gale Goldberg. *Social Service Delivery: A Structural Appproach to Social work Practice*. New York: Columbia University Press, 1974.

Ministerial Advisory Committee on a Maori Perspective for the Department of Social Welfare. *Puao-Te-Ata-Tu The Day Break Report*. Wellington: Department of Social Welfare, 1986.

Ministerial Review Committee. *Report on the Social Work Training Council*. Wellington: Department of Social Welfare, 1985.

Ministerial Task Force on Social Welfare Services. *Social Welfare Services*. Wellington: Department of Social Welfare, July,1986.

______. *Social Welfare Services: The Way Ahead*. Wellington: Department of Social Welfare, July,1987.

Miringoff, Marc L. *Management in Human Service Organizations*. New York: Macmilan Publishing, 1980.

Mishra, R. *The Welfare State in Crisis*. Brighton: Wheatsheaf, 1984.

Mishra, Ramesh. *The Welfare State in Capitalist Society: Policies of Re-trenchment & Maintenance in Europe, North America & Australia*. Toronto: University of Toronto Press, 1990.

Mohan, Brij. *The Logic of Social Welfare: Conjectures and Formulations*. New York: St. Martin's Press, 1988.

Morales, Armando, and Bradford W. Sheafor. *Social Work: A Profession of Many Faces*. 3rd ed. Boston: Allyn and Bacon, Inc., 1983.

Morgan, Gareth. *Images of Organizations*. Beverly Hills: Sage Publications, 1986.

Morrison, Alastair. "Betrayal of the Social Contract." *The Dominion Newspaper*, 11 May 1989, 17.

Morrison, Alastair. "Putting Profit Before Service." *The Dominion Newspaper*, 10 May 1989, 17.

Nachimas, David, and Chava Nachimas. *Research Methods in the Social Sciences*. 2nd ed. New York: St. Martin's Press, 1981.

Nairn, M., and O. Sutherland. "Auckland Committee on Racism and Discrimination Submission of C & Y P A, No. 378." In *The 1985 Public Submissions on the Review of the Children's and Young Person's Act of 1974*, Wellington: Department of Social Welfare, 1985.

Napier District Office. *Report of the Community Development Team*. Napier: Department of Social Welfare, 1984.

New Zealand Association of Citizens Advice Bureaux (NZACAB). *Handbook on Administration of a Citizens Advice Bureau*. Wellington: NZACAB, 1977.

New Zealand Association of Social Workers (NZASW). *The Third Biennial Conference: Challenge of the 1970s*. Hamilton: NZASW, 1970.

______. *Social Welfare at the Crossroads: Report on Social Welfare in New Zealand*. Wellington: NZASW, 1971.

______. *The Papers Presented at the NZASW Biennial Conference*. Christchurch: NZASW, 1972.

______. *Conference Papers: Report to the Fifth Biennial Conference and Convention*. Wellington: NZASW, 1974.

______. *Social Worker's Conference: Community*. Auckland: NZASWY, 1976.

______. *Biennial Conference: Conference Papers*." Palmerston North: NZASW, 1978.

______. *Biennial Conference: Social Justice, A Social Work Concern for the 1980s*. Wellington: NZASW, 1982.

______. *News and Views*. Wellington: NZASW, July,1986a.

______. *News and Views*. Wellington: NZASW, December, 1986b.

New Zealand Council of Social Services (NZCSS). *Establishing District Councils of Social Services*. Wellington: Department of Social Welfare, 1976.

______. *Sharing Social Responsibility: Report of the New Zealand Council of Social Services on Desirable Development*. Wellington: NZCSS, 1978.

New Zealand Federation of Voluntary Welfare Organisations (NZFVWO). *Managing Your Voluntary Agency in the 1980s: A Resource Kit*. Wellington: NZFVWO, Inc., 1981.

______. *Report of a Seminar on Parallel Development: A Model for Voluntary Agencies (Second Seminar on Biculturalism)*. Wellington: NZFVWO, 1987.

New Zealand Planning Council (NZPC). *New Zealand at the Turning Point: Report of the Task Force on Economic and Social Planning (The Holmes Report).* Wellington: Government Printer, 1976.

______. *A Moment of Truth.* Wellington: Government Printer, 1977.

______. *Planning Perspectives: 1978-1983.* Wellington: Government Printer, 1978.

______. *The Welfare State.* Wellington: Government Printer, 1979.

______. *Directions.* Wellington: Government Printer, 1981.

______. *Who Makes Social Policy*? Wellington: Government Printer, 1982.

______. *The Economy in Transition: Restructuring to 1989.* Wellington: NZPC, 1989.

New Zealand Public Service Association (NZPSA). "Privatisation and the Rise of Monetarism in New Zealand." Wellington: NZPSA, 1989a.

______. "SOE Privatisation: The Next Logical Step?" Wellington: NZPSA, 1989b.

Oakley, A. "Interviewing Women: A Contradiction in Terms." In *Doing Feminist Research*, ed. H. Roberts, 30-61. London: Routledge and Kegan Paul, 1981.

Oliver, Hugh. "The Labour Caucus and Economic Policy Formation, 1981-1984." In *The Making of Rogernomics*, ed. Brian Easton, 11-52. Auckland: University Press, 1989.

______. "Devolution-New Times or Old Times?" *Sites* 20 (1990): 110-116.

Oliver, William. "Origins and Growth of the Welfare State." In *Social Welfare and New Zealand Society*, ed. A. D. Trlin. Wellington: Methuen Publications, N. Z., Ltd., 1977.

______. "Social Policy in New Zealand: An Historical Overview". In *The April Report* , Royal Commission on Social Policy, Vol. 1, 3-45. Wellington: Government Printer, 1988.

Opie, Ann. "Qualitative Methodology, Deconstructive Readings, Appropriation of the 'Other' and Empowerment." Wellington: Victoria University, Department of Sociology, 1989.

Organisation for Economic Co-Operation and Development (OECD). *The Welfare State in Crisis: An Account of the Conference on Social Policies in the 1980s*. Paris: OECD, 1981.

Ostrander, Susan A., Stuart Langton, and Hon Van Til, ed. *Shifting the Debate*. New Brunswick: Transaction Books, 1987.

Papesch, Janette, and Noel Stevens. *Foster Care in Christchurch*. Christchurch: University of Canterbury, Department of Social Work, 1985.

Parry, Noel, Michael Rustin, and Carole Satymurti. *Social Work, Welfare and the State*. London: Edward Arnold Pulishers, 1979.

Patti, Rino J. "Applying Business Management Stategies in Social Agencies: Prospects and LImitations." In *Work, Workers and Work Organizations: A View from Social Work*, ed. Sheila H. Akabas and Paul A. Kurzmen, 147-175. Englewood Cliffs, NJ: Prentice-Hall, 1982.

______. *Social Welfare Administration: Managing Social Programs in a Developmental Context*. Englewood Cliffs, NJ: Prentice-Hall, 1983.

Patti, Rino J., and Herman Resnick. "Changing the Agency from Within." *Social work* 17:4 (1972): 48-57.

Patton, Michael. *Qualitative Research Methods*. Beverly Hills, CA: Sage Publications, 1980.

Pearce, John A. II, and Jr. Richard B. Robinson. *Management*. Singapore: McGraw-Hill International Editions, 1989.

Perrow, Charles. *Complex Organizations*. 2nd ed. Glenview, IL: Scott Foresman and Company, 1973.

Pestoff, Victor A. "Third Sector and Co-Operative Services-An Alternative to Privatization." *Journal of Consumer Policy* 15 (1992): 21-45.

Peters, Michael, and James Marshall. "Social Policy and the Move to Community." In *The April Report*, The Royal Commission on Social Policy, Vol. III: Part II, 679-702. Wellington: Government Printer, 1988.

Piccard, Betty J. *Introduction to Social Work: A Primer*. Homewood, IL: The Dorsey Press, 1975.

Pickvance, Christopher. "Central Government, Local Government, Voluntary Associations and the Welfare State: Some Reflections on Opposition to Recent Public Spending Cuts in Britain." In *Shifting the Debate*, ed. Susan Ostrander, Stuart Langton, and Jon Van Til, 81-96. New Brunswick: Transaction Books, 1987.

Pilalis, J. , S. Opal, and T. Mamea. *Dangerous Situations*. Wellington: Department of Social Welfare, 1987.

Pincus, Allen, and Anne Minahan. *Social Work Practice: Model and Method*. Madison: University of Wisconsin Press, 1973.

Pinker, Robert A. "Appendix B: An alternative view." In *Social workers: Their Role and Tasks*, Barclay Report. London: Bedford Square Press, 1982.

______. "Social Welfare and the Education of Social Workers." In *Approaches to Welfare*, ed. Philip Bean and Stewart Mac Pherson, 150-165. London: Routledge and Kegan Paul, 1983.

______. "Populism and the Social Services." *Social Policy Administration* 18:1 (1984): 89-99.

Pitt, P. H. *Social Processes in New Zealand's Future: The Relevance of European Models*. Prepared at the Request of the Commission for the Future. Wellington: Government Printing Office, 1978.

Porter, Lyman, III Edward E. Lawler, and J. Richard Hackman. *Behavior in Organizations*. Tokyo: McGraw-Hill (Kogakusha, Ltd.), 1975.

Prigmore, Charles S., and Charles R. Atherton. *Social Welfare Policy: Analysis and Formulation* . 2nd ed. Lexington, MA: D. C. Heath and Company, 1986.

Reed, Michael. *Redirections in Organizational Analysis.* London: Tavistock Publications, 1985.

Rees, A. M. *T. H. Marshall's Social Policy in the Twentieth Century.* 5th ed. London: Hutchison, 1985.

Rees, Stuart, and Alison Wallace. *Verdicts on Social Work.* London: Edward Arnold, 1982.

Reid, William J., and Audrey D. Smith. *Research in Social Work.* New York: Columbia University Press, 1981.

Rein, Martin, and Lee Rainwater, ed. *Public/Private Interplay in Social Protection: A Comparative Study.* London: M. E. Sharp, 1986.

Reisman, David. *Richard Titmuss: Welfare and Society.* London: Heinemann, 1977.

Resnick, Herman. "Tasks in Changing the Organization from Within." *Administration in Social Work* 1 (Spring 1978): 29-44.

Resnick, Herman, and Rino J. Patti, ed. *Change From Within: Humanizing Social Welfare Organisations.* Philadelphia: Temple University Press, 1980.

Reynolds, Bertha Capen. *Learning and Teaching in the Practice of Social work.* Classic Edition, 1985. National Association of Social Workers. New York: Russell and Russell, 1942.

Robbins, Stephen P. *Organization Theory: The Structure and Design of Organizations.* Englewood Cliffs, NJ: Prentice-Hall, 1983.

Roberts, H. *Doing Feminist Research.* London: Routledge and Kegan Paul, 1981.

Robson, William A. *Welfare State and Welfare Society.* London: George Allen and Unwin, Ltd., 1976.

Rochford, M. W., and M. J. Robb. *People in the Social Services: A New Zealand Study*. Wellington: New Zealand Social Work Training Council, 1981.

Roper, B. "From the Welfare State to the Free Market: Explaining the Transition, Part II: Crisis, Class, Ideology and the State." In *New Zealand Sociology*, 6. Sociology Department: Massey University, New Zealand, 1991.

Rose, Richard, and Rei Shiratori. *The Welfare State East & West*. New York: Oxford University Press, 1986.

Rosengren, Karl Erik, ed. *Advances in Content Analysis*. Vol. 19. Sage Annual Review of Communication Research. Beverly Hills: Sage Publications, 1981.

Rothman, Jack. "Taking Account of the Workplace in Community Organization Practice." In *Work, Workers and Work Organizations: A View from Social Work*, ed. Sheila H. Akabas and Paul A. Kursman, 176-196. Englewood Cliffs, NJ: Prentice-Hall, 1982.

______, John Erlich, and Joseph G. Teresa. *Promoting Innovation and Change in Organizations and Communities*. New York: John Wiley and Sons, 1976.

Rowe, Andrew. "R. Hadley and Stephen Hatch: Social Welfare and the Failure of the State: A Book Review." *Journal of Social Policy* 11 (1982): 556-557.

Royal Commission on Social Policy. *The April Report*. Wellington: Government Printer,1988a.

______. "Social Provision: Access and Delivery." In *The April Report*, Royal Commission on Social Policy, Vol. II, 773-811. Wellington: Government Printer, 1988b. .

______. "The Funding of Social Provision." In *The April Report*, Royal Commission on Social Policy, Vol. II, 657-724. Wellington: Government Printer, 1988c.

______. "New Directions." In *The April Report,* Royal Commission on Social Policy, Vol. II, 843-868. Wellington: Government Printer,1988d.

Royal Commission on Social Security. *Social Security in New Zealand.* Wellington: Government Printer, 1972.

Rubin, Allen, and Earl Babbie. *Research Methods for Social Work.* Belmont, CA: Wadsworth Publishing Company, 1989.

Salaman, and K. Thompson, ed. *People and Organizations.* London: Longman (for Open University Press), 1973.

Sarri, Rosemary, and Yeheskel Hasenfeld, ed. *Human Service Organizations.* New York: Columbia University Press, 1983.

Schatzman, L., and A. L. Strauss. *Field Research.* Englewood Cliffs, NJ: Prentice-Hall, 1973.

Scott, Bob. "A History of the Interaction Between Maori People and the Social Welfare Institutions of Aotearoa." Auckland: University of Auckland, Centre for Continuing Education1985.

Scott, Robert A. "The Selection of Clients by Social Welfare Agencies: The Case of the Blind." In *Change From Within: Humanizing Social Welfare Organizations*, ed. Herman Resnick and Rino J. Patti, 96-109. Philadelphia: Temple University Press, 1980.

Scott, W. Richard. "The Organization of Environments: Nework, Cultural and Historical Elements." In *Organizational Environments: Ritual and Rationality,* ed. John Meyer and W. Richard Scott, 155-178. Beverly Hills, CA: Sage Publications, 1983a.

______. "Health Care Organizations in the 1980s: The Convergence of Public and Professional Control Systems." In *Organizational Environments: Ritual and Rationality*, ed. John Meyer and W. Richard Scott, 99-114. Beverly Hills, CA: Sage Publications, 1983b.

Seebohm Report. *Report of the Committee on Local Authority and Allied Personal Social Services, Cmnd 3703.* London: HMSO, 1968.

Seldon, Arthur. "The Idea of the Welfare State and Its Consequences." In *The Welfare State and Its Aftermath*, ed. S. N. Eisenstadt and Ora Ahimeir, 59-73. London: Croom Helm, 1985.

Sheafor, Bradford W. *Social Work Practice in New Zealand*. Palmerston North: Massey University, 1982.

Sheafor, Bradford, Robert Teare, Mervyn W. Hancock, and Thomas P. Gauthier. "Curriculum Development through Content Analysis: A New Zealand Experience." *Journal of Education in Social Work* 20-21:3 (1985): 113-124.

Shirley, Ian, ed. *Development Tracks*. Palmerston North: Dunmore Press, 1982.

Siddiqui, H. Y. "Social Policy in the Third World: A Third World Perspective." Palmerston North: Massey University, Department of Social Work,1987.

Silverman, David. *The Theory of Organization: A Sociological Framework*. New York: Basic Books, 1971.

Simkin, Mike. *Trapped Within Welfare*. London: Macmillan Press, 1979.

Siporin, Max. *Introduction to Social Work Practice*. New York: Macmillan Press, 1975.

Skidmore, Rex A. *Social Work Administration: Dynamic Management and Human Relationships*. Englewood Cliffs, NJ: Prentice-Hall, 1983.

Skidmore, Rex A., Milton Thackery, and O. William Farley. *Introduction to Social Work*. 4th ed. Englewood Cliffs, NJ: Prentice-Hall, 1988.

Small, Neil. "Community Social Work in China and Britain." *Social Policy and Administration* 18:2 (1984): 148-155.

Smalley, Ruth Elizabeth. *Theory for Social Work Practice*. New York: Columbia University Press, 1967.

Smith, Brenda and Carolyn Noble-Spruell. "An Overview of Feminist Research Perspectives." In *Gender Reclaimed: Women in Social Work*, ed. Helen Marchant and Betsy Wearing, 134-146. Marrickville, NSW: Southwood Press, Pty., Ltd., 1986.

Smith, Dorothy. "Front Line Organizations of the State Mental Hospital." *Administrative Science Quarterly* 10 (1964): 381-399.

Smith, Gilbert. *Social Work and the Sociology of Organizations.* 2nd ed. London: Routledge and Kegan Paul, 1979.

Social Advisory Council (SAC). *The Extra Years: Some Implications for New Zealand Society of an Ageing Population.* Wellington: Government Printer, 1984a (February).

______. *Report of a Conference for Representatives of District Councils of Social Service.* Wellington: Government Printer, 1984b.

______. *Partnership: The Delivery of Social and Community Services.* Wellington: Government Printer, May, 1986.

Social Work Training Council (SWTC). *Report to the Minister on Training for Community Social Workers.* Wellington: Department of Social Welfare, 1975.

Social Work Training Council (SWTC). *Report of the New Zealand Social Work Training Council: A Report Prepared at the Request of the Minister of Social Welfare.* Wellington: SWTC, 1985.

Social Work Training Council (SWTC). *Competent Social Work Practice: A Resource Document.* Wellington: Department of Social Welfare, 1986.

Specht, Harry, and Anne Vickery, ed. *Integrating Social Work Methods.* London: George Allen and Unwin, 1977.

Spicker, Paul. *Principles of Social Welfare: An Introduction to Thinking About the Welfare State.* London: Routledge, 1988.

Stein, Irma. *System Theory, Science and Social Work.* Metuchen, NJ: The Scarecrow Press, Inc., 1974.

Steiner, Joseph R., Thomas Briggs, and Gerald M. Gross. "Emerging Social Work Traditions, Profession Building and Curriculum Policy Statements." *Journal of Education in Social Work* 20:1 (1985): 23-31.

Steiner, Richard. *Managing the Human Service Organization.* Beverly Hills: Sage Publications, 1977.

Stephens, Vanessa. "Power Goes Back to the Maori Tribes." *The Dominican Newspaper*, 8 April 1989, 11.

Stevenson, Olive. "Personal Social Services." In *In Defense of the Welfare State*, ed. Paul Wilding, 98-126. Manchester: Manchester University Press, 1986.

Sutton, Carole. *Handbook of Research for the Helping Professions.* London: Routledge and Kegan Paul, 1987.

Tabbert, Wynn. *District Executive Committee Evaluation Model.* Wellington: Department of Social Welfare, 1987.

Task Group on Devolution. *Sharing Control: A Policy Study of Responsiveness and Devolution in the Statutory Social Services.* State Service Commission, Wellington: Government Printer, February,1988.

Taylor-Goodby, Peter. "The Politics of Welfare: Public Attitudes and Behaviors." In *The Future of Welfare*, ed. Rudolf Klein and Michael O'Higgins, 72-91. Oxford: Basil Blackwell, Ltd., 1985.

Tennant, Margaret. *Paupers and Providers.* Wellington: Allen & Unwin, N. Z., Ltd., 1989.

Terrybery, S. "The Evolution of Organizational Environments." *Administrative Science Quarterly* 12 (1968): 590-613.

Thomlison, Roy J. "Something Works: Evidence from Practice Effectiveness Studies." *Social Work* 29 (1984): 51-16.

Timms, Noel and Rita Timms. *Perspectives in Social Work.* London: Routledge and Kegan Paul, 1977.

Timms, Noel, and Rita Timms. *Dictionary of Social Welfare.* London: Routledge and Kegan Paul, 1982.

Titmuss, Richard. *Social Policy: An Introduction.* ed. Brian Abel-Smith and Kay Titmuss. London: George Allen and Unwin, 1974.

Titmuss, Richard. *Essays on 'The Welfare State'.* 3rd ed. London: George Allen and Unwin, Ltd., 1976.

Toren, Nina. *Social Work: The Case of a Semi-Profession.* Beverly Hills: Sage Publications, 1972.

Trlin, A. D., ed. *Social Welfare and New Zealand Society.* Wellington: Methuen Publications, N. Z., Ltd., 1977.

Unell, Judith. *Help for Self Help: A Study of a Local Support Service.* London: Bedford Square Press, 1986.

University Grants Committee (UGC). *Social Work Review Committee: The Brownlie Report.* Wellington: Government Printing Office, 1982.

Von Tunzelmann, Adrienne, and Jeannette Johnston, ed. *Responding to the Revolution.* Wellington: Government Printing Office, 1987.

Waldegrave, Charles. "Budget '91: Monetarists' Dream Citizens' Nightmare." *Social Work Review* 4:2-3 (1991): 33-34.

Wallace, G. C. P. *Report to the Secretary for Justice on the Enquiry into ACORD Complaints Concerning Detention of Young Persons.* Wellington: Department of Justice, 1984.

Wasserman, Harry. "The Professional Social Worker In a Bureaucracy." In *Change from Within: Humanizing Human Service Organizations,* ed. Herman Resnick and Rino Patti. Philadelphia: Temple University Press, 1980.

Waterman, R. H., T. J. Peters, and J. R. Phillips. "Structure is Not Organization." *Business Horizon* 23:1-3 (1980): 14-26.

Weatherley, Richard A. "Participatory Management in Public Welfare: What are the Prospects?" *Administration in Social Work* 7:1 (1983): 39-50.

Webb, David. "Themes and Continuities in Radical-Traditional Social Work." *British Journal of Social Work* 11 (1981): 143-158.

Wechsler, Henry, Helen Z. Reinherz, and Donald D. Dobbin. *Social Work Research in the Human Services*. 2nd ed. New York: Human Services Press, 1981.

Weick, Karl. "Sources of Order in Underorganized Systems: Theme in Recent Organizational Theory." In *Organization Theory and Inquiry: The Paradigm Revolution*, ed. Yvonna S. Lincoln, 106-136. Beverly Hills: Sage Publications, 1985.

Weiner, Myron E. *Human Services Management: Analysis and Applications*. Homewood, IL: The Dorsey Press, 1982.

Wilding, Paul. *Professional Power and Social Welfare*. London: Routledge and Kegan Paul, 1982.

Wilding, Paul, ed. *In Defense of the Welfare State*. Manchester: Manchester University Press, 1986.

Wilding, Paul. "The British Welfare State: Thacherism's Enduring Legacy." *Policy & Politics* 20:3 (1992): 201-212.

Wilensky, Harold L., and Charles N. Lebeaux. *Industrial Society and Social Welfare*. 2nd ed. New York: The Free Press, 1965.

Wilkes, Chris. "Development as Practice: The Instrument of Reason." In *Development Tracks*, ed. Ian Shirley, 117-134. Palmerston North: Dunmore Press, 1982.

Wilkes, Chris. "The Art of the State." In *Annual Conference of the Public Service Association in Wellington*. Wellington: PSA, 1989.

Wilson, I. G. *Napier Department of Social Work and Voluntary Work*. Napier Department of Social Welfare, 1976.

Winemann, Steven. *The Politics of Human Services*. Boston: South End Press, 1984.

Wolfenden, Lord. *The Future of Voluntary Organisation: Report of the Committee*. London: Croom Helm, 1977.

Wyn, Helen. *Government Funding of Voluntary Welfare Agencies: A Review of Funding by the Department of Social Welfare*. Wellington: Department of Social Welfare, Social Programme Evaluation Unit, 1984.

Yanay, Uri. "Limits to Professional Practice In Decentralized Systems." *Social Policy and Administration* 23:1 (1989): 48-59.

Zastrow, Charles. *The Practice of Social Work*. 2nd ed. Homewood, IL: Dorsey Press, 1985.

Zey-Farrell, Mary, and Michael Aiken, ed. *Complex Organizations: Critical Perspectives*. Glenview, IL: Scott, Foresman and Company, 1981.

INDEX